Lecture Notes in Computer Science   11350

Commenced Publication in 1973
Founding and Former Series Editors:
Gerhard Goos, Juris Hartmanis, and Jan van Leeuwen

More information about this series at http://www.springer.com/series/7408

Jean-Michel Bruel · Manuel Mazzara ·
Bertrand Meyer (Eds.)

Software Engineering Aspects of Continuous Development and New Paradigms of Software Production and Deployment

First International Workshop, DEVOPS 2018
Chateau de Villebrumier, France, March 5–6, 2018
Revised Selected Papers

 Springer

Editors
Jean-Michel Bruel ⓘ
University of Toulouse
Toulouse, France

Manuel Mazzara ⓘ
Innopolis University
Innopolis, Russia

Bertrand Meyer ⓘ
Innopolis University
Innopolis, Russia

and

Politecnico di Milano
Milan, Italy

ISSN 0302-9743   ISSN 1611-3349   (electronic)
Lecture Notes in Computer Science
ISBN 978-3-030-06018-3   ISBN 978-3-030-06019-0   (eBook)
https://doi.org/10.1007/978-3-030-06019-0

Library of Congress Control Number: 2018967312

LNCS Sublibrary: SL2 – Programming and Software Engineering

This Springer imprint is published by the registered company Springer Nature Switzerland AG
The registered company address is: Gewerbestrasse 11, 6330 Cham, Switzerland

Preface

The study of software development processes has a long and respectable history as a subdiscipline of software engineering, so long and venerable indeed that the field became a bit sleepy and self-complacent when the jolt of agile methods caught it by surprise in the 2000s. Another incentive to question long-established wisdom was the spectacular rise of technologies made possible by the World Wide Web, notably cloud computing and software-as-a-service. No longer could we content ourselves with the well-honed scheme in which a software system is analyzed, then designed, then programmed and tested, then released unto the world, then updated at a leisurely pace as problem reports and requests for new features get filed, weeded out, and patiently implemented. The pace frantically increases: For idea–development–deployment cycles that we used to think of as spreading over months, the timeline now is days, hours, even minutes.

In 2009 Patrick Debois coined the term "Devops" to cover this new framework of software development. He and his colleague Andrew Shafer understood the need to combine the skills of software development and system administration, long considered disjoint. They also realized the critical role of deployment, often considered a secondary matter as compared with development.

Devops poses endless challenges to experts in software engineering: Which of the traditional lessons gained over five decades of the discipline's development stand, and which ones need to be replaced in the dizzying world of immediate deployment? An example of a question that takes on a full new life is quality assurance: The stakes are quite different if you have a V&V (validation and verification) phase of a few weeks to prepare for the next release, as in the old world ("old" in IT means, like, 15 years ago), and in the brave new world of deploying this morning's change in the afternoon for the millions of users of your Web-based offering.

DEVOPS 2018 (https://www.laser-foundation.org/devops/2018/), held during March 5–6, 2018, was one of the first scientific events devoted to the software engineering issues raised by the new development models. The event was kicked off by an outstanding introduction to the field by Professor Elisabetta Di Nitto from Politecnico di Milano, and featured an invited talk by Professor Benoît Combemale from Toulouse to start the education panel. The participants came from diverse organizations, with a strong representation of industry along with academia. This volume gathers their papers, considerably enhanced thanks to the feedback received during the conference. This post-conference proceedings format also enabled us to include precious material that usually does not transpire from conference-based publications: partial transcripts of the insightful discussions in panels.

The contributions cover a wide range of problems arising from Devops and related approaches, current tools, rapid development–deployment processes, effects on team performance, analytics, trustworthiness, microservices and related topics, reflecting the thriving state of the discipline and, as is to be expected in such a fledgling field, raising new questions when addressing known ones. A significant number of contributions cover education, as a number of the authors have to teach the new development paradigms to both university students and developers in companies. These contributions provide a fascinating insight into the state of the art in this new discipline.

DEVOPS 2018 was one of the first scientific events held at the new LASER center in Villebrumier near Montauban and Toulouse, France. Inspired by the prestigious precedent of the Dagstuhl center in Germany (the model for all such ventures), but adding its own sunny touch of *accent du sud-ouest* (the songful tones of Southwest France), the LASER center (http://laser-foundation.org, site of the foundation that also organizes the LASER summer school in Elba, Italy) provides a venue for high-tech events of a few days to a week in a beautiful setup in the midst of a region rich with historical, cultural, and culinary attractions. The proceedings enjoy publication in a subseries of the Springer *Lecture Notes in Computer Science* series.

Several events are planned for 2018–2019, including the next DEVOPS: Participants agreed that the workshop merited another edition, which will take place May 6–8, 2019, again at the Villebrumier center, by invitation (write to any of us if you would like to be invited). We hope that you will benefit from the results of DEVOPS 2018 as presented in the following pages and, who knows, that they might even spur you into participating in DEVOPS 2019.

October 2018   Jean-Michel Bruel
                                                        Manuel Mazzara
                                                        Bertrand Meyer

Organization

Program Committee

Kiyana Bahadori	University of Padova, Italy
Antonio Bucchiarone	FBK-IRST, Italy
Alfredo Capozucca	University of Luxembourg, Luxembourg
Paolo Ciancarini	University of Bologna, Italy
Jürgen Cito	MIT, USA
Benoît Combemale	University of Toulouse and Inria, France
Nicola Dragoni	Technical University of Denmark, Denmark
Schahram Dustdar	Vienna University of Technology, Austria
Mohamed Elwakil	Northern Arizona University, USA
Harald Gall	University of Zurich, Switzerland
Vladimir Ivanov	Innopolis University, Russia
Miguel Jiménez	University of Victoria, Canada
Christopher Jones	Depaul University, USA
Rick Kazman	Carnegie-Mellon University and University of Hawaii, USA
Philipp Leitner	Chalmers — University of Gothenburg, Sweden
Hernan Melgratti	Universidad de Buenos Aires, Argentina
Fabrizio Montesi	University of Southern Denmark, Denmark
Sebastien Mosser	University of Nice-Sophia Antipolis and I3S laboratory, France
Manoj Nambiar	Tata Consultancy Services, India
Alexandr Naumchev	Innopolis University, Russia
Larisa Safina	Innopolis University, Russia
Alberto Sillitti	Innopolis University, Russia
Giancarlo Succi	Innopolis University, Russia
Damian Andrew Tamburri	Jheronimus Academy of Data Science, TU/e, The Netherlands
Andre van Hoorn	University of Stuttgart, Germany

Contents

Design of a (Yet Another?) DevOps Course

Alfredo Capozucca$^{(\boxtimes)}$, Nicolas Guelfi, and Benoît Ries

Faculty of Science, Technology and Communication, University of Luxembourg,
Maison du Nombre, 6, Avenue de la Fonte, 4364 Esch-sur-Alzette, Luxembourg
{alfredo.capozucca,nicolas.guelfi,benoit.ries}@uni.lu

Abstract. DevOps have received marginal attention inside the higher education level curricula despite of its boom in the industrial sector.

This paper presents the design of an academic master-level course aimed at DevOps. The proposed design is based on earlier experiences in teaching DevOps-related topics. The specification of the course design is provided using the SWEBOK Guide and Bloom's taxonomy to enhance the quality of the course design specification, and ease its assessment once delivered.

Keywords: Software engineering · Education · Course design

1 Introduction

A recent study about emerging jobs in the U.S. [1] has found out not only that tech-focused jobs are leading the trend, but also that people holding one of the top emerging jobs, five years ago they were working as software engineers. This provides evidence about the key role played by the software engineering area regarding opportunities in the U.S. labour market.

Actually, this evidence becomes even more important when considering that some of today's top emerging jobs did not exist five years ago. Therefore, teaching software engineering at the higher education level is a must to form people with a relevant set of skills that would allow them to chase the most exciting job opportunities (which today, might not yet exist).

In the large spectrum covered by the software engineering field, agile methods have gained particular attention due to their widespread use on the industrial sector [2]. Moreover, special emphasis is currently being given to DevOps[1] initiatives as a means to ease the achievement of certain agile's principles, in particular those related to iterative development, testing and team collaboration.

Since there is not official standard definition for DevOps [3], there exist many of them out there [4]. However, it can be stated with certain level of certainty that the aim of DevOps is to facilitate the interaction between Development and

---

[1] Abbreviation for the interactions between Dev (Development) and Ops (Operations).

© Springer Nature Switzerland AG 2019
J.-M. Bruel et al. (Eds.): DEVOPS 2018, LNCS 11350, pp. 1–18, 2019.
https://doi.org/10.1007/978-3-030-06019-0_1

Operations to shrink the time since a modification is made by a developer until it makes into production without sacrificing quality.

Contrary to agile methods, which have gained their own place inside the higher education level curricula, DevOps-related subjects have received marginal attention [5]. Thus, there is a clear need to enhance computer science curricula with content oriented to DevOps such that graduates can be better prepared to tackle the industrial sector needs.

The aim of this paper is to present the design of a master-level[2] course aimed at DevOps. The design of this course is based on earlier experiences in teaching topics associated with DevOps, but from a different viewpoint. This design is described providing not only the course's objectives, expected learning outcomes, and grading system, but also how the scheduled activities allow students to reach the expected learning outcomes. The expected cognitive level to be reached by students for each learning outcome is also indicated in the course design description by means of the well-known Bloom's taxonomy. Moreover, it is also indicated the parts of the *Guide to the Software Engineering Body of Knowledge Guide (SWEBOK)* [6] that are covered by each of the course's activities. This allows the reader to have a vision of the coverage offered by the course regarding such standard. This way of providing the description of a course may be also considered as a contribution brought by the paper.

The reader can find information about the SWEBOK and Bloom's taxonomy in Sect. 2, where it is also explained the course's context. Section 3 contains information about the former version of the course and its origins, whereas Sect. 4 reports the teaching experiences for such a version. The description of the new course design can be found in Sect. 5. The paper closes with some discussions about this new proposed design (Sect. 6).

2   Context and Background

2.1   The MiCS

Started in September 2010, the *Master in Informatics and Computer Science (MiCS)* [7] is a 2 years full-time programme (120 ECTS[3]) offered at the University of Luxembourg[4] (UL).

The MiCS's objectives are to introduce students to state-of-the-art computing knowledge in modern and relevant fields, as well as laying the groundwork for either working in high-level industry-oriented environment or continuing PhD studies.

The MiCS courses, which are fully taught in English, are organised in four semesters (S1, S2, S3 and S4). In S1 courses are common to all students as the aim is twofold: to provide a solid foundation on computer science and act as

---

[2] In this paper "master-level" and "graduate" terms are used interchangeably.

[3] European Credit Transfer and Accumulation System.

[4] Created in 2003 and characterised by its multilingual and intercultural environment.

orientation for the courses to pursue in the next semesters. It is in S2 and S3 when students select courses based on available *profiles*.

Each profile is a set of *required* and *elective* courses related to a particular field. A student accomplishes a profile once he has validated all *required* courses. Notice that this distinction between required and elective courses is what allows students to have the chance of following multiple profiles, if desired. It is necessary (but not sufficient) to accomplish at least one profile to obtain the degree. Thus, the way the programme is organised lets students decide their own path through the degree, which is in line with the student-centred education principle promoted by the Bologna process.

Today, there are five available profiles: Adaptive Computing, Communication Systems, Information Security, Intelligent Systems, and Reliable Software Systems. The list of profiles is regularly assessed according to student, professor or industry needs. The course described in this paper belongs to the *Reliable Software Systems* profile and it is taught in S3.

The official MiCS programme description[5] states that, regardless the chosen profile, students who have validated (at least one) profile and collected the 120 ECTS would be able to (sic): *master general and specific topics in computer science, build bridges between several computer science subjects via different profiles, demonstrate a broad understanding of both fundamental and specialised areas of information technologies, stay abreast of the fast technological changes in the rapidly evolving IT sector, work effectively in multinational teams being exposed to the culture diversity of the very international master studies, tackle complex technical problem in IT by productively using a wide range of tools.* These learning outcomes should be key points to be considered when designing a MiCS's course.

2.2   SWEBOK Guide and Bloom's Levels

Today, there is not (in the scientific community) common agreement about the definition of DevOps [4] nor acknowledged standard that can be used as fundamental building block for clarifying what it means and covers [3].

Despite of this lack of common agreement in the community, it is already possible to glimpse with an important level of confidence that contributions brought by DevOps drop into the software engineering field. Therefore, it makes perfect sense to rely on the *Guide to the Software Engineering Body of Knowledge Guide (SWEBOK)* [6] as reference to present the intended knowledge to be covered by a course that addresses software engineering concerns. After all, it was one of the objectives for which it was conceived: *"to provide a foundation for curriculum development and for individual certification and licensing material"*. Therefore, the SWEBOK Guide's content, which is a characterisation of the generally accepted[6] software engineering knowledge, can be used as reference when designing software engineering-related curricula.

---

[5] See *Learning outcomes* at [7].

[6] *"Means the knowledge and practices described are applicable to most projects most of the time, and there is consensus about their value and usefulness"* [6].

The characterisation provided by the SWEBOK Guide is organised in 15 knowledge areas (KAs), representing each of them a chapter of the Guide. This structure is aimed to scope and clarify the place of software engineering regarding other disciplines like Mathematics and Computer Science. Each KA is decomposed in topics (TPs), sometimes also named subareas. Since the aim of TPs is to ease the way readers may find references to the actual body of knowledge, they are also broken down in sub-topics (STPs). Each STP provides a short description including one or more references. In total, the SWEBOK Guide has 100 TPs and 395 STPs. For course design purposes, a coverage course description with respect to the SWEBOK Guide could fairly being done relying on TPs, only. This is exactly the SWEBOK Guide usage intention for the purposes of this paper.

There are others well known curriculum guidelines which could be used to assess the knowledge coverage of a course (or even an entire programme). The closest alternative to the SWEBOK Guide would be the *Curriculum Guidelines for Graduate Degree Programs in Software Engineering* [8] as the others target undergraduate programmes [9,10]. However, one of the main advantages of the SWEBOK Guide is its periodic updating and revision.

While the SWEBOK Guide (or any other standard curriculum guidelines) can be used to clearly indicate the knowledge elements to be covered by a particular course, it is still necessary to specify the expected minimum level of attainment for these targeted knowledge elements. A widely used classification system for such a purpose is the Bloom's taxonomy [11][7] corresponding to the *cognitive* domain[8]. This domain, also known as knowledge-based, is concerned with the acquired knowledge and how such a knowledge it is acquired by a learner.

In particular, the Bloom's taxonomy for the cognitive domain was used in the SWEBOK Guide version 2004 (Appendix D) [13] to determine the levels of learning a software engineering graduated with four years of experience should have on each topic. Thus, the widely usage of Bloom's taxonomy when organising levels of acquired knowledge along with its use in the Guide (version 2004) justify the use of such taxonomy in this paper.

For recalling purposes and to make the paper self-contained, a short description of the Bloom's taxonomy (adapted from [13]) for the cognitive domain is presented in Table 1.

It is worth mentioning that the levels listed and described in Table 1 are hierarchical: reaching learning objectives at a higher level depends on having attained knowledge at the lower levels. For example, a learner aimed at attaining a level L3 will need first to attain levels L1 and L2, in that order.

In this paper, the SWEBOK Guide and the Bloom's taxonomy are used to indicate the KAs/TPs covered by new proposed course's along with the expected level of attainment for each course's learning outcome, respectively.

---

[7] The work has been revised in [12].

[8] The other domains are *affective* and *psychomotor*.

Table 1. Bloom's taxonomy for cognitive domain.

Taxonomy level	Description of level
(L1) Knowledge	Recall data
(L2) Comprehension	Basic understanding without knowing its full implications
(L3) Application	Use a concept learned in the classroom in a new concrete situation
(L4) Analysis	Structure information such that its organisational structure may be understood
(L5) Synthesis	Rely on previous knowledge to produce new knowledge
(L6) Evaluation	Make judgments about ideas using concrete and valid evidence

2.3   Existing DevOps Courses

As mentioned in the introduction, currently DevOps-related courses at the higher education level are the exception rather the rule. At the moment of writing this paper, only four courses have been found matching the following criterion[9]: course targeting graduate students, delivered by an academic institution in the context of a programme oriented to either software engineering, computer science or informatics.

The first of these found courses corresponds to the one delivered by Len Bass at Carnegie Mellon University (USA) since 2016 [14]. Its title is *DevOps: Modern Deployment*, it lasts one semester and counts for 5 ECTS. The course covers both theoretical and practical aspects: beside regular lectures, students have to complete assignments. The course is focused on the implementation of DevOps principles from a software engineering viewpoint, only (i.e. soft-skills are not considered). The text book of reference is *DevOps: A Software Architect's Perspective* [15]. Major topics covered by the course are: DevOps overview, virtualisation (virtual machines and containers), deployment pipeline (continuous integration, continuous delivery), microservice-based architecture, the cloud as platform, basics on security related to networking, and monitoring.

It is at North Carolina State University (USA) where other of the found courses is being offered. It is delivered by Christopher Parnin since (spring) 2015 [16]. The course's title is *DevOps: Modern Software Engineering Practices*, it lasts one semester, and counts for 5 ECTS. The course combines lectures with in-class workshops. Students work in teams to accomplish a project aimed at building a continuous delivery pipeline from scratch. This project is delivered in several milestones. In-class workshops are meant to ease the achievement of each project's milestone. Main topics covered in the course are virtualisation (virtual machines, provisioning, and infrastructure as code), continuous delivery (configuration, build, test, and deploy management), monitoring and analysis. This course is enclosed in graduate programme with professional orientation.

---

[9] Paper's authors are pretty much sure that more courses would match this criteria by the time the paper sees the light of day.

That may explain large number of tools covered through the intensive technical in-class workshops.

The participation at the DevOps18 workshop [17] allowed knowing two other courses addressing DevOps-related topics: one delivered at Polytech Nice-Sophia (France) by Mosser et al. [18], and other at DePaul University (USA) by Jones [19].

The course at Polytech Nice-Sophia, named *Introduction to Software Architecture & DevOps*, is available to students since 2015. It is offered as an optional full semester course that counts for 5 ECTS. Students work in groups over a project where they exercise the topics presented during lectures interleaved with in-class practical work. DevOps-related topics covered by the course are continuous integration, testing frameworks, and containers. The project also requires students to develop. That means, they face with real interactions problems during the execution of the project. This allows students to learn soft-skills to deal with such as problems.

It has been reported that despite of being offered as an optional course, it is close to its full capacity since it was started. This is because students are very aware of the advantages of having DevOps-related skills when applying for a job.

The course delivered at DePaul University, named *Continuous Delivery and Devops*, is a full semester course being offered since (spring) 2015. The course forms part of a programme designed to let students attend the courses while working. It counts for 5 ECTS[10] and the main topics covered are: virtualisation, cloud technologies, and deployment pipeline (i.e. continuous integration, building, deploy, and testing), and configuration management. Beside the technical topics, the course also covers non-technical aspects related to organisational transformation and economics of DevOps, team organisation, collaboration, and software development practices. The course uses as book of reference *Continuous Delivery: Reliable Software Releases Through Build, Test, and Deployment Automation* [20].

3   The Course

3.1   Origins

In early 2012 the paper's authors started a research project in the domain of software engineering. More precisely, the project's goal was to provide a software engineering methodology oriented to students aimed at learning software engineering. Such methodology, was supposed to come along a tool aimed at providing direct support to ease the implementation of such methodology. As result of this research project, the methodology *Messir* and the tool *Excalibur* [21] saw the light of the day by middle 2014[11].

---

[10] This information could not be officially confirmed by the instructor at the writing of the article.

[11] Newer versions of the tool were released after this year, as both the methodology and the tool are under continuous improvement.

The software environment required to manage the *Messir* requirements elicitation process while developing prototypes and beta versions of *Excalibur* was evolving proportionally to the visibility and maturity of the expected outcomes. Thus, the initial software environment made of a simple IDE, some console applications and intensive use of emails turned into a much more complex environment. Figure 1 shows the software environment produced at the moment of releasing the first official version of *Excalibur*. It is worth mentioning that such software environment is still under use and maintenance to handle the delivery of every new *Excalibur* release.

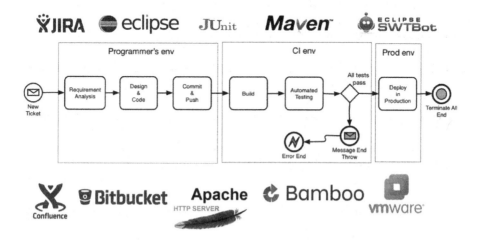

Fig. 1. The *Excalibur* deployment pipeline.

It was in early 2015 when the idea came: teach to students of the MiCS the problems faced, decisions made and lessons learnt during the process that led to the *Excalibur* software development environment. The final objective behind such idea was that at the end of the course students should be capable to specify, design and better implement the necessary means for supporting software engineering when either joining to an ongoing project, or starting one from scratch. The idea became concrete in September of the same year with the implementation of the course entitled *Software Engineering Environments*.

3.2 Initial Design

The request to the MiCS programme's director to deliver such a course ended up with the assignment of a weekly 1.5 hs course in the second year's winter semester (i.e. S3), counting for 4 ECTS and a duration of 14 weeks. It was part of the initial request to make the course part of the *Reliable Software Systems* profile. The course's ECTS, place into the programme, and schedule were set based on the MiCS's curriculum. They are not supposed to change unless the profile is modified, or a restructuring of the MiCS programme takes place (something that has never happened, so far).

The course was designed as a series of lectures and practical sessions. At the beginning of the course, 2 regular lectures were used to (1) recall the fundamentals of software engineering (e.g. definition, phases of software development life cycle, etc.), (2) give a panorama about the categories of tools aimed at supporting the life cycle of a software development project[12], and (3) describe the product quality model introduced in the ISO/IEC 25010:2011 Standard [22] along with its use when assessing both the software under development and the software engineering environment that supports its development. Last, but not least (4), both the *Excalibur* tool and its associated software development environment (see Fig. 1) were used to show the role played by each tool regarding the phase of the software development life cycle and the targeted quality model attributes.

Once presented the theoretical framework, each student was assigned with an individual project. The project was aimed at enhancing the *Excalibur* software engineering environment regarding one (or more) quality attribute. Thus, each student had to start analysing the current status of the given software engineering environment from the targeted quality attribute, and then perform a market analysis regarding the project's goals to choose some tools that would allow such as goals to be reached. Finally, a proof-of-concept implementation using the selected tools had to be made.

An example of a given project was to explore the use of containers as a mechanism to ease the maintenance of the different required environments (development, testing, production), while enhancing the performance compared to virtual machines.

Based on the course's ECTS, the load for an average student was stipulated in 8 weekly hours. From the third week, and until the end of the course, each student had a 1 h individual practical work session to present to his project supervisor[13] the advances achieved with respect to the objectives set in the previous week, and the impediments faced (if any). Support to solve the faced impediments was given by the project supervisor during the practical work session (office hours were also organised in case of more time was required to deal with the impediment). After 3 practical work sessions, each student gave a talk (knows as checkpoint) to the whole class presenting the current status of his project along with a plan of activities to achieve the remaining project's objectives. That made a total of 3 delivered talks for each student.

A report evaluating the work done in the project from a qualitative viewpoint had to be also delivered along with the project's technical artifacts. This report counted for 25% of the final grade, whereas the technical artifacts counted for

---

[12] *Tools* for supporting any single task of the software development project life cycle, *workbenches* which combine in an integrated way two or more tools to cover a subpart of the software development project life cycle, and *environments* which combine tools and workbenches in order to cover the full software development project life cycle.

[13] One of the teaching staff members.

50%. The 3 interleaved talks counted for 12.5% of the final grade. A final wrap-up project presentation, delivered for each student during the exam session, was the last component of the final grade (12.5%). While the report and the project's technical artifacts were only evaluated for the project supervisor, the talks and the final presentation were graded by all teaching staff members[14].

At the end of this course students were expected to attain the following learning outcomes: define the requirements of the software engineering environment required for a particular software development project (LO1); analyse and classify tools based on certain quality attributes (LO2); use, integrate and/or improve existing development tools (LO3); write a report of scientific and technical quality (LO4); and handle (i.e. plan, coordinate, and report activities) a project (LO5).

4   Facts, Feedback and Reflections

Three editions of the course were delivered. These editions were delivered by the same teaching staff composed of one professor and two teaching assistants. The profile of the students remained the same on each edition of the course: 70% got their undergraduate (i.e. bachelor) degree one year ago (20% were graduated at the UL, whereas 80% came from central and east Europe), very few students had industrial experience, and most of them were not used to doing projects. In general, they had good technical abilities, but poor scientific skills.

The first edition (i.e. academic year 2015–2016) resulted in 4 students passing the course, 2 failures and 1 drop out. Students' feedback collected through general discussions organised at the end of checkpoint sessions and individual interviews made during the project follow-up sessions confirmed agreement about the following facts: "hard time to get into the project's subject", "very hard work to get the project done", "high effort vs. course ECTS", and "unbalance between practical and theoretical work".

The student's claims were acknowledged by the teaching staff based on the many office hours given to students to help them to move the projects ahead. As reflection of the first edition, the teaching staff concluded that a more detailed initial project description would be provided to each student, and in particular a clear description of the technical-related objectives to be met. It was also added as requirement to provide management-related information (e.g. track weekly working hours for each working package and report them at each checkpoint). Both measures were aimed at decreasing the risk of getting students lost and/or working overtime on non-relevant tasks. Last, but not least, the teaching staff reviewed the material of the initial theoretical lectures aimed at clarifying how concerns like product under development, software engineering environment, tools, and quality attributes were related to each other, and particularly, their role on the student's projects. Obviously, the teaching staff had to invest a

---

[14] Average of the given grades.

non-negligible time in the preparation of the second edition of the course, in particular in the project descriptions to achieve a equal level of complexity among them (very challenging task).

The second edition of the course (i.e. academic year 2016–2017) resulted in 5 students passing the course, 1 failure and 2 drops out. The student's feedback again gave as result a high agreement about the claims "very hard work to get the project done", and "high effort vs. course ECTS". Despite some punctual facts as overtime work and request for office hours (of some students) by the end of the semester, not real evidence was found by the teaching staff supporting these two claims. Extra inquires revealed that students' claims were based on comparing the requested working load of the course with respect to other programme's course with the same ECTS. Thus, the fact the course was actually requesting the maximum allowed budget for each given ECTS (i.e. 30 h/semester for each given ECTS), plus the execution of a project as part of the requirements to pass it, were (from the student viewpoint) valid concerns when choosing and assessing the course. However, for the teaching staff, both the requested working load and project-based approach were (and still are) non-negotiable items in the design and execution of the course.

The same feedback revealed that much less effort was required by students to get into the project and understand its objectives. Moreover, a better alignment between practice and theory was achieved by the results presented by students during their checkpoints and in the final report. Therefore, the investment made by the teaching staff paid off. However, the time spent by the teaching staff on the course was over the average mainly due to: tough task of defining equally complex projects[15], and their respective supervision.

The third (and last) edition (i.e. academic year 2017–2018) was a game changer for the course's life cycle. The course started with 6 students, but, after four weeks, only 2 students remained coming to the weekly project follow-up meetings. Through informal discussions with the "survivor" students it was confirmed that students quit the course because of its (expected) workload and evaluation mechanism (continuous project-based assessment). This resulted not only in a 4-project description effort discarded, but also in a questioning process about what to do with the course.

It must be mentioned that for one of the two remaining students, the course was elective as he was formally registered in a different profile. This is an important fact to highlight as it shows that (fortunately) there are still motivated students that decide to attend a course based on the expected learning outcomes rather its exigencies. Therefore, based on the willingness to contribute in the development of such kind of students and to continue supporting the MiCS's mission, it was decided to keep delivering the course, but only after redesign it.

---

[15] The number of projects was directly proportional to the number of students registered to the course.

4.1 Objectives for the New Version

The reason for redesigning the course was not only to (1) make its content more DevOps-oriented, but also to (2) achieve an organisation and execution that were more independent of the number students. While the first point was motivated by the need to bring DevOps into the classroom as a first-class subject to better prepare students to modern software industry, the second one's was to minimise the impact of drops out in the course execution, as faced in its last edition. Notice that achieving a course organisation and execution that is (up to certain level) independent of the number of participants helps not only when the numbers decreases, but also increases.

It has to be recognised that the fact of redesigning the course allowed advertising it as a sort of "new course" covering a trending topic as DevOps. This, may help having more registered students, but definitely not to avoid their later drop out. Thus, the new version of the course had to be designed to favour interactivity and student engagement.

The next session describes the new design of the course aimed at attaining the objectives earlier mentioned while coping with the challenges imposed by the context: students (very often) not motivated, with weak analytical and technical skills, and not used to doing project-based courses that require regular continuous work.

5 New Version

5.1 Activities and Organisation

Here it is explained what are the activities to be done by teachers and students during the course such that the objectives can be reached. Before presenting these activities along with their respective descriptions, it is worth explaining that most of the types of such as activities are taken from the course's initial design. This is because project-based teaching, blended with traditional lectures and tutoring sessions has already proved to be successful as knowledge transfer mechanism.

Project Presentation: activity performed by the teaching staff at the inaugural lecture of the course. The project plays a central role in the course as it is the chosen pedagogical vehicle to let student construct knowledge and skills based on the tasks required to be performed by themselves in order to reach the project's objectives. The success of this pedagogical approach (clearly confirmed in the course's previous editions as due reported) depends on the precision and clarity of the project's objectives description. Thus, a clear presentation relying on the *Excalibur* case study is given to let students understand what is a deployment pipeline as this is the aim of the project: implement a deployment pipeline based on open source technologies that work on a unix-based OS. Any other conditions that may apply over the project (like that the product to pass through the pipeline has to be a web app) are also clearly stated. It is emphasised that the intention is to achieve a proof-of-concept deployment pipeline, so aspects like performance or reliability will not be evaluated. That, however, does not impede students to take into consideration such concerns when developing the project.

It is not part of the project the development of the product to demonstrate the working of the pipeline. This means that each group has to pay special attention when choosing the product: it has to help achieving the project's goal rather than adding complexity. The selected product would make each project unique with respect to each other, regarding the technical solution to be provided. However, the overall project's objectives and conditions are the same for each group, regardless the chosen product (i.e. a common project for all the groups). The project is done in groups, and students are free to decide about the group's composition.

Lecture: activity performed by the teaching staff once the project has been presented. Lectures are aimed at teaching the relevant concepts associated to DevOps used in the project. However, it is not the interest of the course's lectures to teach how a particular tool works, but the concepts associated to the use of such a tool, in particular highlighting the requirements that such tool aims to tackle. A total of six lectures are delivered along the semester. The first three weeks of the course are mainly aimed at lectures. The remaining ones are separated two/threes weeks each other as other project-related activities start being interleaved. The initial condensed number of lectures are aimed at presenting the DevOps theoretical background that scopes the project. They will later leave place to sessions oriented to management and follow-up of the project. The topics covered by the lectures are aligned with the project's objectives. Thus, after introduced DevOps to present its definition(s), principles, practices, its role on the software engineering life cycle, and the different roles and responsibilities (first lecture), the deployment pipeline concept (architecture, environments, tools and selection criterion) is presented (second lecture). It is also part of this lecture to introduce the notion of quality[16] and how such notion applies both to the pipeline and the product(s) that will go through it. The remaining lectures focus on the pipelines concerns, so configuration management (third lecture), build management (fourth lecture), test management (fifth), and deploy and release management (sixth lecture) are the covered topics. The project's objectives (and then, covered topics) were chosen based on the recommendations given in [5,17], teaching staff's experience and context's constraints (i.e. course duration and assigned workload). The books given as main references to the students (and required to consult) are [15] and [20]. Other extra relevant references (but not required during the course) are [23] and [24].

---

[16] It is planned to keep using the ISO/IEC 25010:2011 Standard [22] to introduce the notion of product quality model.

Short Product Presentation: activity assigned to each group, and performed by one (or more) member of the group as an informal presentation. This activity is given as assignment for the second week. Each group has to present a list of possible products to be used with the deployment pipeline. The presentation's form is free, and it is followed by a open discussion. This should help each group to choose the best product. The main aim of this activity, beside an early selection of the product, is to foster students interaction and engagement with the project. It is a non-graded activity.

Project Follow-Up Session: activity performed by students and the teach staff in joint way. Each group is supervised by a member of the teaching staff (aka project supervisor). A member of the group chairs the session. The chair opens the session handling a (free) document that reports the time spent: coding, designing, using a particular tool, learning about a particular tool, and coordinating with members of the group. These times[17] have be detailed for each group member. The aim of requesting students to track these times is twofold: detect students' overtimes/downtime; and assess actual project workload (very useful for improving future editions of the course). The session continues with the report of work done, and what to do for the next session. The last part of the session is used to resolve the encountered impediments, if any. There are five follow-up sessions scheduled such that there is always one before a checkpoint. The chairing of the session is a rotating post among group's students. The supervisor grades each session based on the quality of the information provided and formulation of the encounter impediments.

Checkpoint: activity assigned to each student's group, which consists in presenting the advances of the group's project. This presentation consists in a 10–15 min talk where one single member of the group reports the work done by the group. There are three checkpoints, so each group's student has to deliver (at least) one presentation[18]. The first checkpoint takes place in the fifth week. There are four weeks between each consecutive checkpoint. In the first checkpoint the group is aimed at presenting the product to be used to demonstrate the functioning of the deployment pipeline. A first design of such pipeline, including candidate tools and quality attributes to be addressed must also be included. In the second checkpoint the group should present how virtualisation and provisioning tools are used to setup the different environments. It is also in this checkpoint that the presence and correct functioning of a continuous integration server (i.e. commits in a version control system end up in launching a build plan). The final checkpoint is devoted to present the final version of the deployment pipeline architecture, selected tools, and quality attributes addressed. A demo of a feedback loop[19] provided by the deployment pipeline is a must in the final

---

[17] Tracking times taken from [14].

[18] While the conditions would allow it, groups will be made of up to 3 students.

[19] Commit, build, automated test cases execution, deploy (if all test cases have passed).

checkpoint. Each checkpoint is graded by the teaching staff. The project deliverables (i.e. scripts, source code, test cases, readme file, ...) have to be submitted in the morning of the last checkpoint's day.

Report Writing: activity assigned to each student's group and expected to be performed in a collaborative manner by all members of the group. The report has to describe the objectives of the project executed by the group, requirements, assumptions, and constraints. Special emphasis has to be given not only in the description of the proposed solution, but also in the justification of the choices led to such solution. It is expected that students write the report in a scientific manner (e.g. precise description of the problem, its context, found evidence, ...), but still providing relevant technical information about the developed solution. The report must contain between 3000 and 4000 words, and have a lesson learnt section. It has to be submitted two weeks after the official end of course.

Report Reviewing: activity performed both for each teaching staff member and students. This activity consists in reviewing the report to check the accuracy of its content from the technical and scientific viewpoint according to the given report's objectives. While each teaching staff member has to review every single report, a student is expected to review only one non-authored report. A report is reviewed for every teaching member and two students, providing each of them a grade (that is differently weighted). The report's grade goes to each of its authors. Note that this activity introduces peer-assessment. Depending on how good (or bad) the student performs his review he may gain (loss) extra points to his individual grade. More details are provided below in the grading section. Each student has one week to perform the review of the report.

5.2   Grading

Students are evaluated based on the activities they perform. Except for the assessment of the project report review (where the student is evaluated individually), the other evaluations are group-based: i.e. the same grade is given to every group member. Below, it is detailed how the final grade of a particular student is computed:

- Project deliverables: 50%
- Report: 25% (includes peer reviewing)
- Checkpoints: 12.5%
- Project management: 12.5% (the capability to report the tracking indicated times, along with the working plan (done/to-do/impediments)).

The peer-reviewing grading system deserves an explanation in itself. The assessment of the report, which counts for 25%, is made by the teaching staff and two non-authored students. Below it is shown how this 25% is decomposed depending on the person's profile:

- Average (Teaching staff): 40%
- Student 1: 30%
- Student 2: 30%

The peer-reviewing activity made by a student is "paid" in points for his grade. Depending on the quality of the performed review, he may either win or loss points. Thus, a teaching staff member will assess the student's review to decide how many points he gets (from −30% to 30% of the report's grade).

5.3   Learning Outcomes

The execution of the activities described in the previous section would let students attain the following learning outcomes: design and implement a deployment pipeline for a particular software development project (LO1); classify tools based on certain quality attributes (LO2); use, and integrate existing tools (LO3); write a report of scientific and technical quality (LO4); and plan, coordinate, and report activities in a multi-participant project (LO5). It is not surprising that several learning outcomes are the same as in course's previous edition since some type of activities were kept in the new course design.

Table 2 shows how each of the activities performed along the course contributes to the achievement of the claimed learning outcomes. Moreover, the same table describes the covered SWEBOK knowledge by each activity, allowing to get an overall idea of the coverage provided by the course with respect to such standard. Table 3 complements the mapping activity-learning outcomes with information about the cognitive level reached by each student passing the course with regard each of the claimed learning outcomes.

6   Discussion

Making the course oriented to DevOps was not a random or marketing choice. Former editions of the course have already covered some subjects related to DevOps like virtualisation, continuous integration and automated testing. The new version not only better organises these subjects, but also introduces others to show how they could be efficiently integrated to achieve a pipeline that covers continuous integration, building, testing, and deployment. Thus, the previous experiences on teaching and working (i.e. *Excalibur* case study) with these subjects provides certain guaranties about the mastering level of the subjects to be taught. Moreover, the topics covered by the course justifies the claimed MiCS's learning outcome that students once have completed the programme would *"stay abreast of the fast technological changes in the rapidly evolving IT sector"* and be able to *"tackle complex technical problem in IT by productively using a wide range of tools"*.

DevOps is not only about advanced technical aspects related to the software engineering, but also about culture and organisation [14]. The project-based pedagogical methodology allows to achieve a holistic approach that encloses the

Table 2. Mapping between activities, SWEBOK knowledge areas/topics, and addressed learning outcomes.

Activity	SWEBOK coverage	Addressed learning outcome
Introduction to DevOps (Lecture)	KA1: TP1	LO1, LO3
	KA8: TP1, TP2	
	KA11: TP2, TP3	
Deployment pipeline (Lecture)	KA2: TP3	LO1, LO2, LO3
	KA3: TP1	
	KA4: TP1, TP2	
	KA6: TP1	
	KA10: TP1	
Configuration management (Lecture)	KA6: TP1, TP2, TP3	LO1, LO3
Build management (Lecture)	KA6: TP6	LO1, LO3
Test management (Lecture)	KA4	LO1, LO3
Deploy and release management (Lecture)	KA6: TP6	LO1, LO3
Short product presentation (Talk)	KA1: TP4	LO2, LO5
	KA2: TP3	
	KA3: TP4	
	KA4: TP1, TP2, TP6	
Project follow-up session (Meeting)	KA1: TP5, TP6	LO1, LO2, LO3, LO5
	KA11: STP1.9, TP2, TP3	
Deployment pipeline implementation (out of class work)	KA2:TP3	LO1, LO2, LO3, LO5
	KA3: TP3	
	KA6	
	KA10	
	KA15: TP1, TP4	
Checkpoint (Talk)	KA7: TP2, TP3	LO1, LO2, LO3, LO5
	KA11: TP2, TP3	
Report writing (out of class work)	KA11: TP2, TP3	LO4, LO5
Report reviewing (out of class work)	KA11: TP3	LO4

three dimensions. This teaching approach, already used in the previous editions of the course, is reinforced in the new edition by requesting students to work in groups. This decision expects to enhance interaction and recreate social environments where soft skills can be developed. Due to the multicultural environment that characterises the MiCs, team work guarantees the achievement of the claimed programme's learning outcome: *"students would be able to work effectively in multinational teams being exposed to the culture diversity"*. Notice, that people with such skill are very valuable in any professional sector.

Table 3. Bloom's level reached for each learning outcome.

Learning outcome	Bloom's level
LO1	Application (L3)
LO2	Analysis (L4)
LO3	Application (L3)
LO4	Synthesis (L5)
LO5	Application (L3)

Assigning the same project to every group let the teaching staff avoid the challenge task of producing different projects but with equal complexity. This choice also helps to ensure consistency when evaluating groups' work.

Yet another advantage of working on a common project is related to the organisation and execution of the course as it is not any more dependent on the number of registered students (what was the case in former editions of the course). Based on earlier experience, a teaching staff composed of two people[20] can handle a class of up to 12 students without quality lost.

A novelty introduced in the new design is peer-assessment. This was decided to foster the academic dimension of the master programme: reviewing articles is part of the duties of a researcher. Moreover, it is believed that such activity may help enhancing student's motivation and engagement with the course.

The use of the SWEBOK and Bloom's taxonomy not only bring clarity over the specification of a course, but also, they can be used later to assess the execution of the course. Based on the executed activities and student's performance (grades, feedback) it can be judged whether the SWEBOK's TPs were covered and the learning outcomes attained as expected, respectively.

It is expected that, despite of the context-specific constraints, the design of the course presented in the paper could be taken as reference by other instructors when facing with the challenging task of teaching DevOps.

References

1. LinkedIn Economic Graph Team: LinkedIn's 2017 U.S. Emerging Jobs Report, December 2017. https://economicgraph.linkedin.com/research/LinkedIns-2017-US-Emerging-Jobs-Report

2. VersionOne: 11th annual state of agile report (2017). https://explore.versionone.com/state-of-agile/versionone-11th-annual-state-of-agile-report-2

3. Standard, N.I.: DevOps - standard for building reliable and secure systems including application build, package and deployment (2016). https://standards.ieee.org/develop/project/2675.html

4. Jabbari, R., bin Ali, N., Petersen, K., Tanveer, B.: What is DevOps?: a systematic mapping study on definitions and practices. In: Proceedings of the Scientific Workshop Proceedings of XP 2016. XP 2016 Workshops, pp. 12:1–12:11. ACM, New York (2016)

---

[20] Teaching staff composition to deliver the new version of the course.

5. DevOps Educator Workshop: First DevOps Educators Workshop, November 2016. https://github.com/devopseducator/2016workshop
6. Society, I.C., Bourque, P., Fairley, R.E.: Guide to the Software Engineering Body of Knowledge (SWEBOK(R)): Version 3.0, 3rd edn. IEEE Computer Society Press, Los Alamitos (2014)
7. MiCS: Master in information and computer sciences (2010). https://mics.uni.lu
8. Pyster, A., et al.: Graduate software engineering 2009 (GSwE2009) curriculum guidelines for graduate degree programs in software engineering. Stevens Institute of Technology (2009)
9. Joint Task Force on Computing Curricula, Association for Computing Machinery (ACM) and IEEE Computer Society: Computer Science Curricula: Curriculum Guidelines for Undergraduate Degree Programs in Computer Science. ACM, New York (2013). ACM Order Number: 999133
10. The Joint Task Force on Computing Curricula: Curriculum guidelines for undergraduate degree programs in software engineering. Technical report, New York, NY, USA (2015)
11. Bloom, B.: Taxonomy of Educational Objectives: The Classification of Educational Goals. Mackay, New York (1956)
12. Anderson, L., Krathwohl, D., Bloom, B.: A Taxonomy for Learning, Teaching, and Assessing: A Revision of Bloom's Taxonomy of Educational Objectives. Longman, New York (2001)
13. IEEE Computer Society: Guide to the software engineering body of knowledge 2004 version. SWEBOK 2004 Guide to the Software Engineering Body of Knowledge (2004)
14. Bass, L.: DevOps: Modern Deployment (2017). http://mse.isri.cmu.edu/software-engineering/Courses/17-611-DevOps-Modern-Deployment.html
15. Bass, L., Weber, I.M., Zhu, L.: DevOps: A Software Architect's Perspective. Addison-Wesley Professional, New York (2015)
16. Parnin, C.J.: DevOps: modern software engineering practices, August 2017. https://wolfware.ncsu.edu/courses/details/?sis_id=SIS:2018:1:1:CSC:519:001
17. DEVOPS18: First international workshop on software engineering for continuous development and new paradigms of software production and deployment (2018). https://www.laser-foundation.org/devops/2018/
18. Mosser, S., Pinna-Déry, A.-M., Collet, P., Molines, G.: Introduction to software architecture and DevOps (2017). https://github.com/mosser/isa-devops
19. Jones, C.: Continuous delivery and DevOps (2017). https://www.cdm.depaul.edu/academics/pages/classinfo.aspx?Term=20182&ClassNbr=21100&fid=258484
20. Humble, J., Farley, D.: Continuous Delivery: Reliable Software Releases Through Build, Test, and Deployment Automation, 1st edn. Addison-Wesley Professional, New York (2010)
21. Guelfi, N., Capozucca, A., Ries, B.: Website of the Messir Method and the Excalibur Environment (2014). https://messir.uni.lu
22. ISO/IEC: ISO/IEC 25010 - Systems and software engineering - Systems and software Quality Requirements and Evaluation (SQuaRE) - System and software quality models. ISO/IEC 13211-1 (2011)
23. Davis, J., Daniels, K.: Effective DevOps: Building a Culture of Collaboration, Affinity, and Tooling at Scale, 1st edn. O'Reilly Media, Inc., Sebastopol (2016)
24. Httermann, M.: DevOps for Developers, 1st edn. Apress, Berkely (2012)

Stepwise Adoption of Continuous Delivery in Model-Driven Engineering

Jokin Garcia[1](✉) and Jordi Cabot[2](✉)

[1] IK4-IKERLAN, Arrasate, Spain
jgarcia@ikerlan.es
[2] ICREA-UOC, Barcelona, Spain
jordi.cabot@icrea.cat

Abstract. *Continuous Delivery* (CD) and, in general, *Continuous Software Engineering* (CSE) is becoming the norm. Still, current practices and available integration platforms are too code-oriented. They are not well adapted to work with other, non text-based, software artifacts typically produced during early phases of the software engineering lifecycle. This is especially problematic for teams adopting a *Model-Driven Engineering* (MDE) approach to software development where several (meta)models (and model transformations) are built and executed as part of the development process. Typically, (part of) the code is automatically generated from such models. Therefore, in a complete CD process, changes in a model should trigger changes on the generated code when appropriate.

A step further would be to apply CD practices to the development of modeling artefacts themselves. Analogously to "traditional" CD, where the goal is to have the mainline codebase always in a deployable state, the aim would be to have the modeling infrastructure always ready to be used. Those models could be the final product themselves or an intermediate artifact in a complete CSE process as described above.

Either way, a tighter integration between CD and MDE would benefit software practitioners by providing them with complete CSE, covering also analysis and design stages of the process.

Keywords: Continuous Evolution · Continuous Delivery ·
Model-Driven Engineering

1 Introduction

Gone are the days when developing projects required a mere compiler. Nowadays, software engineering is much more complex and heterogeneous, often involving several stacks, languages, and frameworks.

Software building tools have evolved accordingly and we have gone from *make* to *Gradle*, passing through *Ant* and *Maven*. Besides, agile practices and specifically *Continuous Delivery* (CD) has encouraged a more frequent software integration and testing. This philosophy of faster release cycles has expanded to

© Springer Nature Switzerland AG 2019
J.-M. Bruel et al. (Eds.): DEVOPS 2018, LNCS 11350, pp. 19–32, 2019.
https://doi.org/10.1007/978-3-030-06019-0_2

the organizational level (e.g. for a rapid time-to-market and quality feedback) in what it is known as *Continuous Software Engineering* (CSE).

Unfortunately, so far this trend has left aside another parallel trend in software engineering: *Model-Driven Engineering* (MDE) [5]. MDE advocates for the rigorous use of models as key artifacts in all software engineering activities. Though this idea is far from new and we are still learning how to best effectively apply it in practice, recent studies suggest an increasing uptake of MDE and a more widespread use than commonly believed [22], specially when taking MDE on a broad sense (e.g. models beyond code-generation approaches, for instance, models used for communication purposes or software documentation).

Therefore, it is evident that software models play some role in most software development projects. Challenges for MDE adoption include social and organizational factors but also tool-related ones [23] such as synchronization problems between models and code. Clearly, a tighter integration between CD and MDE would benefit software practitioners by providing them with a more complete CSE, covering also analysis and design stages of the process. This integration is what we call Continuous Model-Driven Engineering.

This paper will be looking at this integration at two different levels. First, it will discuss how to add modeling artifacts as standalone executable components in a standard CD pipeline aimed at releasing a new software version.

Then, it will cover a more complex scenario where the target of the CD is a MDE artifact itself built as the result of a collaboration in a MDE ecosystem (a.k.a. megamodel in literature). Indeed, in many projects, the "modeling side" is a combination of models (possibly conforming to different metamodels, where each metamodel defines the possible set of well-formed models to be created with that language, similar to the relationship between programs and language grammars), model-to-model and model-to-text transformations (for the former, input and output are models, for the latter, the output is a text file, e.g. a piece of code generated from a model). Transformations can also be regarded as models on their own and conform to specific model transformation languages. As for the modeling languages, projects usually combine general modeling languages like UML with several *Domain-Specific Languages* (DSLs). DSLs can be reused from other projects or be developed adhoc for the current one, which implies creating their abstract syntax (grammar) and concrete syntax (notation) as part of the project itself.

Figure 1 tries to sketch how these elements relate to each other. As shown in Fig. 1, model *Ma* is transformed into model *Mb* using a M2M transformation, and then model *Mb* is transformed into code through a M2T transformation. As can be seen from the number of relationships, CD of a MDE artifact is a complex task where changes on one artifact can trigger changes on several others that need to co-evolve together. This process requires tools for model comparison, merging, testing,... that react accordingly to (meta)model changes. While specific couples of on-demand evolution scenarios have been studied (metamodels-models [8], metamodels-transformations [12] and metamodels-editors [9]) no holistic and global approach has been proposed so far.

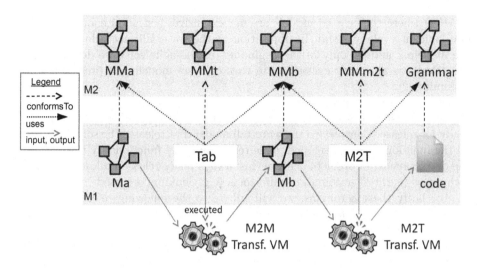

Fig. 1. MDE architecture

The remainder of the paper is structured as follows. Section 2 tries to clarify the glossary of terms that the mixture of Continuous* and Model-Driven domains entails. In Sect. 3 we analyze how can models can be integrated in CD processes and tools. Then, in Sect. 4 it is proposed to use CD practices to manage the evolution of MDE artifacts. Section 5 exposes related work; and finally, in Sect. 6 we conclude with a summary and future challenges.

2 Background

The Agile Manifesto was born in 2001. This manifesto claimed four values and twelve principles. The values are well-known: individuals and interactions over processes and tools, working software over comprehensive documentation, customer collaboration over contract negotiation and responding to change over following a plan. The principles are as well described in the manifesto [4].

In this agile context, and opposite to what it could be thought, teams are more likely to model than in traditional methodologies [23], as modeling supports many of their principles, as communication, rapid feedback or quality. MDE is a paradigm that uses models to develop software. Models conform to metamodels, and are transformed to other models or to code, building an ecosystem of related artifacts (Fig. 1). These models can be used in workflows where they can be: validated, merged, compared, transformed, etc. [18]. These tasks are not in solitary confinement: they need to be integrated in heterogeneous projects managed with CD methodologies.

Rooted in the spirit of the manifesto, the Agile Model Driven Development (AMDD) method was conceived to ensure the emergence of effective architectures, requirements and designs. As the name suggests, AMDD is an agile version of MDD where the created models are not extensive, just good enough for the development cycle at hand. In opposition to the waterfall methodology where the modeling is done only in the beginning, in the agile software development lifecycle there are many cycles and in each of them modeling is present at the beginning [2].

The last step is introducing as well agility in the release step. Continuous Delivery is a subset of agile that emphasizes the need for software to be always ready for release. Contrary to the waterfall model that releases the software once all the functionality is developed, agile releases partial functionality throughout the development. In order to achieve this always-ready release philosophy, some techniques (e.g. test automation) and tools (e.g. Jenkins) are used.

To clarify these acronyms, we will adhere to the following reference terminology [15]: *Continuous Integration (CI)* is the frequent integration of code by all the members of a project. Build and tests are accomplished automatically in order to detect integration errors as soon as possible. *Continuous Delivery (CD)* is an extension of CI where it is guaranteed that the mainline is always in a deployable state, and that this deployment can be done in "one click". Opposed to CD where the deployment is manual, in *Continuous Deployment*, every time there is a commit, the software is automatically deployed to production. Continuous Software Engineering (CSE) is the organizational and cultural attempt to connect development with business strategy. All these practices are encompassed in what is known as Continuous*. In this paper we are going to use the term Continuous Delivery (CD), as it is closest to our proposal of always keeping the MDE infrastructure ready to be executed.

In order to achieve this automatic deployment, these techniques are based on the automation of the build. Specifically, a *deployment pipeline* divides and executes automatically different stages of the build; which are generally compilation, tests and deployment. This stages are, as well, broken up into jobs. This pipeline provides visibility of the whole process.

3   Integration of MDE Tools in CD

In most software development projects, there is some degree of model use [22]. MDE components must collaborate with each other but also interface with other non-MDE tools, including CD servers [19], in a global CSE context.

This section looks at whether this integration is possible, focusing on the basic scenario of individual MDE artifacts used as part of a larger software development CD scenario. The key requirement of CD servers like Jenkins[1] is that an IDE cannot be used to build the software, as it does not guarantee a repeatable build. To be part of a CD pipeline, MDE tools must be able to be wrapped as jobs to be executed standalone, i.e. without human intervention, when called by the CD server.

Therefore, at its simplest level, integration of MDE in CD will be possible if we find at least one MDE tool, for each major MDE activity, offering some

---

[1] https://jenkins-ci.org/.

kind of external interface (via API or shell access) that allows its integration in CD pipeline. And indeed, we do. Table 1 lists examples of such tools for each activity.

Table 1. Example of available tools for each modeling task

Modeling task	Tool example
Modeling framework	EMF[a]
Model to model transformation	ATL, Epsilon ETL, QVT
Model to text transformation	Acceleo, Epsilon EGL, Xpand
Model comparison	EMFCompare, Epsilon ECL
Model weaving/composition/merge	AMW, Epsilon EML
Model injection/extraction	Xtext, EMFText
Model validation	EMFtoCSP, Epsilon EVL

[a]One difference of running EMF standalone is that the application is unaware of plug-ins, so registrations have to be done now in the code

This alone is powerful enough to build CD pipelines for (model-based) development projects.

Illustrating Example

As an example of MDE infrastructure, we are going to use a very common *Forward Engineering* (FE) process, where models are used to design a solution that is later automatically transformed into a CRUD-based web application. This scenario is illustrated in Fig. 2:

1. The left-bottom part shows a UML class diagram depicting the need to store information about books and bookshops.
2. A transformation uses this schema definition to generate a navigation model [6] with the usual CRUD pages as default website structure.
3. A final model-to-text transformation generates the code corresponding to the forms, pages and tables for the example.

The class diagram conforms to the UML language while the navigation model is represented as an object diagram conforming to a small DSL called sWML (*Simple Web Modeling Language* [5], inspired in IFML [6]). The transformation is written in ATL and describes how to generate sWML models from UML ones. The upper rule bootstraps the sWML model while the lower one iterates through the UML model and, for each class it founds, it creates the corresponding CRUD pages. More details on this example can be found in [1].

This transformation chain (from UML to sWML and from sWML to code) is implemented in the CD server (Jenkins) by creating two new jobs, one per transformation (see the last two jobs in Fig. 3). This way we enable: the chaining

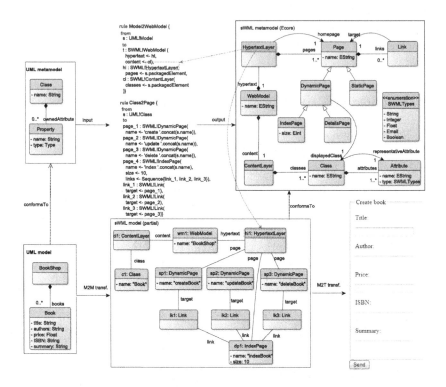

Fig. 2. Example of a model-based software process

of modeling tasks (M2T is automatically executed when M2M finalizes), visualization of their status (if there is any error in the execution or resulting model or code) and the immediate re-execution of the process when a model is updated (either at the UML or sWML levels). Reactivity is achieved thanks to a hook between the SCM and Jenkins[2], that allows the execution of jobs as triggers after an update in the software repository.

Still, this integration is straightforward but quite dumb in the sense that the CD server sees models as pure text/XML artifacts and therefore is unable to use the model semantics to better manage the pipeline, for instance by preventing triggering the transformations when the model update does not have any real impact in the rest of the chain. We discuss a more advanced integration in the next section.

4   Continuous Evolution of MDE Infrastructure

All MDE elements in the previous example are a software product on its own that have followed as well a build and deploy process, and therefore may benefit

---

[2] https://wiki.jenkins-ci.org/display/JENKINS/Git+Plugin.

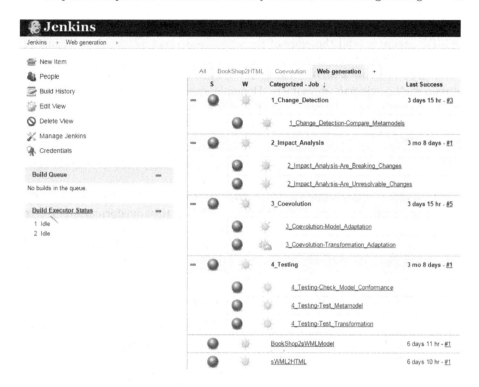

Fig. 3. Jenkins pipeline of the co-evolution process

from being the target of a CD process themselves to bring all CD benefits to the MDE domain (or to best exploit them when part of a more global CD process). These benefits include:

- Reactivity: The co-evolution process does not have to be launched by the developer manually anymore. Everytime a new change is committed in the repository, the process will be triggered automatically.
- Parallelization: Different co-evolution solutions are given depending on the affected artifacts. Instead of applying them one by one, a CD server allows to execute in the same time all of them.
- Visibility: of the process and its state.
- Time saving: Co-evolution and testing is only executed if the impact analysis determines that it is actually needed.
- Flexibility: We may not need the modeling expert. The domain expert can execute the whole process alone.

Due to the complex and non-linear nature of MDE ecosystems, we must deal with changes at two different levels: the model level but also the metamodel one, not usually the case when developing more traditional software products where the grammars and libraries imported in the project hardly ever change during the development; instead in MDE, the DSLs change much more often.

Covering this scenario is important to ensure the long-term maintainability of the MDE artifacts (and therefore of the software depending on them) as part of a *Continuous Evolution* [11] effort.

When co-evolving a MDE ecosystem, we must take into account the coupling between each single pair of artifacts. Dependencies between different artifacts in a MDE ecosystem can be seen in Fig. 1. These are the most common coupling cases, that happen when the metamodel, which is the cornerstone of the ecosystem, evolves:

- Metamodel - model: When a metamodel evolves, instances of that metamodel have to be adapted to changes [8].
- Metamodel - transformation: Transformations are defined between metamodel elements, so when any of the metamodels of the transformation (source or target) evolves, it has to be adapted to that evolution as well [12].
- Metamodel - editors: When the metamodel defining the abstract syntax of an editor changes, the rest of the editor artifacts are affected [9].

4.1 Evolution Scenario: An Example Implementation

Coming back to our example of Fig. 2, we propose a simple evolution scenario: the sWML metamodel evolves, renaming the name of the type *HypertextLayer* to *NavigationLayer*. This change forces us to change the references to that type in the transformations using it as input/output element and update all model elements that instantiate that type to reclassify them. We can see these impacts as dotted arrows in the figure.

In a naive MDE - CD integration (as the one sketched in the previous section), any change on a MDE artifact will trigger an update on all the depending elements which in turn could fire further changes down the lane. Ideally, the CD server should be smarter than that and be able to understand enough the MDE artifacts it manages in order to optimally coevolve them.

Figure 3 shows how our CRUD-based example has been implemented as a fully automated pipeline in a CD server (Jenkins). For clarity, jobs have been divided into phases:

1. **Change detection:** analyzing and classifying the kind of changes that have occurred after every update by comparing the two versions of the artifact. When the new version of the metamodel is committed, the process is triggered. Both metamodel versions will be compared by calling the tool EMF-Compare in charge of generating a difference model that represents the differences between the two versions of the metamodel. In this case, it will result in a *Rename Class* type of change. Notice that in this step, a textual comparison tool is not enough: a tool that deals with model semantics is needed.
2. **Impact analysis:** it is assessed what parts of the system are likely to be affected by a change on the related artifacts running an impact analysis algorithm. It decides, for each depending artifact, whether the changes should be classified into:

- *Non Breaking Changes (NBC)*: changes that do not have any impact.
- *Breaking and Resolvable Changes (BRC)* changes that have an impact but that can be resolved automatically.
- and *Breaking and Unresolvable Changes (BUC)* changes that have an impact that requires human intervention.

As we can see in Fig. 3, there is one job for detecting breaking changes and another for unresolvable changes. The impact analysis has been implemented as an ATL transformation wrapped in Java. The *Rename Class* would be classified as a BRC type.

3. **Synchronization:** Once we know the affected artifacts (and the kind of changes relevant to them), they are synchronized: for NBCs, the CD server should not propagate anything, for BRCs it should evolve the depending element automatically and for BUCs mark it as in an erroneous state for manual reviewing. This step is implemented via an ATL transformation wrapped in Java. In the example, as it is a BRC, the co-evolution jobs will adapt both the models conforming to the *sWML* metamodel and the model to model transformation. In the case of models, *HypertextLayer* elements will be renamed; and in the ATL transformation, elements of type *OclModelElement* will be renamed as well. This is because there is a coupling between *EClass* element in Ecore and *OclModelElement* in ATL metamodel. As we can see in the pipeline, there is one job for coevolving models and another one for coevolving transformations.

4. **Testing** the results. Conformance verifications have been implemented using EMF default checking mechanisms. In the pipeline, there are several testing jobs, one per artifacts: model, metamodel and transformation.

The corresponding jobs have been linked using the *post-build* section mechanism provided by Jenkins, where all elements are tested after any change and feedback is provided if any error is detected (see [1] for the full details).

As we can see, this smarter integration would save a lot of time and, potentially, many unnecessary redeployments in any non-trivial system. In the case of Forward Engineering scenarios where code is generated, we avoid all the generation and testing of code.

Nevertheless, from the naive to the smart integration approaches we have a full range of intermediate solutions depending on the characteristics of the project and the availability of the model-based components required for each of the four previous tasks in the specific project context.

4.2   Adoption Levels

Therefore, a step-wise adoption of Continuous MDE for software companies could follow the phases described next, which progressively raise the level of adoption:

Using Generic Support. Without any specific model support, the CD server treats models as plain text and is not aware of their structure at all. Dependencies

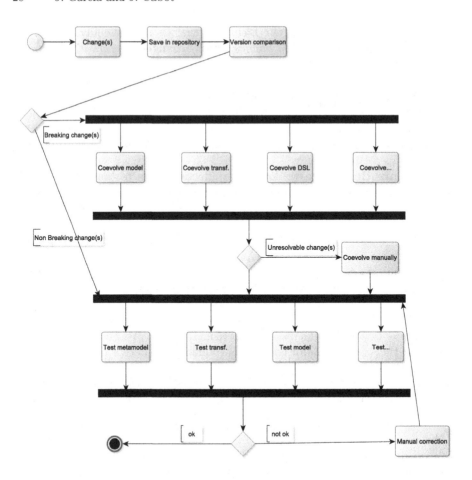

Fig. 4. Conditional and parallel execution of coevolution jobs

between jobs have to be manually added and co-evolution is limited to alerting developers when an element needs to be manually reviewed. Any new model version triggers all depending jobs.

With Co-evolution Support. We can add co-evolution support for coupled MDE artifacts. As described in the evolution scenario and (see also the generic process described the Fig. 4), a model comparison job is triggered to interpret model changes for a given artifact when a new version of the model is saved in the repository.

– If there are breaking changes, co-evolution jobs (one for each coupled element type) take care of processing those changes and determining whether the depending elements need to be resynchronised. Those jobs are parallelizable.

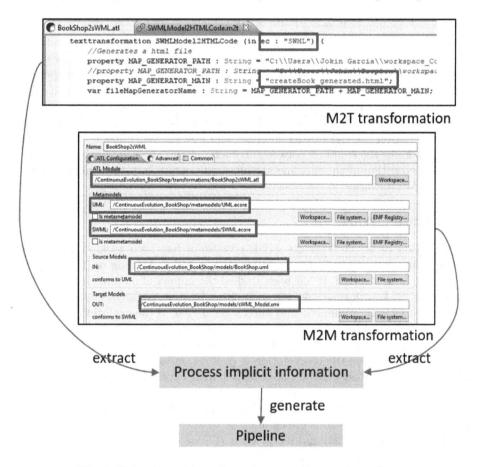

Fig. 5. Extraction of transformation execution configurations

Then, if there was any unresolvable change, developers will be notified to do a manual co-evolution. After that, tests will be executed in parallel.

– If there are not breaking changes, tests are executed directly, without passing through the co-evolution step.

This conditional and parallel execution shortens the deployment time. The limitation of this approach is that jobs are still manually added as part of the pipeline definition phase but the pipeline is automatically executed (except for BUCs) afterwards.

Automatizing the Process. As a final step in the integration between MDE and Continuous Delivery, we could automate the definition of the pipeline itself. The initial configuration of the CD server can be generated programmatically. For instance, the pipeline feature in Jenkins 2.0 (or Job DSL plugin[3] in previous

---

[3] https://wiki.jenkins-ci.org/display/JENKINS/Job+DSL+Plugin.

versions of Jenkins) allows to build Jenkins jobs using a simple DSL on top of Groovy, which can be integrated in version control systems. This script, in turn, could be generated based on the analysis of the (implicit or explicit) dependencies between artifacts like a transformations configuration launch with specific reference to the input/output metamodels. In Fig. 5 we can see the implicit process information in the m2t and m2m transformations regarding the relation between transformation, metamodels and models. We could take advantage of this information for the impact analysis and co-evolution phases, where it is needed to know the coupling between artifacts. In this scenario, both the definition and execution of the pipeline are fully automated. Implementing this part is left as future work.

5   Related Work

Co-evolution of artifacts in the MDE ecosystem has been tackled in several works, where specific solutions have been proposed depending on the type of artifact to be co-evolved. It has been studied the impact of metamodel evolution on models [8], transformations [12] and editors [9]. But, as far as we know, there are not works with an holistic and automatized view of the evolution. They are limited to an on-demand and manual co-evolution between pairs of artifacts. Using those evolution tools as building blocks, we are proposing a more ambitious approach where the co-evolution is reactive, automatic and parallelizable. Moreover, the process can be implemented with existing tools, integrating all the modeling tasks that are standalone.

The most basic premise in order to apply any kind of Continuous* practice is that all the artifact versions are committed to a Version Control System. VCSs [7,14,16], comparison [21] and merge tools [17] for models have been proposed.

There are also methodologies based on *Ant* to chain MDE operations [18] but they have not been proposed as part of a CD process.

Papers studying the synergies between CD and MDE for specific domains have also been presented. In [3], authors provide a model-based approach to generate TOSCA blueprints (that supports the definition of deployments as code), allowing the quick (re) deployments of cloud applications. Also in the domain of cloud computing, [20] proposes a model-driven approach to abstract and automate a continuous delivery process of cloud resources. This is done with a tool that uses a Domain Specific Language (DSL) to model the cloud infrastructure and a transformation that from that model creates scripts to manage different Configuration Management Tools. Similarly, in [10], a developer team can specify a model of the deployment of its application and automatically enact it in a test environment. Finally, in [13], authors present a prototype that uses a model-driven generator combined with CI server. They report on an empirical evaluation that shows the benefits of using MDE in combination with a CI server.

Complementary to these approaches, our work provides a more generic solution and studies the benefits of using CD processes and tools in the maintainability of MDE infrastructures themselves.

6   Conclusions and Future Research Directions

We have sketched the integration of MDE artifacts as first-class citizens in continuous software engineering, ranging from a direct use of current integration platforms to advanced coevolution scenarios, depending on the needs of the project and the role MDE plays in it. This benefits developers of both software artifacts (that can benefit from MDE) and MDE artifacts (that can benefit from CSE in their work).

Nevertheless, to achieve a complete and smooth support for MDE in CSE, we need to extend the state of the art in several directions. First, MDE technologies themselves need to become more mature. While some (e.g. model transformations) are reliable and ready-to-use in complex industrial scenarios, others (e.g. model merging) require more work to provide automatic solutions and/or professional tools. Secondly, CI components should be model-aware, providing default support for some model management operations (like model comparison for well-known types of models, e.g. UML class diagrams) or at least standard extension points to provide that. Finally, brand new research proposals should target some of the co-evolution scenarios and smarter dependency and impact analysis algorithms that have not been addressed so far and that would enable a better CSE automation for MDE projects.

We hope to see progress in these directions in the coming years.

References

1. https://github.com/jokingarcia/ContinuousEvolution. Accessed 9 July 2018
2. Ambler, S.W.: Agile software development. In: Encyclopedia of Software Engineering, pp. 29–46. Taylor & Francis (2010)
3. Artač, M., Borovšak, T., Di Nitto, E., Guerriero, M., Tamburri, D.A.: Model-driven continuous deployment for quality DevOps. In: Proceedings of the 2nd International Workshop on Quality-Aware DevOps (2016)
4. Beck, K., et al.: Manifesto for Agile Software Development (2001)
5. Brambilla, M., Cabot, J., Wimmer, M.: Model-Driven Software Engineering in Practice. Morgan & Claypool Publishers (2012)
6. Brambilla, M., Fraternali, P.: Interaction Flow Modeling Language. Morgan Kaufmann, Burlington (2015)
7. Brosch, P., et al.: Adaptable model versioning in action. In: Modellierung (2010)
8. Demuth, A., Riedl-Ehrenleitner, M., Lopez-Herrejon, R.E., Egyed, A.: Co-evolution of metamodels and models through consistent change propagation. J. Syst. Softw. **111**, 281–297 (2016)
9. Di Ruscio, D., Lämmel, R., Pierantonio, A.: Automated co-evolution of GMF editor models. In: Malloy, B., Staab, S., van den Brand, M. (eds.) SLE 2010. LNCS, vol. 6563, pp. 143–162. Springer, Heidelberg (2011). https://doi.org/10.1007/978-3-642-19440-5_9
10. Ferry, N., Solberg, A.: Models@Runtime for continuous design and deployment. In: Di Nitto, E., Matthews, P., Petcu, D., Solberg, A. (eds.) Model-Driven Development and Operation of Multi-Cloud Applications. SAST, pp. 81–94. Springer, Cham (2017). https://doi.org/10.1007/978-3-319-46031-4_9

11. Fitzgerald, B., Stol, K.-J.: Continuous software engineering: a roadmap and agenda. J. Syst. Softw. **123**, 1–14 (2015)
12. García, J., Diaz, O., Azanza, M.: Model transformation co-evolution: a semiautomatic approach. In: Czarnecki, K., Hedin, G. (eds.) SLE 2012. LNCS, vol. 7745, pp. 144–163. Springer, Heidelberg (2013). https://doi.org/10.1007/978-3-642-36089-3_9
13. García-Díaz, V., Espada, J.P., Núñez-Valdéz, E.R., García-Bustelo, B.C.P., Cueva Lovelle, J.M.: Combining the continuous integration practice and the model-driven engineering approach. Comput. Inf. **35**, 299–337 (2016)
14. Holmes, T., Zdun, U., Dustdar, S.: MORSE: a model-aware service environment. In: 4th IEEE Asia-Pacific Services Computing Conference (2009)
15. Humble, J., Farley, D.: Continuous Delivery: Reliable Software Releases through Build, Test, and Deployment Automation. Pearson Education, London (2010)
16. Koegel, M., Helming, J.: EMFStore: a model repository for EMF models. In: International Conference on Software Engineering (2010)
17. Kolovos, D.S., Paige, R.F., Polack, F.A.C.: Merging models with the epsilon merging language (EML). In: Nierstrasz, O., Whittle, J., Harel, D., Reggio, G. (eds.) MODELS 2006. LNCS, vol. 4199, pp. 215–229. Springer, Heidelberg (2006). https://doi.org/10.1007/11880240_16
18. Kolovos, D.S., Paige, R.F., Polack, F.A.C.: A framework for composing modular and interoperable model management tasks. In: MDTPI Workshop (2008)
19. Paige, R.F., Matragkas, N., Rose, L.M.: Evolving models in model-driven engineering: state-of-the-art and future challenges. J. Syst. Softw. **111**, 272–280 (2016)
20. Sandobalin, J., Insfrán, E., Abrahão, S.: An infrastructure modelling tool for cloud provisioning. In: International Conference on Services Computing, pp. 354–361 (2017)
21. Toulmé, A.: Presentation of EMF compare utility. In: Eclipse Modeling Symposium (2006)
22. Whittle, J., Hutchinson, J., Rouncefield, M.: The state of practice in model-driven engineering. IEEE Softw. **31**, 79–85 (2014)
23. Whittle, J., Hutchinson, J., Rouncefield, M., Burden, H., Heldal, R.: Industrial adoption of model-driven engineering: are the tools really the problem? In: Moreira, A., Schätz, B., Gray, J., Vallecillo, A., Clarke, P. (eds.) MODELS 2013. LNCS, vol. 8107, pp. 1–17. Springer, Heidelberg (2013). https://doi.org/10.1007/978-3-642-41533-3_1

A Proposal for Integrating DevOps into Software Engineering Curricula

Christopher Jones$^{(\boxtimes)}$

School of Computing, DePaul University,
243 S. Wabash Avenue, Chicago, IL, USA
`christopher.jones@depaul.edu`

Abstract. The "2017 State of DevOps Report" asserts that 27% of its respondents work on devops teams, an increase of almost 23% from 2016 and almost 69% from the 2015. Devops practices are intended to improve an organization's software development throughput by reducing the cycle time needed for a software change to reach its users. Although the skills needed for effective devops are in demand, it is challenging to integrate it into a academic curriculum for several reasons. First, software development curricula often only take students through the delivery stage of software development and do not spend meaningful time on operational activities, making it difficult to recruit faculty with the requisite IT operations experience. Second, many of the applications and their environments that can most benefit from devops are extremely complex, making it difficult to provide an appropriate learning environment. Third, many requirements for successful devops are not technical but instead emphasize the human and organizational aspects of our craft. Fourth, for many students, the problems addressed by devops are abstract. In this paper we look at these challenges in more detail and review one proposal for integrating devops into existing curricula in light of current devops maturity models, disciplines, and industry trends.

1 Introduction

The "2017 State of DevOps Report" [1], jointly produced by PuppetLabs and DevOps Research and Assessment (DORA), reports that 27% of its respondents currently work for a devops team. This is almost a 23% increase from the 2016 and nearly a 69% increase from the 2015 editions of the same report. Theses findings are supported when we look at the number of Google searches for "devops" over the last 5 years, shown in Fig. 1. Devops jobs are also on the rise. One SDTimes article found that, based on data from Indeed.com, there was a 225% increase in the number of job postings for the role of "DevOps Engineer" between January, 2015 and April, 2016 [2]. Based on these observations, as well the volume of devops-related subjects at industry conferences, and the number of devops-related books, it is clear that the subject of devops is important to the software development community. The very creation of this workshop is a further testament to devops' influence on software development.

© Springer Nature Switzerland AG 2019
J.-M. Bruel et al. (Eds.): DEVOPS 2018, LNCS 11350, pp. 33–47, 2019.
https://doi.org/10.1007/978-3-030-06019-0_3

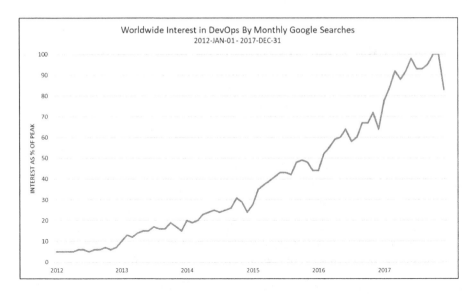

Fig. 1. Monthly Google searches for "devops" (2012-JAN-01 through 2017-DEC-31)

1.1   Challenges of Devops Education

Devops education is challenging for several reasons. First, much of the devops literature emphasizes the development and quality assurance (QA) aspects of the software delivery lifecycle but does not address many of the concerns of IT operations, especially those that occur beyond the software deployment and release stages of the SDLC. This can make it difficult to find faculty with relevant IT operations experience. This makes intuitive sense: since it is difficult to teach the operational aspects of software, that subject may be omitted from academic curricula, thus making it unnecessary to attract faculty with the relevant background in IT operations, thus perpetuating the cycle.

Second, any application and its associated runtime environments that could benefit from devops is typically much more complex than those demanded for most courses. Applications used in academic courses are often designed to be relatively limited in scope and to emphasize particular topic or technique in comparative isolation. In contrast, many of the challenges addressed by devops practices are only visible when the complexity of an application and its runtime environments reach a certain scale. This is particularly true of modern microservice based applications in which multiple services must collaborate to realize more complex business processes. Such architectures can be complex not only in terms of their technical stack, but also their ownership, their evolution, and their deployment models. This complexity is rarely if ever visible in traditional classroom applications.

Third, many of the existing devops offerings focus primarily on the technical aspects of the art. While these are practical to study in the classroom, they are often not the most critical elements of devops success. The most beneficial aspects of devops such as culture, organizational change, and collaboration, are much more difficult for students to practice. These may also prove to be the least interesting subjects to students who may be much more excited about working with interesting (and marketable) technologies rather than in learning how to communicate and work with business people, operators, or infrastructure specialists, individuals with whom they commonly have little interaction.

Finally, many of the problems addressed by devops can be difficult for students to understand without related experience. For example, it is easy to understand continuous integration in principle, but it is much harder to truly grasp its benefits unless one has worked on complex integrations spanning hours, days, or even weeks. Similarly, it can be difficult to learn about organizational transformation when one is comparatively new to one's career and lacks the insight and influence to help effect change, assuming there is recognition that change is necessary at all and what that change should be.

1.2   Scope of Devops Education

In this paper we treat devops as the most comprehensive set of processes within the SDLC, which means that when we discuss devops we can also discuss supporting processes such as agile development, continuous integration, continuous delivery, and release engineering. The mapping of these processes onto a basic SDLC is shown in Fig. 2. Devops has traditionally been regarded as the intersection of the three independent yet related disciplines shown in Fig. 3: development, IT operations, and quality assurance. Security is beginning to mature as a fourth discipline, although we do not consider it here. Informal definitions for each of these disciplines are provided below, but each discipline plays essentially the same role under devops that it played pre-devops. However, under a devops mindset these roles are neither independent nor isolated, but are instead interdependent and mutually reinforcing.

Development	Plans, architects, designs, and constructs software such that it is ready to be handed over to the Quality Assurance (QA) team for testing. Under devops, development teams may take on the role of QA by adopting automated testing.
QA	Confirms that the software is fit for use and fit for purpose. QA not only locates functional discrepancies, but also identifies possible problems in the software's ability to meet its service-level objectives. QA under devops often becomes less about running tests and more about mentoring the development team in testing practices.
IT Operations	Operates the software within its runtime environment. IT operations often performs activities such as provisioning new hardware, managing the environment's configuration, enables business continuity like backups and disaster recovery, and assisting in resolving unplanned events such as outages.

In their 2016 book, "Effective DevOps", [3] Davis and Daniels argue that collaboration and affinity are "pillars" of devops just as much as tools and technology. We see a similar emphasis in other literature. For example, in "Continuous Delivery and DevOps: A Quickstart Guide" [4], Swartout dedicates several chapters to organizational change, measurements, metrics, culture, and behavior. Of its seven chapters, only one is dedicated to tools and technology. This is a significant departure from prior works where the constructive use of technology as a devops enabler was often the central focus. This invites us to consider that effective devops has a much broader impact than the traditional three dimensions of Fig. 3. One way to gauge this scope of impact is to identify industry perception of the most important devops disciplines. We thus turn our attention to some of the influences on devopscurricula.

2   Influences on Devops Curricula

Many factors can influence which topics of devops should be incorporated into a curriculum and how they are introduced. In this paper we consider only three: industry maturity models, technical foundations, and IT operations foundations.

2.1   Maturity Models

Several devops maturity models have been proposed. Forrester Research [5] defined a maturity model that incorporated common devops practices into CMMI [6]. 2013 and 2014 whitepapers from InfoQ [7] and IBM [8] respectively, define five continuous delivery maturity levels, which are different from those of CMMI, but which serve the same basic purpose. In contrast, a 2013 IBM DevOps maturity model [9] defines only four maturity levels emphasizing the adherence to standards, the use of automation, and the documentation of practices. The maturity levels themselves are not of primary interest to us here. Instead, we focus on the dimensions of devops evaluated by those maturity levels and how they contribute to a foundation suitable for defining the devops practices and principles that we wish our curricula to address.

Some standards bodies are currently attempting to define standards around devops practices. For example, IEEE project 2675 seeks to

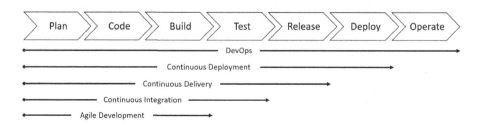

Fig. 2. Devops evolution mapped onto a basic software development lifecycle

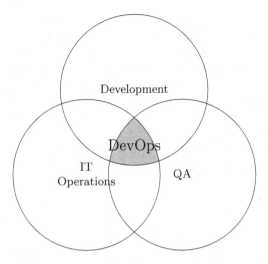

Fig. 3. Devops forces the convergence of traditionally separate disciplines

"...specify required practices for operations, development and other key stake-holders to collaborate and communicate to deploy systems and applications in a secure and reliable way" [10]. However, most devops maturity models are being drafted by industry groups. One continuous delivery maturity model [8] considers the following areas to be of interest in assessing devops maturity: building, deploying, testing, and reporting. InfoQ [7] instead assesses: culture and organization; design and architecture; build and deploy; test and verification; and information and reporting. Because these were maturity models for continuous delivery only, any reference to the maturity of operational practices is notably absent. This reflects a tendency of maturity model authors to emphasize the software delivery facets of devops rather than addressing the complete SDLC. For example, IBM's devops maturity model [9] has "Monitor/Optimize" as one of their model's capabilities, and yet monitoring and optimization are only a small fraction of the operational activities with which an organization must contend. Disaster recovery, notification and escalation, and incident and event management are all essential operational practices that must be considered.

There are also maturity models that address IT infrastructure and operations (I&O). One model from Gartner [11], the *ITScore for Infrastructure and Operations (ITSIO)*, suggests that I&O maturity be assessed against five levels based on the management of: processes; people; technology; and business. The CERT Resilience Management Model (CERT-RMM) [12] looks at operational resilience based on the management dimensions of: engineering; operations; enterprise; and process. These dimensions overlap with Gartner's proposed ITScore model. While not a true maturity model, the IT Infrastructure Library (ITIL) [13] defines core areas: service strategy, service design, service transition, service operation, and continual service improvement. Taken together these areas capture most of the same disciplines of maturity as the other models examined previously. Some maturity models have even been developed for ITIL such as [14] and [15]. The implication is that maturity in the broader ITIL practices will necessarily make an organization more mature in terms of devops practices since devops practices are subsumed within the broader ITIL practices.

Thus from a devops education perspective, the guidance provided by these various maturity models suggests that we should address: business; process; technology; measurements and metrics; and continuous improvement. We will see these subjects again in Sect. 3.

2.2   Technical Foundations

Technical considerations are often the most obvious ones when discussing devops, especially in the area of traditional software development. The challenges of defining software delivery pipelines that can take, in their most comprehensive form, each code commit and deploy the resulting artifacts with zero downtime deployments, is an enticing technical problem with compelling organizational benefits. In their seminal work, "Continuous Delivery", Humble and Farley [16] take up much of the book with purely technical topics like continuous integration, test data management, and build and deployment scripting. In fact, technology is such an important element of all devops efforts, that the company, XebiaLabs, provides their "Periodic Table of DevOps Tools[1], showing dozens of tools spanning a variety of subject areas, each of which can contribute to the smooth operation of a devops initiative. Figure 4 shows one generation of their periodic table. This table defines 15 categories of tools across five different licensing models from open source through enterprise.

Because schools of computing are adept at teaching development, these foundations are in many ways the easiest to build. Easy access to virtualization and cloud resources makes it comparatively simple to define a software delivery pipeline that exhibits continuous integration, delivery, and deployment, addressing at least the Development and QA disciplines from Fig. 3. Existing approaches to devops education such as DevOpsEnvy [17] provide support through the practice of continuous deployment. However, such approaches ignore the operational aspect of devops education instead focusing almost exclusively on the software delivery aspects. Additionally, placing too much emphasis on technology can actually undermine the efforts at adopting devops practices. While it is undeniable that technology is a significant devops enabler, it is a mistake to think it the most important one. If devops was nothing more than a series of technical challenges, then its education would be, if not straightforward, at least amenable to traditional teaching methods and programs. However, the non-technical challenges of devops are significant enough that the 2016 and 2017 "State of DevOps Reports" [1,18] have focused on non-technical aspects of devops such as transformational leadership and the return on investment of devops adoption.

---

[1] https://xebialabs.com/periodic-table-of-devops-tools/.

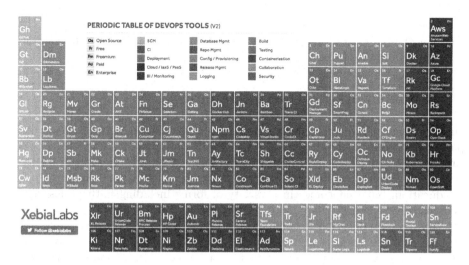

Fig. 4. XebiaLabs' periodic table of DevOps tools

2.3   IT Operations Foundations

One complexity of devops education is the fact that many IT Operations activities can only be examined once the software has been deployed and is in operation, sometimes for an extended period of time. Most software engineering curricula only take software through the "deploy" phase of the Fig. 2 model. While this assuredly involves some aspects of IT Operations, those activities are hardly representative of the breadth of responsibilities that such teams generally wield. Similarly, the teaching of "infrastructure as code" often requires a sound knowledge of infrastructural elements including networking, computing, and storage. Added to these basic components are larger and larger SaaS offerings from cloud providers such as Amazon Web Services (AWS) and Microsoft. While these offerings are undoubtedly useful, they require expertise to setup and configure in a cost-efficient way. They also require expertise to architect the software to take advantage of those offerings. The technical and operational complexity is often significant enough that most major cloud providers define some kind of certification process so that individuals can demonstrate a degree of competency with the provider's services and capabilities. For example, Amazon defines certifications such as the AWS Certified Solutions Architect and AWS Certified SysOps Administrator (emphasizing the development and IT operations disciplines respectively). Microsoft and Google both offer similar certifications for its cloud platforms.

Major cloud providers like AWS do not themselves take on the burden of common operational tasks such as defining monitors and their thresholds, specifying the notification structure for the team that is ultimately responsible for the availability of the service, and defining, codifying, and exercising major activities such as disaster recovery. Yet the livelihoods of many businesses may depend on these activities being performed consistently and well. This suggests that the study of IT operations, alongside development and QA, should be a major consideration in all devops education.

3   A Framework for DevOps Education

One significant challenge to devops education is that devops impacts many disparate disciplines, something many students, even after years of experience, will simply not have. This is not inherently a problem – full lifecycle software delivery is, of necessity, a collaborative effort. Filling this experience gap is the role of education, but that comes in a variety of forms including both professional and academic models.

Professional education is common and often considered more cost-effective by organizations because of the comparatively short time frames to complete the training as well as a perception that the training might be more "practical" rather than "academic". There are many options for professional devops training such as the "DevOps Foundation" certification from the DevOps Institute[2] or the "DevOps Certification Training" from online provider Linux Academy[3]. Several publicly available devops courses are offered by providers such as OSU [19] or Coursera. Some firms that consult in the field of devops also offer some kind of devops training. As with the rest of devops however, there is often little agreement on exactly what to teach. Some vendors may choose to adopt a technical approach that emphasizes the tools with which they themselves are most familiar or the vendors with whom they have strategic partnerships. While there is nothing wrong with this *per se*, we believe it is important to differentiate devops training from technical training. Technical training can be comparatively focused and discrete but because of its much broader scope, we believe that devops education must be more expansive and holistic, highlighting the interdependencies between its constituent disciplines.

To fully understand the interdependencies between the various devops disciplines in an academic setting, a devops curriculum might benefit from following the same educational model used for many Management in Business Administration (MBA) programs. For example, the 2016 Association of MBAs (AMBA) MBA Accreditation [20] advises that students should gain an understanding of several key areas of business knowledge including:

- Accounting
- Finance
- Marketing
- Micro- and macro-economics
- Operations
- Organizational theory

---

[2] https://devopsinstitute.com/certifications/devops-foundation/.

[3] https://linuxacademy.com/devops/courses.

In addition to these foundational areas, MBA students are typically free to choose an area of concentration, which might introduce more advanced studies in the aforementioned topics or additional topics that are more specialized than the above general business knowledge. This model, when combined with the discussion in Sect. 2.1, suggests that a devops education should consider the following disciplines:

- Agile Development Frameworks
- Architecting for Devops
- Infrastructure and Automation
- Configuration Management
- IT Operations
- IT Security
- Organizational Transformation
- Software Delivery Automation
- Software Economics
- Software Testing

Each of these topics is large and this list is clearly not inclusive since it assumes that prerequisite topics such as programming, data structures, and computer organization are covered elsewhere. One of the most import aspects of these disciplines is that they reinforce one another.

Agile Development Frameworks	Agile development frameworks allow for new capabilities to be rapidly incorporated into software or its environments. Such changes are carefully prioritized and planned. Because of the comparatively rapid pace of delivery, "Configuration Management" is a critical supporting subject. Agile development emphasizes common techniques such as unit testing and continuous integration, which are necessary to realize more advanced forms of release such as continuous delivery and continuous deployment.
Architecting for Devops	Devops is intended to support the rapid delivery of working software without compromising on software quality [21]. However, applications must be architected to support those goals. The involvement of both the IT operations and QA disciplines may in fact result in architectural changes that will better support those disciplines [22]. Architecting applications that enable devops requires an understanding of nearly every other topic in this list.
Infrastructure and Automation	Understanding the major infrastructural elements of compute, memory, and networking is critical in understanding how to effectively evaluate and select amongst alternative application architectures. Understanding how data centers function is critical to architecting effective solutions that lend themselves to devops adoption as well as in making decisions about the utility and appropriateness

of cloud providers. Knowing how cloud providers monetize their offerings is critical for understanding the economics of cloud-based software and the architectures used for them. Practitioners must understand the shared security models between the cloud provider and the cloud consumer. devops has a goal of treating infrastructure as code. A study of automation techniques and technologies is essential to reaching that goal.

Configuration Management
A key principle of devops is that almost everything should be stored in source code. This is the premise of infrastructure-as-code, but it can be expanded to include other things such as code delivery pipelines [23]. Furthermore, the techniques used for configuration management such as trunk based development [24] or feature toggles [25] can impact our ability to deliver software rapidly and reliably.

IT Operations
The use of cloud infrastructure does not obviate the need for sound operational activities including: monitoring, notification, escalation, and disaster recovery. Moreover, such concerns can radically impact an application's architecture. Designing the process that allow an application to honor its recovery time and recovery point objectives can be essential to avoiding violations of the service-level agreements generally defined as part of all software service contracts.

IT Security
Devops has been slowly evolving to include security, resulting an a broader topic known as "devsecops". While security has been an important topic for years, the adoption of devops practices makes it even more critical. As product development teams are given more control and responsibility for provisioning and managing their own infrastructure, knowledge of security considerations will directly impact their ability to meet compliance, regulatory, and auditing requirements imposed by clients and governmental regulatory agencies.

Organizational Transformation
The adoption of devops requires significant organizational change. This is especially true in organizations where technology teams wield little authority or where the applications or their technologies are considered "legacy". The use of software economics can be used to create a business case for the gradual adoption of devops practices from the other subjects. What sets this subject apart from the others is a focus on people and soft skills such as: listening, negotiation, business communication, persuasion, and patience.

Software Delivery Automation
Successful devops typically requires significant automation across the major processes. Such automation enables the rapid delivery of working software and can be integrated

	with the automation required to provision and configure cloud hardware such that the software and its assorted runtime environments can all be treated as code.
Software Economics	Each devops decision is subject to economic realities. The study of software economics ensures that the adoption of devops solutions balance the economic costs of violating availability, recovery time, or recovery point objectives with the economic gains of mitigating those same risks.
Software Testing	Testing corresponds to the QA discipline of devops. Software delivery pipelines require different kinds of tests to ensure that the various functional, capacity, and acceptance criteria have been met. In this case it does not include activities such as penetration or fuzz testing although if this model was extended to include DevSecOps, then it undoubtedly would.

While a comprehensive university program comparison is beyond the scope of this paper, we can say that we see elements of these subjects in existing university devops programs such as "DevOps: Modern Deployment" from Carnegie Mellon University [26], "Continuous Delivery and DevOps" at DePaul University [27], and "DevOps Software Development" from Johns Hopkins University [28]. Letterkenny Institute of Technology offers an MS degree in DevOps [29]. These programs address some common elements including virtualization, containerization, software delivery pipelines, basic cloud technologies, and certain operational activities like monitoring. There are also areas of divergence. For example, [26] spends additional time on security and architecture, whereas [27] addresses topics like devops economics, build automation, and the use of automated testing frameworks within the software delivery pipeline. Because devops covers a large number of topics, any one-semester class will likely be deficient in some aspect of the subject, either because there is simply not time or because the topic is covered in other courses. Obviously of those other courses are not taken, then students of a single devops course will necessarily have corresponding gaps in their education. This reinforces our belief the devops requires a holistic curriculum rather than only a single course.

4 Discussion

The ACM 2014 Curricula Recommendations for Software Engineering [30] mentions many, although not all, of the subjects we identified in Sect. 3 along with proposed hours of instruction. As shown in Table 1, the guidelines do not directly reference anything to do with IT operations. Similarly, architecture is defined loosely and doesn't directly address operational concerns although it does address common concerns associated with deploying code to cloud environments.

Based on these estimates, and to say nothing of whether or not the amount of time is actually sufficient to the need, we see that the ACM guidelines suggest almost 180 h of instruction across these topics, which do not even address all of

Table 1. ACM suggested instruction hours by devops discipline

Hours	Discipline
24	**Agile Development Frameworks** Process implementation, process evolution, and planning and tracking
51	**Infrastructure and Automation** Systems engineering and architecture and the evaluation of the design. Computer architectures, operating systems, and network protocols
6	**Configuration Management** Release management, revision control, software deployment, and software configuration management processes. Some elements of these guidelines address Software Delivery Automation
0	**IT Operations** This discipline is not significantly addressed by the ACM guidelines
20	**IT Security** Security fundamentals, encryption and cryptography, social engineering, computer and network security, developing secure software
23	**Organizational Transformation** Group dynamics, stakeholder interaction, communication skills, team and group communication, and presentation skills
0	**Software Delivery Automation** Parts of this discipline are addressed as part of Software Configuration Management, but do not address concepts like infrastructure automation
8	**Software Economics** The economics of software development and delivery
47	**Software Testing** Software verification, validation, and quality. This does not directly address the verification or validation of the runtime environment
179	**Total Suggested Instructional Hours**

the subjects in our proposed list. For example, we include course on computer organization, operating systems, and networking within the "Infrastructure and Automation" category. While these topics are important, they do not generally suffice to teach "IT Operations", which is more concerned with developing processes and practices to eekp an operating environment stable. This provides a strong indication that a single devops course is unlikely to meet all of the needs of a holistic devops education.

Christenson [31] describes an approach by which many aspects of devops are taught within a single 7-week course, "Cloud Computing and Architecture." During the course, students focus on the practical implementation of common devops disciplines that cover many of the subject areas mentioned above including: Agile Development; and Cloud Infrastructure and Automation. The course also exhibits some elements of Operations. It is an architecture course and emphasizes architecting for the cloud although it is not clear whether it emphasizes architecting for devops. Similarly, while testing is undoubtedly an element of this class, it is unclear what kinds of testing are emphasized. Christenson's course also benefits from the rapid feedback from trained assistants using appropriate automation as needed to simulate a variety of failure modes.

Other approaches attempt to ease the burden of devops education both on the student and the instructor. DevOpsEnvy [17], a devops education support system mentioned above, does this through the use of Docker containers of common open source tools commonly used by organizations that embrace devops. The system also provides instructors will common metrics to assist their student evaluations. As mentioned before, however, this approach does not address other aspects of devops such as IT operations. Neither does it address the human factors that are necessary for adoption to succeed. Approaches such as DevOpsEnvy are necessary for devops education, but they are not sufficient.

5   Conclusion

Devops is exciting. The IT industry is embracing its practices in an effort to optimize their software delivery models. There is a lack of sound and impartial devops education that roots its practices firmly in the existing disciplines of computer science and software engineering, while also teaching our students how those practices can be adapted to support the increased agility and speed desired by software providers.

We have looked at some approaches to teaching devops. While there are many industry-driven devops training programs, academic institutions have been slower to provide devops education. Some of the reasons for that include the need for a breadth of skills not always available to faculty, especially those who have not worked in an operations capacity; the need for realistic runtime environments with which to teach the operational aspects of devops; the fact that devops requires many non-technical skills for successful adoption; and the fact that many of the problems solved by devops may be fairly abstract to students who have not worked on a project of meaningful size and complexity.

We have revisited devops as the intersection of the traditional three disciplines of development, QA, and operations and discussed why this view is too limited. Various devops maturity models can be used to provide insight into the various disciplines that the industry at large perceives to be important to devops practice. Based on such models, we propose one set of disciplines that make devops holistic: agile development frameworks, architecting for devops, cloud infrastructure and automation, configuration management, IT operations, IT security, organizational transformation, software delivery automation, software economics, and software testing. Based on industry trends and the demand for skilled devops practitioners, we have made the case that the breadth of material warrants a complete curriculum for devops rather than simply a course.

We have seen the emergence of different devops classes, some from academia, but even more from industry. We have made that case that while these programs are a reasonable starting point the devops mindset must ultimately be interwoven throughout a computing curriculum if devops practitioners are ultimately going to be able to effectively apply its principles, practices, and techniques.

References

1. Forsgren, N., Kim, G., Humble, J., Brown, A., Kersten, N.: 2017 state of devops report. Technical report, PuppetLabs and DORA (DevOps Research and Assessment) (2017)
2. Moore, M.: Report: software architect, devops engineer among top paying jobs in industry, April 2016. https://sdtimes.com/report-software-architect-devops-engineer-among-top-paying-jobs-industry/
3. Jennifer Davis, K.D.: Effective DevOps. O'Reilly UK Ltd., Farnham (2016)
4. Swartout, P.: Continuous Delivery and DevOps: A Quickstart Guide. Packt Publishing, Birmingham (2012)
5. Forrester Consulting, Inc.: Continuous delivery: a maturity assessment model. Technical report, Forrester Consulting, Inc. (2013)
6. CMMI Institute: What is capability maturity model integration (CMMI)®? January 2018. http://cmmiinstitute.com/capability-maturity-model-integration
7. Rehn, A., Palmborg, T., Boström, P.: The continuous delivery maturity model, February 2013. https://www.infoq.com/articles/Continuous-Delivery-Maturity-Model
8. Minick, E.: Continuous delivery maturity model, February 2014. https://developer.ibm.com/urbancode/docs/continuous-delivery-maturity-model/
9. Bahrs, P.: Adopting the IBM DevOps approach for continuous software delivery, October 2013. https://www.ibm.com/developerworks/library/d-adoption-paths/index.html
10. Aiello, R.: Devops - standard for building reliable and secure systems including application build, package and deployment, August 2016. https://standards.ieee.org/develop/project/2675.html
11. Holub, E.: ITScore for Infrastructure and Operations. Tech Report, Gartner Inc., October 2016
12. Caralli, R., Allen, J., White, D.: CERT Resilience Management Model: A Maturity Model for Managing Operational Resilience. Addison-Wesley Professional, Boston (2010)
13. Axelos: What is ITIL® best practice? https://www.axelos.com/best-practice-solutions/itil/what-is-itil
14. Axelos Limited: ITIL Maturity Model, October 2013. https://www.axelos.com/Corporate/media/Files/Misc%20Qualification%20Docs/ITIL-Maturity-Model.pdf
15. Orbus Software: Measuring maturity: The ITIL Maturity Model, July 2015. https://www.orbussoftware.com/resources/downloads/measuring-maturity-the-itil-maturity-model/
16. Humble, J., Farley, D.: Continuous Delivery: Reliable Software Releases through Build, Test, and Deployment Automation. The Addison-Wesley Signature Series. Addison Wesley (2011)
17. Rong, G., Gu, S., Zhang, H., Shao, D.: DevOpsEnvy: an education support system for DevOps. In: 30th IEEE Conference on Software Engineering Education and Training, CSEE&T 2017, Savannah, GA, USA, 7–9 November 2017, pp. 37–46 (2017)
18. Brown, A., Forsgren, N., Humble, J., Kersten, N., Kim, G.: 2016 state of DevOps report. Technical report, PuppetLabs and DORA (DevOps Research and Assessment) (2016)

19. Oregon State University Open Source Lab: DevOps Bootcamp (2017). https:// devopsbootcamp.osuosl.org/
20. Association of MBAs: MBA Accreditation Criteria (2016). https://www.mbaworld. com/-/media/files/accreditation/mba-criteria-for-accreditation.ashx?la=en
21. Bass, L., Weber, I., Zhu, L.: DevOps: A Software Architect's Perspective. SEI Series in Software Engineering. Addison Wesley (2015)
22. Shahin, M., Babar, M.A., Zhu, L.: The intersection of continuous deployment and architecting process: practitioners' perspectives. In: Proceedings of the 10th ACM/IEEE International Symposium on Empirical Software Engineering and Measurement, ESEM 2016, pp. 44:1–44:10. ACM, New York (2016)
23. Jenkins: Pipeline as code with jenkins, July 2018. https://jenkins.io/solutions/ pipeline/
24. Hammant, P., Smith, S., et al.: Trunk based development: Introduction (2017). https://trunkbaseddevelopment.com/
25. Tiwari, A.: Decoupling deployment and release- feature toggles, October 2013. https://abhishek-tiwari.com/decoupling-deployment-and-release-feature-toggles/
26. Carnegie Mellon University, School of Computer Science, Institute for Software Research: 17–611 DevOps: Modern Deployment. http://mse.isri.cmu.edu/ software-engineering/Courses/17-611-DevOps-Modern-Deployment.html
27. DePaul University, School of Computer Science, College of Computing and Digital Media: SE-441 Continuous Delivery and DevOps. http://www.cdm.depaul.edu/ academics/pages/courseinfo.aspx?CrseId=014273
28. Johns Hopkins University, Whiting School of Engineering: 605.409 DevOps Software Development. https://ep.jhu.edu/programs-and-courses/605.409-devops-software-development
29. Letterkenny Institute of Technologys: Master of science devops, July 2018. https:// www.lyit.ie/CourseDetails/D202/LY_KDVOP_M/DevOps
30. Association of Computing Machinery: Software engineering 2014. Technical report, Association for Computing Machinery, February 2015
31. Christensen, H.B.: Teaching devops and cloud computing using a cognitive apprenticeship and story-telling approach. In: Proceedings of the 2016 ACM Conference on Innovation and Technology in Computer Science Education, ITiCSE 2016, pp. 174–179. ACM, New York (2016)

Omniscient DevOps Analytics

Damian Andrew Tamburri[1(✉)], Dario Di Nucci[2], Lucio Di Giacomo[3],
and Fabio Palomba[4]

[1] TU/e - JADS, 's-Hertogenbosch, The Netherlands
`d.a.tamburri@tue.nl`
[2] Vrije Universiteit Brussel, Brussels, Belgium
[3] Guardia di Finanza di Trento, Trento, Italy
[4] University of Zurich, Zürich, Switzerland

Abstract. DevOps predicates the continuity between Development and
Operations teams at an unprecedented scale. Also, the continuity does
not stop at tools, or processes but goes beyond into organizational practices, collaboration, co-located and coordinated effort. We conjecture
that this unprecedented scale of continuity requires predictive analytics
which are *omniscient*, that is (i) transversal to the technical, organizational, and social stratification in software processes and (ii) correlate all
strata to provide a live and holistic snapshot of software development, its
operations, and organization. Elaborating this conjecture, we illustrate a
set of metrics to be used in the DevOps scenario and overview challenges
and future research directions.

Keywords: Predictive analytics · DevOps quality ·
Organizational and technical aspects

1 Introduction

Omniscient - [om-nish-uh nt], adjective— *"having complete or unlimited knowledge,
awareness, or understanding; perceiving all things."*—[Cit. Oxford Dictionary]

DevOps is a set of practices aimed at accelerating the lead-time between a
change and its operational availability to end-users [1]. On one hand, since its
early inception, DevOps has radically shifted the way of conceiving software processes as well as the production of software artifacts; sample DevOps practices
include the incremental or radical intermix of Dev- and -Ops professionals in
the same team, using application lifecycle automation tools to enable continuous delivery, or designing failure-first software architectures to learn a "proper"
architecture from runtime operations monitoring. On the other hand, tracking
and evaluating the effective monetary, technical, organizational, and social gains
connected to any single DevOps practice over others, or compared to the previous way of working is still a challenge for several reasons. For example, there
is still no definite way to shift from classical software engineering practices to

© Springer Nature Switzerland AG 2019
J.-M. Bruel et al. (Eds.): DEVOPS 2018, LNCS 11350, pp. 48–59, 2019.
https://doi.org/10.1007/978-3-030-06019-0_4

DevOps lest by incurring in great costs[1] that cannot be estimated up-front. Moreover, there is still a lack of actionable metrics to measure the impact, risks, and gains connected to every single practice let alone any of their combinations. Conversely, a proliferation of *ad-hoc* measurement and monitoring solutions exist mainly configured to sustain each organizational scenario in each company.

We argue that, given the scope of its proclaimed shifts, DevOps also deserves a radical shift in the means and mechanisms that software people need to employ in tracking DevOps pains and gains. In fact, we observe the following. First, DevOps practices altogether aim at improving all aspects of software production, operation, and evolution, with small, and steadfast devices of technical (*e.g.*, tools), organizational (*e.g.*, co-operation practices), and social (communication practices) nature. Second, achieving DevOps involves a shift of culture towards *failure*—products should fail fast, fail observably, fail quantifiably, fail safely, and more. In summary, we observe that DevOps: (a) entails changes along all possible activities in all possible layers around software (see Fig. 1), and (b) focuses on failure. From this observation we conclude that DevOps requires measurable, fine-grained, complete, constant awareness over every*thing* and every*one*, to achieve an understanding of what dimension (social, organizational, or otherwise) is influencing what else, for the purpose of constant, continuous improvement.

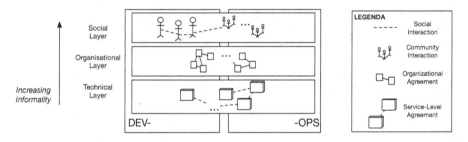

Fig. 1. Omniscient DevOps analytics, an overview - a social layer accounts for the people and communities to be monitored; an organizational layer accounts for the organizational agreements and protocols to be tracked; a technical layer accounts for the product variables to be observed

We refer to the above awareness condition with the term *omniscience* and argue that omniscience can be achieved via specific predictive analytics [2] frameworks that: (i) are able to constantly analyze sensory data over all contracts, agreements, and measurable quantities from layers in Fig. 1; (ii) constantly and statistically relate the elicited analyses at multiple levels of granularity (*e.g.*, person vs. team vs. unit vs. organization) and transversally to all layers.

The ultimate goal of such omniscient DevOps analytics toolkits shall be to sustain the perpetual improvement cycles at the basis of the DevOps philosophy,

---

[1] https://jaxenter.com/true-cost-devops-adoption-138287.html.

offering at every step, a clear overview over what needs to be improved along which measurable improvement dimension, and in which layer.

Structure of the Paper. Section 2 presents the background. Section 3 describes *DevOps Omniscient Analytics* with a scenario-based example, while Sect. 4 provides a set of organizational- and technical-related metrics tailored for *DevOps Omniscient Analytics*. Section 5 overviews a set of challenges and future research directions. Finally, Sect. 6 concludes the paper.

2   Background

The concept of *omniscience* in the context of DevOps refers to being able to monitor, track, and receive feedback from the three layers of complexity along which software development and operations are carried out, namely, social, organizational, and technical.

On the one hand, from a social and organizational perspective there exists no standard and well-known/evaluated framework to account for *community quality*—intended as the fitness for purpose of an organizational structure to its intended organizational goal or software mission [3]. Although several attempts were made (*e.g.*, consider the emerging CHAOSS initiative from the open-source software foundation[2]), no definitive solution has been evaluated to date. Our work has the main goal of providing a holistic view of the quality of software projects, which takes into account all the aspects that play a role in the development. To this aim, we plan to provide a set of metrics and methodologies able to characterize the three aforementioned complexity layers.

On the one hand, from a technical perspective several software quality frameworks [4,5] were proposed since before the 90's [6], and at various abstraction levels (Architectural, modularization, class, method-level, etc.). For instance, Crispin [5] investigated whether and the extent to which test-driven development influences the quality of source code, while other researchers (i) studied how and why source code quality degrades over time [7–16] and (ii) devised methods and tools to improve source code quality in the context of software maintenance and evolution [17–27]. Despite the notable advances of the recent years, we can notice that most of the work done so far only considers the technical aspects of a software system independently from the surrounding environment, *i.e.*, without considering the additional social and organizational complexities emerging in the context of DevOps. On this front, we believe that further research is strictly needed in order to enable a proper management of the whole development DevOps process: for this reason, we propose a omniscient view that, through software analytics, puts together the three main layers composing the typical development in a DevOps context.

---

[2] https://chaoss.community/.

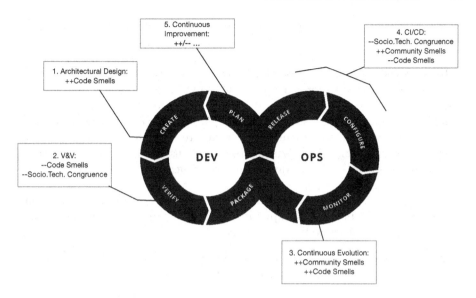

Fig. 2. Omniscient DevOps analytics explained - a '++' sign means that the dimension or factor may be improving while a '−' sign means the dimension or factor is worsening; specific analytics for the factors in the figure (e.g., Socio-Technical Congruence) are omitted for the sake of brevity.

3   DevOps Omniscient Analytics

To flesh out what we mean with Omniscient DevOps analytics we employ a simple and intuitive scenario-based counter-example, tailored from of a real-life industrial situation. The scenario in question is recapped in Fig. 2 and illustrates a pre-DevOps situation in which a classical hand-off between development and operations teams takes place, consequently causing a series of events that, in the context of DevOps can and must be tracked for continuous improvement over the entire cycle. More specifically, the scenario illustrates the following.

1. During *Architectural Design* [28] software designers and developers sit together to create a first rough image of the architecture and start drafting prototypical code, employing design patterns as they see fit; the first version of the application prototype normally contains a number of code smells [29]. The underlying assumption behind this quick and dirty version of the working application is that, during *2. Verification and Validation*, code smells are discovered and removed appropriately, to keep technical debt [30] at an acceptable maximum.
2. During *Verification & Validation*, code smells are removed by refactoring the architectural design and severely changing the modularization structure—the changes in the structure change also the way in which people in the development (and hence, operations) teams also communicate and collaborate—as a consequence, community smells [3] emerge.

3. In a classical *Continuous Evolution* loop, an incremental and iterative maintenance and evolution phase is bootstrapped which essentially reiterates on items 1 and 2 above: *this is where omniscient DevOps analytics come in.*
4. To break the classical cycle, continuous evolution is instrumented with appropriate automations to form a *CI/CD* phase which creates synergy between development and operations teams following the guidelines and tactics part of the DevOps menu [1]—as part of this phase, however, the organization is studied jointly with the architectural structure such that, for example, low levels of socio-technical congruence (see previous section) can be detected, community smells can be addressed, and technical as well as social debt [3] can be managed.
5. Finally, a *Continuous Improvement* phase enacts all of the above points continuously for the purpose of improving the product, the organizational structure [31] around it, as well as its technical baselines. .

We argue that a set of Omniscient DevOps Analytics might support the overall activities carried out to develop a software system in a DevOps scenario.

4   Omniscient DevOps Metrics

In the following we provide a non-exhaustive list of metrics that were explored in the state of the art which could be considered as fitting the purpose of tracking the quality of organizational and technical structures for DevOps omniscience. The list in question serves as a sample starting list to outline and flesh out DevOps omniscient analytics. In particular, we suggest some organizational- and technical-related metrics in the scope of DevOps, considering that these families of metrics are complementary [32].

4.1   Organizational-Related Metrics

Several metrics have been proposed to assess the quality of the organization behind a software system. The most investigated and most considered ones are reported and discussed below:

– **Truck-Factor.** Originally formulated as "The number of people on your team who have to be hit with a truck before the project is in serious trouble"[3] and established in software engineering literature as well [33–35]. We operationalize truck-factor based on core and peripheral community structures identified by CodeFace, as the degree of ability of the community to remain connected without its core part. Further details on how core and periphery members are determined can be found in the work of Joblin [36].
– **Socio-Technical Congruence.** Paraphrased from previous work [37] as "the state in which a software development organization harbors sufficient coordination capabilities to meet the coordination demands of the technical products under development" and operationalized in this study as the number of

---

[3] http://www.agileadvice.com/2005/05/15/agilemanagement/truck-factor/.

development collaborations that do communicate over the total number of collaboration links present in the collaboration network.

- **Core-Periphery Ratio.** This ratio has been confirmed to regulate communities [36]. We operationalize it as the ratio between the median centrality of periphery members and the median centrality of the core members. In other words, we considered the importance of core developers with respect to periphery ones.
- **Community Member Turnover.** This quantity reflects the amount of people who migrate from the community across subsequent 3-month time-windows of our analysis [38–40]:

$$TO(CommNet, CollNet) = \frac{Leaving}{(Populus + Size)/2} * 100\%$$

where, *CommNet* and *CollNet* are conjuncted using a 1-Elementary Symmetric Sum between adjacency matrices [41], *i.e.*, $(V_m \cup V_c, E_m \cup E_c)$ in the notation above. Variables in the formula above are as follows: (i) *Leaving* is the number of members who left the project in the analysed window; (ii) *Populus* is the total number of members who populated the community in the previous analysis window; (iii) *Size* is the total number of members populating the community in the currently analyzed window. Similar formulations of turnover exist [42,43] but we chose the formulation above since it matches the definition of turnover and, by the way in which CODEFACE computes the formula variables, our formulation accounts for both core and periphery member turnover; this differentiation is previously absent in literature and the easiest to operationalise with our available tooling, *e.g.*, CODEFACE determines *Populus* for both core and periphery communities, combining both into one after a normalization based on amount of contribution.
- **Smelly-Quitters.** This ratio reflects the amount of people P who were part of a community smell C_X (that is, a reportedly harmful anti-pattern found in the community structure [3]) for two subsequent time windows T_1 and T_2 but then left the community for the remaining time windows (T_{2+y} where $Y > 0$) in the available range of data for the total set of community smells found, *i.e.*, C. More formally:

$$P = \frac{\sum P(C_X)}{C}$$

The quantity in question is tailored from the social-networks analysis metrics also used for Social Network Disorder measurement [44,45].

4.2   Technical-Related Metrics

While the organization view reports important information on how community members work and collaborate with each other, the technical properties of software systems represent the core of the development and, therefore, deserve the investigation of how well-known and less-known metrics relate to the organizational aspects. In the following, we report and discuss some of those metrics.

- **Lines of Code.** LOC of a class is widely recognized as a relevant factor to study the quality of a technical component, as it represents a proxy metric to assess quality-related aspects such as, for instance, software cohesion [46,47]. We believe that this metric can strongly impact the DevOps style development, as less cohesive classes might require more organizational efforts for developers.
- **Coupling Between Object Classes.** The number of external dependencies of a class might represent an important factor that influences the maintainability of software systems [48]. Indeed, the higher the number of relationships with other classes, the lower the ability of developers to consistently manage the complexity of a technical product [46]
- **Code Change Process.** The way a source code component changes over time might impact its size and complexity [49], thus possibly decreasing the overall maintainability of a software project as well as increasing the efforts required at an organizational level. To account for this aspect, some metrics such as (i) number of lines of code added or modified in the class over different releases of a code component (a.k.a., code churn) and (ii) number of commits performed on such component over time should be carefully taken into account.
- **Developer-related Factors.** Besides structural and process metrics, also *who* touches a source code component might influence the management effort in the context of DevOps applications [50,51]. For instance, the number of developers who committed changes related to a certain component may reveal precious information on the organizational effort required to maintain it. At the same time, experience metrics (*e.g.*, the number of commits performed by a developer on a codebase) are highly relevant to study the quality of the overall development process.
- **Runtime Maintainability Measures.** Previous work showed that code components affected by problems in the past are more likely to be problematic in the future [52]. Thus, metrics like the presence/persistence of design issues [53] or the emergence of defects [19] might provide additional useful information to enable a comprehensive view of the quality of the development process.
- **Operations Factors.** Previous work in operations has focused mostly over performance, throughput and similar metrics, however, the need emerges currently for metrics that account for architectural characteristics that make services more monitorable or *observable* [54]. Such factors are yet to be fully explored and evaluated in action.

5   Research Roadmap

In the scope of our future research agenda and while discussing the above concepts and findings with the LASER DevOps community[4] in an open focus-group

---

[4] https://www.laser-foundation.org/devops/2018/.

of 92 min, we confirmed the following valuable research directions in pursuit of Omniscient DevOps analytics.

1. *Investigate the Cross-Reference between known software quality indicators and metrics with respect to known organizational and socio-technical metrics.* In this respect, for example, practitioners as well as academics need to confirm the validity of metrics currently established for the evaluation of software development artifacts quality in the context of DevOps pipelines.

2. *Investigate the relation between software systems observability [54] and software technical, organizational, and socio-technical quality.* In this respect, for example, software practitioners and academics need to evaluate the degree to which software development as well as software operations artifacts can in fact be monitored by common monitoring technology or whether specific technology and metrics must be devised and evaluated.

3. *Investigate the relation between macro-phenomena in the organizational structure and micro-phenomena emerging in the software code.* In this respect, for example, organizational structures research as well as software engineering research reports on many macro-phenomena occurring at the level of the organizational structure (*e.g.*, think of Conway's law [55], or Lehman's laws of software evolution [56] or the social reflexivity theory [57–59] and more) that may influence the software development as well as operations codes

4. *Investigate the quality of software-related organizational and socio-technical decisions, beyond the current level of understanding over software design decisions as well as their decision-making process.* In this respect, further research needs to capture and find ways to measure the cognitive frame in which software developers and software operators make and disseminate decisions in their respective operational areas such that a common knowledge flow and transfer mechanism can be devised.

5. *Investigate ways to concretize and quantify the additional project cost connected to sub-optimal software organizational structures, i.e., social debt [60].* In this respect, with the aim of further improving the organizational and socio-technical aspects within DevOps pipelines, further research shall concentrate on defining formally established and evaluated means to measure *social debt* [60] at the same time that technical debt is measured as well.

6. *Investigate the quality of software operations artifacts and code as much as software development artifacts and code have been studied up to this point.* In this respect, it must be noted that we currently know very little in the ways of measuring and assessing software operations code quality, as well as any design patterns (or even anti-patterns, for that matter) thereof. Further research shall concentrate on finding and carefully evaluating, both qualitatively and quantitatively, their validity and applicability at large.

7. *Evaluate and investigate metrics for the level of continuity between development artifacts and people with operations artifacts and people.* In this respect, it should be noted that one of the key drivers and foundations behind the original DevOps movement is the creation and maintenance of synergy between development and operations—maintaining that synergy requires ways to measure the continuity between Dev and Ops beyond simple *speed* metrics (*e.g.*,

release rate, build-success or failure rates, etc.) but rather, metrics that look more holistically at the entire DevOps pipeline from the 3 perspectives highlighted in Fig. 1 need to be devised and evaluated.

6   Conclusions

In this paper, we introduced the concept of *Omniscient DevOps Analytics*, that refers to the use of software analytics to support a holistic view of the development process that takes into account social, organizational, and technical aspects of software systems. We illustrate a set of metrics that can be exploited to enable such a view, also providing a use-case scenario where omniscience can be achieved and effectively exploited by developers. Finally, we overview a set of challenges and future research directions that would enable the generation of theory, methods, and tools for Omniscient DevOps Analytics. Such future directions and open challenges represent the main points of our research agenda, which is focused on improve the quality of the whole DevOps development process.

References

1. Bass, L., Weber, I., Zhu, L.: DevOps: A Software Architect's Perspective. SEI Series in Software Engineering. Addison-Wesley, New York (2015)
2. Yang, Y., Falessi, D., Menzies, T., Hihn, J.: Actionable analytics for software engineering. IEEE Softw. **35**(1), 51–53 (2017)
3. Magnoni, S., Tamburri, D.A., Di Nitto, E., Kazman, R.: Analyzing quality models for software communities. Communications of the ACM (2017, under review)
4. Software Quality Connection: Software quality connection (2015)
5. Crispin, L.: Driving software quality: how test-driven development impacts software quality. IEEE Softw. **23**(6), 70–71 (2006)
6. Watts, R.: Manufacturing Software Quality. NCC Publications, Manchester (1987)
7. Bavota, G., De Lucia, A., Di Penta, M., Oliveto, R., Palomba, F.: An experimental investigation on the innate relationship between quality and refactoring. J. Syst. Softw. **107**, 1–14 (2015)
8. Palomba, F., Zaidman, A.: Does refactoring of test smells induce fixing flaky tests? In: 2017 IEEE International Conference on Software Maintenance and Evolution (ICSME), pp. 1–12. IEEE (2017)
9. Palomba, F., Zaidman, A., Oliveto, R., De Lucia, A.: An exploratory study on the relationship between changes and refactoring. In: 2017 IEEE/ACM 25th International Conference on Program Comprehension (ICPC), pp. 176–185. IEEE (2017)
10. Palomba, F., Panichella, A., Zaidman, A., Oliveto, R., De Lucia, A.: The scent of a smell: an extensive comparison between textual and structural smells. IEEE Trans. Softw. Eng. **44**, 977–1000 (2017)
11. Palomba, F., Bavota, G., Di Penta, M., Fasano, F., Oliveto, R., De Lucia, A.: On the diffuseness and the impact on maintainability of code smells: a large scale empirical investigation. Empir. Softw. Eng. **23**(3), 1188–1221 (2018)
12. Palomba, F., Bavota, G., Di Penta, M., Fasano, F., Oliveto, R., De Lucia, A.: A large-scale empirical study on the lifecycle of code smell co-occurrences. Inf. Softw. Technol. **99**, 1–10 (2018)

13. Tufano, M., et al.: When and why your code starts to smell bad (and whether the smells go away). IEEE Trans. Softw. Eng. **43**(11), 1063–1088 (2017)
14. Tufano, M., et al.: An empirical investigation into the nature of test smells. In: 2016 31st IEEE/ACM International Conference on Automated Software Engineering (ASE), pp. 4–15. IEEE (2016)
15. Spadini, D., Palomba, F., Zaidman, A., Bruntink, M., Bacchelli, A.: On the relation of test smells to software code quality. In: Proceedings of the International Conference on Software Maintenance and Evolution (ICSME). IEEE (2018)
16. Vassallo, C., Panichella, S., Palomba, F., Proksch, S., Zaidman, A., Gall, H.C.: Context is king: the developer perspective on the usage of static analysis tools. In: 2018 IEEE 25th International Conference on Software Analysis, Evolution and Reengineering (SANER), pp. 38–49. IEEE (2018)
17. Catolino, G., Palomba, F., De Lucia, A., Ferrucci, F., Zaidman, A.: Enhancing change prediction models using developer-related factors. J. Syst. Softw. **143**, 14–28 (2018)
18. Di Nucci, D., Palomba, F., Tamburri, D.A., Serebrenik, A., De Lucia, A.: Detecting code smells using machine learning techniques: are we there yet? In: 2018 IEEE 25th International Conference on Software Analysis, Evolution and Reengineering (SANER), pp. 612–621. IEEE (2018)
19. Di Nucci, D., Palomba, F., De Rosa, G., Bavota, G., Oliveto, R., De Lucia, A.: A developer centered bug prediction model. IEEE Trans. Softw. Eng. (2017, to appear)
20. Di Nucci, D., Panichella, A., Zaidman, A., De Lucia, A.: Hypervolume-based search for test case prioritization. In: Barros, M., Labiche, Y. (eds.) SSBSE 2015. LNCS, vol. 9275, pp. 157–172. Springer, Cham (2015). https://doi.org/10.1007/978-3-319-22183-0_11
21. Di Nucci, D., Palomba, F., Oliveto, R., De Lucia, A.: Dynamic selection of classifiers in bug prediction: an adaptive method. IEEE Trans. Emerg. Top. Comput. Intell. **1**(3), 202–212 (2017)
22. Moha, N., Guéhéneuc, Y.G., Duchien, L., Meur, A.F.L.: DECOR: a method for the specification and detection of code and design smells. IEEE Trans. Softw. Eng. **36**(1), 20–36 (2010)
23. Palomba, F., Bavota, G., Di Penta, M., Oliveto, R., Poshyvanyk, D., De Lucia, A.: Mining version histories for detecting code smells. IEEE Trans. Softw. Eng. **41**(5), 462–489 (2015)
24. Palomba, F., Panichella, A., De Lucia, A., Oliveto, R., Zaidman, A.: A textual-based technique for smell detection. In: 2016 IEEE 24th International Conference on Program Comprehension (ICPC), pp. 1–10. IEEE (2016)
25. Palomba, F., Zanoni, M., Fontana, F.A., De Lucia, A., Oliveto, R.: Toward a smell-aware bug prediction model. IEEE Trans. Softw. Eng. (2017). https://ieeexplore.ieee.org/document/8097044
26. Palomba, F., Zaidman, A., De Lucia, A.: Automatic test smell detection using information retrieval techniques. In: International Conference on Software Maintenance and Evolution (ICSME). IEEE (2018, to appear)
27. Tsantalis, N., Chatzigeorgiou, A.: Identification of move method refactoring opportunities. IEEE Trans. Softw. Eng. **35**(3), 347–367 (2009)
28. Bass, L., Clements, P., Kazman, R.: Software Architecture in Practice. SEI Series in Software Engineering. Addison-Wesley, Boston (2012)

29. Palomba, F., Bavota, G., Penta, M.D., Oliveto, R., Lucia, A.D.: Do they really smell bad? A study on developers' perception of bad code smells. In: Proceedings of the International Conference on Software Maintenance and Evolution (ICSME), pp. 101–110. IEEE Computer Society (2014)
30. Kruchten, P., Nord, R.L., Ozkaya, I., Visser, J.: Technical debt in software development: from metaphor to theory report on the third international workshop on managing technical debt. In: ACM SIGSOFT Software Engineering Notes, vol. 37, no. 5, pp. 36–38 (2012)
31. Tamburri, D.A., Lago, P., Vliet, H.V.: Organizational social structures for software engineering. ACM Comput. Surv. 46(1), 3:1–3:35 (2013)
32. Palomba, F., Tamburri, D.A., Serebrenik, A., Zaidman, A., Fontana, F.A., Oliveto, R.: How do community smells influence code smells? In: Proceedings of the 40th International Conference on Software Engineering: Companion Proceedings, pp. 240–241. ACM (2018)
33. Williams, L., Kessler, R.R.: Pair Programming Illuminated. Addison Wesley, Boston (2003)
34. Avelino, G., Passos, L.T., Hora, A.C., Valente, M.T.: A novel approach for estimating truck factors. In: 24th IEEE International Conference on Program Comprehension, ICPC 2016, Austin, TX, USA, 16–17 May 2016, pp. 1–10. IEEE Computer Society (2016)
35. Ferreira, M.M., Valente, M.T., Ferreira, K.A.M.: A comparison of three algorithms for computing truck factors. In Scanniello, G., Lo, D., Serebrenik, A. (eds.) Proceedings of the 25th International Conference on Program Comprehension, ICPC 2017, Buenos Aires, Argentina, 22–23 May 2017, pp. 207–217. IEEE Computer Society (2017)
36. Joblin, M., Mauerer, W., Apel, S., Siegmund, J., Riehle, D.: From developer networks to verified communities: a fine-grained approach. In: Bertolino, A., Canfora, G., Elbaum, S.G. (eds.) Proceedings of International Conference on Software Engineering (ICSE), pp. 563–573. IEEE Computer Society (2015)
37. Valetto, G., Helander, M., Ehrlich, K., Chulani, S., Wegman, M., Williams, C.: Using software repositories to investigate socio-technical congruence in development projects. In: International Workshop on Mining Software Repositories, p. 25 (2007). IEEE Computer Society, Los Alamitos. http://doi.ieeecomputersociety.org/10.1109/MSR.2007.33
38. Lin, B., Robles, G., Serebrenik, A.: Developer turnover in global, industrial open source projects: insights from applying survival analysis. In: Proceedings of the 12th International Conference on Global Software Engineering, pp. 66–75. IEEE Press (2017)
39. Nassif, M., Robillard, M.P.: Revisiting turnover-induced knowledge loss in software projects. In: 2017 IEEE International Conference on Software Maintenance and Evolution (ICSME), pp. 261–272. IEEE (2017)
40. Rigby, P.C., Zhu, Y.C., Donadelli, S.M., Mockus, A.: Quantifying and mitigating turnover-induced knowledge loss: case studies of chrome and a project at Avaya. In: Proceedings of the 38th International Conference on Software Engineering, pp. 1006–1016. ACM (2016)
41. Macdonald, I.G.: Symmetric Functions and Hall Polynomials. Oxford University Press, Oxford (1998)
42. Vasilescu, B., et al.: Gender and tenure diversity in GitHub teams. In: Begole, B., Kim, J., Inkpen, K., Woo, W. (eds.) Proceedings of the 33rd Annual ACM Conference on Human Factors in Computing Systems, CHI 2015, Seoul, Republic of Korea, 18–23 April 2015, pp. 3789–3798. ACM (2015)

43. Constantinou, E., Mens, T.: Socio-technical evolution of the ruby ecosystem in GitHub. In: Pinzger, M., Bavota, G., Marcus, A. (eds.) SANER, pp. 34–44. IEEE Computer Society, Washington, DC (2017)
44. van den Eijnden, R.J.J.M., Lemmens, J.S., Valkenburg, P.M.: The social media disorder scale. Comput. Hum. Behav. **61**, 478–487 (2016)
45. Mislove, A., Marcon, M., Gummadi, K.P., Druschel, P., Bhattacharjee, B.: Measurement and analysis of online social networks (2007)
46. Kitchenham, B., Pickard, L., Pfleeger, S.L.: Case studies for method and tool evaluation. IEEE Softw. **12**(4), 52–62 (1995)
47. Zhou, Y., Leung, H., Xu, B.: Examining the potentially confounding effect of class size on the associations between object-oriented metrics and change-proneness. IEEE Trans. Softw. Eng. **35**(5), 607–623 (2009)
48. Moha, N., Gueheneuc, Y.G., Duchien, L., Le Meur, A.F.: DECOR: a method for the specification and detection of code and design smells. IEEE Trans. Softw. Eng. **36**(1), 20–36 (2010)
49. Munson, J.C., Elbaum, S.G.: Code churn: a measure for estimating the impact of code change. In: 1998 Proceedings of International Conference on Software Maintenance, pp. 24–31. IEEE (1998)
50. Di Nucci, D., Palomba, F., De Rosa, G., Bavota, G., Oliveto, R., De Lucia, A.: A developer centered bug prediction model. IEEE Trans. Softw. Eng. **44**, 5–24 (2017)
51. Hassan, A.E.: Predicting faults using the complexity of code changes. In: Proceedings of the 31st International Conference on Software Engineering, pp. 78–88. IEEE Computer Society (2009)
52. Ostrand, T.J., Weyuker, E.J., Bell, R.M.: Predicting the location and number of faults in large software systems. IEEE Trans. Softw. Eng. **31**(4), 340–355 (2005)
53. Palomba, F., Bavota, G., Di Penta, M., et al.: On the diffuseness and the impact on maintainability of code smells: a large scale empirical investigation. Empir. Softw. Eng. **23**, 1188 (2018). https://doi.org/10.1007/s10664-017-9535-z
54. Tamburri, D.A., Bersani, M.M., Mirandola, R., Pea, G.: DevOps service observability *by-design*: experimenting with model-view-controller. In: Kritikos, K., Plebani, P., de Paoli, F. (eds.) ESOCC 2018. LNCS, vol. 11116, pp. 49–64. Springer, Cham (2018). https://doi.org/10.1007/978-3-319-99819-0_4
55. Conway, M.E.: How do committees invent. Datamation **14**(4), 28–31 (1968)
56. Lehman, M.M.: Laws of software evolution revisited. In: Montangero, C. (ed.) EWSPT 1996. LNCS, vol. 1149, pp. 108–124. Springer, Heidelberg (1996). https://doi.org/10.1007/BFb0017737
57. Vass, J., Munson, J.E.: Revisiting the three Rs of social machines: reflexivity, recognition and responsivity. In: Gangemi, A., Leonardi, S., Panconesi, A. (eds.) WWW (Companion Volume), pp. 1161–1166. ACM, New York (2015)
58. Coleman, J.S.: Foundations of Social Theory. Harvard University Press, Cambridge, London (1990)
59. Han, S.: Theorizing new media: reflexivity, knowledge, and the Web 2.0. Sociol. Inq. **80**(2), 200–213 (2010)
60. Tamburri, D.A., Kruchten, P., Lago, P., et al.: Social debt in software engineering: insights from industry. J. Internet Serv. Appl. **6**, 10 (2015). https://doi.org/10.1186/s13174-015-0024-6

Teaching DevOps at the Graduate Level
A Report from Polytech Nice Sophia

Benjamin Benni[1][✉], Philippe Collet[1], Guilhem Molines[1,2], Sébastien Mosser[1], and Anne-Marie Pinna-Déry[1]

[1] Université Côte d'Azur, CNRS, I3S, Sophia Antipolis, France
{benni,collet,mosser,pinna}@i3s.unice.fr, guilhem.molines@unice.fr
[2] IBM France Lab, Paris, France
guilhem.molines@fr.ibm.com

1 Introduction

The massive evolution of IT development towards new Web architectures, from service-oriented to micro-services, clouds and containers, call for changes in the way software is developed, deployed and maintained. DevOps has emerged as a set of practices bridging software development (*Dev*) with software operations (*Ops*) [1]. DevOps makes up a model in which development, quality assurance, releasing, deployment, operation with infrastructure management, and maintenance are integrated and automated as much as possible. With automation and monitoring present at all stages, a DevOps approach is supposed to reduce the time between a change (*e.g.*, a commit) and its availability in production, while mastering quality.

From a teaching perspective, hiring companies for software engineering students are currently in the middle of a technological transformation to introduce DevOps pipelines in their organizations, while agile and continuous integration practices are still in the process of being digested. It is clearly necessary for our students to be aware of such practices to complement their background in software engineering and architecture, and also to make a difference at recruitment time. At first sight, it seems easy to integrate DevOps principles with software development projects and other courses dealing with large software systems or software architectures. Still, different issues arise when materializing the course. As DevOps mainly deals with a technological pipelines, a trade-off must be found between using a complete and relevant stack, and understanding the DevOps principles and its pillars: platform, deployment, testing, and people [2]. Furthermore, using toy examples over the isolated elements of a DevOps pipeline would transform the course in a set of basic tutorials, missing a comprehensive point of view of both the principles and the end-to-end technological hands-on.

In this paper, we report on a course dedicated to "*N-tiers Architectures and DevOps*", which aimed at introducing DevOps while tackling these identified issues. It is taught at the graduate level at Polytech Nice Sophia since 2015. The target audience is 4th year (graduate) students specialized in software engineering and architecture. In the remainder of this paper, we discuss the identified

J.-M. Bruel et al. (Eds.): DEVOPS 2018, LNCS 11350, pp. 60–72, 2019.
https://doi.org/10.1007/978-3-030-06019-0_5

challenges to construct this course, as well as the vision to implement it. We then give some details on the course content and on the used case studies. We conclude by summarizing results and discussing future development.

2   Challenges and Vision

We believe that Software Architecture and DevOps are two sides of the same coin: one needs DevOps concepts to properly implement and deliver complex architectures, and complex architectures justify such an approach. The course follows a project-based approach to support both parts and we rely on the development dimension of the project to create a continuum between architecture and operations. When materializing the course, we then identified the following challenges:

- Even if the technological stack can be hard to apprehend and deploy, tools are just a means to an end, and the course must focus on the pillars associated to DevOps: platform, deployment, testing, and people [2]. As a consequence, the course must focus on the concepts, and use tools only as an illustration. Moreover, coupling architecture to DevOps is important as both approaches complement each others, and the course must smoothly merge these two dimension to support a fully-fledged curriculum.
- We defend that toy examples are not enough, and delivering such a content using isolated labs cannot lead to the comprehensive point of view we envisioned. It is important to rely on a project-based approach where students will be confronted to real-life choices, at architectural, development and operation levels.

As a consequence, the course must provide theoretical concepts for architecture design, software development and operational deployment around a shared project that will be used as a backbone during lab assignments. To simulate real-life software engineering, the labs must be defined thanks to an open and informal specification expressed in business terms, and it will be up to the students to design the right architecture, implement it in an iterative way and support its deployment thanks to a continuous delivery pipeline.

3   Course Content

In the school of engineering, the presented course is taught to 4th year students (graduate level) that have chosen a specialization in software engineering and architecture. It is thus an optional course in the master curriculum with a capacity of 50 students per year.

3.1   Overall Organization

The presented version is the result of merging two course slots, each one over a half-day along a full semester, so that the course is scheduled on each Friday for the spring session. It notably enables to easily and dynamically focus a day or half of it to a specific topic, *i.e.*, a software architecture topic or an element of the DevOps pipeline, or to give time for the main project development (cf. Fig. 1).

Week	Friday Morning		Friday Afternoon		
	08:00 - 09:00	09:15 - 12:15	13:30 - 14:30	14:45 - 17:45	
6	Introduction to Software Architecture		DevOps Overview	Mutation Testing Lab	Kick-off
7	Poly'Event Architecture definition (unsupervised)		Arch. for Testing	Mutation Testing Lab	
8	Mutation Testing Lab (unsupervised until further notice)		Func. & Int. Tests	Poly'Event Architecture definition	
9	Soft. Components	Poly'Event Project	Arch Dojo #1	Poly'Event Project	
10	Winter break				
11	Interoperability & WS	Poly'Event Project	Cont. Integration	Poly'Event Project	Poly'Event Project Implementation
12	Cont. Integration	Poly'Event Project	Build plan & Pipeline	Poly'Event Project	
13	Technical interview (Minimal & Viable Product)		Poly'Event Project (unsupervised)		
14	Persistence	Poly'Event Project	Deployment	Poly'Event Project	
15	Arch Dojo #2	Poly'Event Project	Soft. Containers	Poly'Event Project	
16	Q&A, Stepback	Poly'Event Project	Scaling	Poly'Event Project	
17	Easter Break				
18	Poly'Event Project (unsupervised)		Technical Interview (Almost-final Product)		
19					
20		Architecture Exam (3 hours)		DevOps Exam (3 hours)	

Fig. 1. 2018 planning of the "N-tiers Architectures and DevOps" course

Prerequisites for the course are the following:

- A strong background in object-oriented programming, with fluency in Java;
- The knowledge of some software engineering principles and tooling, *i.e.*, life-cycle, code versioning (Git), unit testing (JUnit), automated construction (Maven);
- Notions of design and UML, mainly to abstract from the associated project code through component and deployment diagrams.

These prerequisites are all coming for the mandatory courses defined by the graduate program followed by the attendees.

The teaching team has slightly evolved over time, but it has been constantly led by a full-time professor and an industrial partner who holds a part-time position in the school in addition to his daily job as a software architect. The team is completed by two other teachers, making a specialized pair for each axis, software architecture and DevOps. This enables each pair to easily follow student project development according to each axis. Students are organized in teams of four, and the course is known to require a strong investment in software development from them. The same case study is addressed under the two different and complementary axes, and students have to work on the development of a system that implements the specifications associated to the chosen case study as lab assignment.

To support the development of such a system, we implemented a reference system named *The Cookie Factory* (TCF) [3] (see Sect. 4.1 for details). In the first weeks, the course focuses on the concepts associated to n-tiers architectures and the pre-requisites associated to DevOps, *i.e.*, understanding modularization and testing. To support this task, students are asked to analyze the implementation of TCF. They quickly identify that it is implemented as a single monolith that needs to be modularized at all levels (business implementation, test, and deployment). This step helps them to get confidence with the project technological stack, as well as to identify why and how a DevOps approach is a good fit for such class of systems.

In the following sections, we describe the content of each course axis and show how the reference case study and developed project help in building a consistent solution to the identified challenges.

3.2   Software Architecture

For the software architecture part, we focus on the definition of an n-tiers architecture using software components (implemented as EJBs using the Java EE framework). A part of the architecture is also developed in .Net, emphasizing the need to support system interoperability using Web Services. An introductory course is setting up the work context and the technological stack (cf. Fig. 2), while the next courses introduce several principles and some associated technologies using the TCF case study as an illustration:

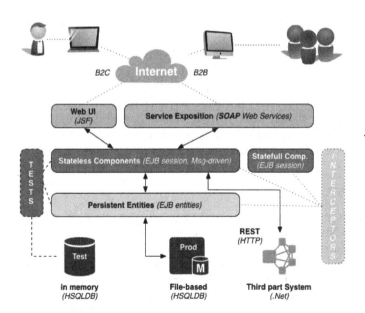

Fig. 2. Technological stack for the architectural axis

- Notions of software architecture, layers, and diagrams to represent them;
- The many architectural viewpoints, with focus on functional (work at the interface level), development (modularity and dependency management), and deployment viewpoints;
- *Object-relational mapping* (ORM) variants, and related architectural patterns;
- Introduction to *Enterprise Java Beans* (EJBs), with an overview of the bean types (entity, session, message), their business focus, as well as the principles of inversion of control and dependency injection;
- A focus on session beans, defining a 3-tiers architectures, and introducing stateful and stateless principles and impacts on an architecture;
- Introduction to the notion of services (being different from Web Services technical implementation), contracts and the impact of their different kinds (no contract, light form, strong contract), discussion on bad practices (*e.g.*, REST **is** different from CRUD);
- Focus on domain-driven design, and its implementation through entity beans, issues in modeling relationships, lazy loading, query languages in ORMs, etc.
- Architectural MVC pattern with its implementation in JSF over Java EE, the messaging paradigm and its implementation in JMS, light form of aspect-orientation and its implementation in Java EE interceptors.

As shown on the planning (Fig. 1), the conduct of the successive lectures follows the design and development of their own architecture for their project (*Poly'Event* project on the planning). Students should propose an initial architecture with only the introduction, trying to build something consistent with their own background. Then each new lecture enables to criticize their successive propositions, using the TCF case study during the lecture (*e.g.*, with *architecture dojos* where students and professor co-define an architecture respecting several properties during the lecture), and on their own project during the labs. This enables to mix the learning of many technological elements with the different notions of software architecture, their impacts and the necessary trade-offs a software architect should master in her day-to-day work. The TCF case study brings both a starting point for the project and an existing architecture to criticize and evolve as the course progresses.

3.3 DevOps

For the DevOps dimension, the aim is to address the problem of aligning a *development* (dev) team with the *operational* one (ops) to build a given piece of software. Addressed issues are notably how to slice the code into independent modules that can be compiled, tested and deployed in a continuous way, and how to properly test the integration between such loosely coupled components.

This part of the course is organized in a slightly different way. While the students starts to define their own project architecture, the first part of DevOps introduces theoretical concepts and aims at applying them in a separate lab on mutation testing [4]. The organization of this part is as follows:

- Introduction on software delivery, lifecycle and pipelines;
- Reminder on quality assessments, introduction on the different types of tests, how to architect and run them;
- Focus on functional and integration testing, and on what should be considered when running them.

With these lectures, several labs are targeted at building a mutation testing pipeline over a Java project, using Maven, scripts, and a Java source code transformation library[1]. The objective is to make concrete the creation of a pipeline using a software project to build other artifacts, run other tasks (compiling the mutant projects separately), get results (deciding whether a mutant project is passing existing tests or not).

The rest of the lectures focus on introducing the principles and technologies related to the DevOps pillars:

- continuous integration, with build on servers, separated components, their dependencies, notions of artifacts, and necessary repositories, Jenkins[2] and Artifactory[3] being chosen as technological support;
- other subjects related to continuous management, i.e., quality assessment through static code analysis, code branching for a better organization;
- deployment, with the main differences between testing and production environments, as well as test orchestration;
- software containers and virtual machines, focusing on the Docker[4] light container ecosystem, with its composition and scalability mechanisms.

As this part of the course progresses, the students have to apply the principles with the proposed technology to their projects. Considering the *platform* pillar, the tools selected by the students (*e.g.*, continuous integration server, testing framework, containers) must be justified and used accurately *w.r.t* the needs associated to their own project. At the *deployment* level, it is up to the students to mitigate the constraints from the development team, the operational context and the customer's expectations to create the right build plan. For the *testing* pillar, students know about unit tests and the course introduces integration and acceptance tests. Students must justify that the built product is rightly tested at these different levels. Finally, considering the *people* pillar, they have to modularize their code (and the associated tests, build plans,...) in a way that fits their development team and their business objectives [5].

This organization enables the DevOps part of the course to provide real practice of industrial tools applied to a non-toy N-tiers architecture that students are extending at the same time, and also to focus on application of the different principles and pillars of DevOps.

---

[1] Spoon, http://spoon.gforge.inria.fr/.

[2] Jenkins, https://jenkins.io/.

[3] Artifactory, https://jfrog.com/artifactory/.

[4] https://www.docker.com/.

3.4   Evaluation

The evaluation of the course is organized around multiple milestones and deliveries:

– after two weeks a first *Minimum Viable Product* (MVP) architecture should be provided by the student teams, for feedback only.
– After two other weeks, an architecture-report must be provided. It contains the following elements: use cases diagrams, business objects definition as class diagram, associated persistent-schema and object-relational mapping definition, interfaces pseudo-code definition (*e.g.*, Java like), components described by a component diagram, deployment of the defined components as a deployment diagram. Each artifact must be justified with respect to its relevance in the proposed architecture.
– At the same time, the mutation testing pipeline should be delivered (through a tagged commit on the provided Git repository). A small report is also delivered, answering the following questions: what are your directory structure and language/script choices? How are mutators compiled and applied to your target project? Which mutations did you write, and why? What issues did you run into, and how did you solve them? What characterizes good mutators?
– At mid-term, demos of the minimal viable product architecture and its associated DevOps tooling are conducted through technical interviews driven by a team of two teachers, one per axis. At that stage, the key-point in architecture is to demonstrate a walking skeleton of the technical stack, from the input entered by the user, sending a request to the Java EE component backend through a Web Service, with an interaction with a third-party service simulated in .Net. For DevOps, the focus is on demonstrating that *Continuous Integration* (CI) is mastered, compiling the project in a way that respects the dependencies among modules, relying on an artifact repository to store the produced binaries. A CI server is expected, so to support the build process and artifacts storage, through inter-dependent build plans.
– Similar demos are also conducted near the end of the course. Technical interviews are conducted by teams, switched from the previous demos. On the architecture side, students should demonstrate a comprehensive architecture, going from the persistence layer to the exposition one (*i.e.*, web services, JSF). They must be able to defend strengths of their architecture, as well as discuss its limitations and evolution capabilities. For DevOps, the pipeline should have evolved from a CI system to a fully instrumented *Continuous Delivery* (CD) pipeline, ensuring software quality through various levels of testing, and generating the product deliverables as composable Docker images.
– Codes and reports should be finally delivered before the exams.

The lab and project evaluations are completed by two final exams, one per axis. Exam subjects mix small targeted questions with a large question on a given case study, evaluating the students capability to step back on the development and DevOps practices. Each axis has also its own marking breakdown:

– Software architecture part: architecture report: 15%; intermediate demonstration: 10%; final presentation: 15%; project (code and report): 20%; final exam: 40%.
– DevOps: mutation testing: 15%; intermediate demonstration: 15%; final presentation: 15%; project (code and report): 15%; final exam: 40%.

4   Case Studies

We describe here the main reference case study, showing its features, architecture and the *kind* of complexity it exhibits to support our teaching approach. We also give a brief description of the projects submitted to students in the past years.

4.1   Reference Case Study: The Cookie Factory (TCF)

The Cookie Factory[5] is an imaginary major bakery brand in the USA, providing a plausible context to the creation of the software system. The *Cookie on Demand* (CoD) system is an innovative service offered by TCF to its valued customers. They can order cookies online thanks to an application, and select when they will pick-up their order in a given shop. The CoD system is supposed to ensure to TCF's happy customers that they will always retrieve their prepaid warm cookies on time.

As shown on Fig. 3, the system is defined as layers:

– A remote client, that will run on each customer's device;
– An EJB kernel, implementing the business logic of the CoD system;
– An external partner (simulating a Bank, implemented in .Net);
– An interoperability layer between the kernel and its partners. Communication with the client is supported by an RPC (SOAP) service, and communication with the bank as a REST one.

To deliver the expected features, the CoD system defines the following internal interfaces (Fig. 4):

– `CartModifier`: operations to handle a given customer's cart, like adding or removing cookies, retrieving the contents of the cart and validating the cart to process the associated order;
– `CustomerFinder`: a finder interface to retrieve a customer based on her identifier (here simplified to her name);
– `CustomerRegistration`: operations to handle customer's registration (*e.g.*, users profile)
– `CatalogueExploration`: operations to retrieve recipes available for purchase in the CoD;
– `OrderProcessing`: process an order (kitchen order lifecycle management);

---

[5] https://github.com/polytechnice-si/4A_ISA_TheCookieFactory.

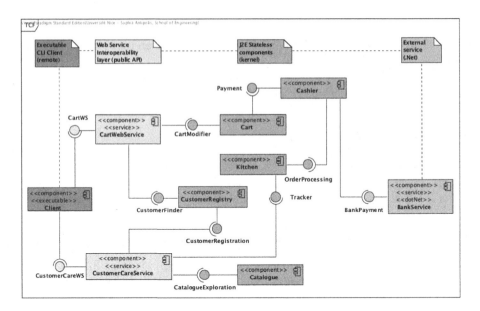

Fig. 3. Component diagram of the Cookie on Demand system

- **Payment**: operations related to the payment of a given cart's contents;
- **Tracker**: order tracker to retrieve information about the current status of a given order.

To ease comprehension by the students, the business objects are simple (Fig. 5): Cookies are defined as an enumerate, binding a name to a price. An Item models the elements stored inside a cart, *i.e.*, a given cookie and the quantity to order. A customer makes orders thanks to the CoD system, and an order stores the set of items effectively ordered by the associated customer (bidirectional association).

The implementation of TCF is made of 102 Java Classes, representing approximatively 3,000 lines of code. As the focus of the course is an introduction to software architecture, we made the choice to go as lightweight as possible with respect to the tooling. We thus decided not to deploy a real set of application servers and use embedded artifacts instead. This is the very justification of using TomEE+ as Java EE container (instead of a classical Tomcat or Glassfish container) and Mono as .Net implementation (instead of the classical Visual Studio technological stack). We advocate that the execution details are not important when compared to the complexity of designing the right system. In addition, mapping this demonstration to existing application servers is pure engineering, with no added value.

4.2   Case Studies to be Developed by Students

As previously mentioned, each year, a different product case study is proposed for the development stage, each being presented like the TCF specification part,

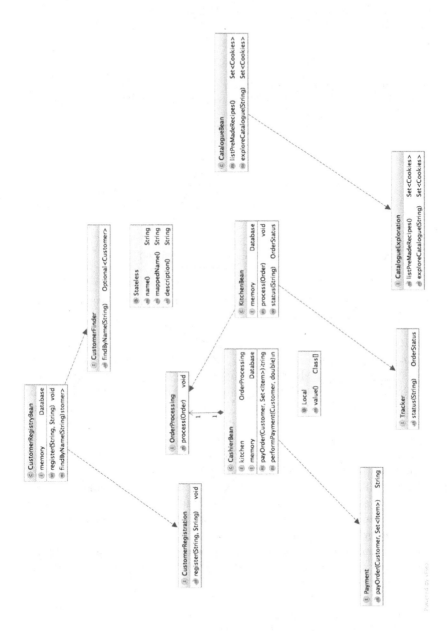

Fig. 4. Interface details of the Cookie on Demand system

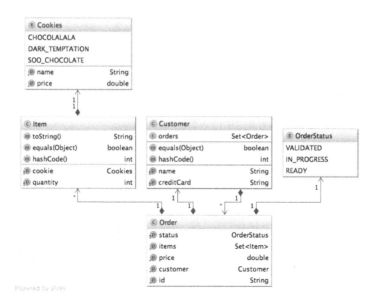

Fig. 5. Business objects of the Cookie on Demand system

with a product vision, examples, personas and related epics. We give here a brief description of these projects:

– *PolyEvent* is an event management system at the scale of an academic campus, events being internal or external, with booking of premises, possible catering, etc. The system should be generic enough to target different campuses, and should handle both the planning stages and the event day and six personas are defined (logistics manager, premises manager, accounting manager, an external event organizer, cleaning company contact, campus event manager).

– A *Disloyalty card* is a loyalty card targeting a specific commercial zone instead of a retail chain, with a sponsoring from the town council of the zone (*e.g.*, gifts, parking discount with any purchase) to encourage customers to visit as many shops as possible in the area. This kind of card boosts local shops and reward customers who shop in the promoted zone. The developed system should be deployable in medium to large cities, with few changes between a deployment to another. The system card can be used as a payment method for small amounts, and frequent buyers get a VIP status with more advantages. Personas are different kinds of buyers, *e.g.*, a town employee and a shop manager.

– *Isola 3000* is a ski resort management system for a company owning two resorts, the main feature being lift tickets selling and automatic access control to the ski lifts. A ticket is an NFC card and lifts are connected with different means to the main resort (ethernet, wifi, radio waves, nothing at all). Outdoor screens show slope availability and are connected in real-time with connected lifts and patrolmen. Tickets are sold online or at counters, many pre-built offer are proposed with different discounts, premium statuses, and specific durations or area restrictions. As these offer might evolve, statistics over sales are necessary.

– *PolyTweet* is a social-network based solution to solve communication problems between students, faculty members and administrative staff within the school. The system should foster information sharing, by publishing short messages to channels, the school exposes several "public" channels available to external users (for integration purpose with the public website), files can be attached to messages (*e.g.*, pictures, lab descriptions). Communication channels can be created as open internal channels, with moderators. To evaluate the return on investment, metrics over the whole system usage should also be computed and displayed.

5 Conclusion

Results. The course is close to its full capacity since 2015 (137 students out of 150 slots on 3 years). It is evaluated by the project delivery (code, report and oral defense), complemented by two exams (case study, 3 hours). We push students to stop being consumers of tools, and instead become DevOps architects able to identify what is necessary and how tools from the state of practice can be assembled to support a given project. The discussions and interviews made with partners' contacts and interns' tutors are strongly positive on that point. Recruiters clearly state that such a knowledge makes a strong difference between candidates at recruitment time (interns or permanent positions). At the student level, the course received a highly positive feedback in evaluations. Student expressed as comments their surprise about the importance of the *people* pillar. We also noticed that even students who do not specialize into software architecture after the course are introducing the DevOps philosophy in their projects.

From an academic research point of view, building this course also led to interesting questions about service containerization from a software engineering point of view that lead to a publication in the domain of software composition [6].

Future Development. In the future, we naturally plan to continue to improve the content and organization of the course. Next year, we will change the way the different elements of the pipeline are introduced. The mutation testing pipeline is not perceived by students as useful as we envisioned, while this organization pushes the application of advanced concepts as containers to the end of the timeline. This prevents students from stepping back from their DevOps realization, and transitively from their software architecture as well. Our plan is then to introduce all principles and pillars of DevOps earlier, together with basic realizations for each part, i.e. a basic pipeline with deployment and a simple *dockerization*, so that they can be applied to the project. Then the advanced concepts, and related technological elements, will be introduced and applied. By using this course as a prerequisite for some specialization course, we aim to deliver to students specialized skills (*e.g.*, micro-service development, user experience) while keeping in mind the close relationship that exists between development and operations, leveraging our experience in teaching agility and user experience.

References

1. Bass, L., Weber, I., Zhu, L.: DevOps: A Software Architect's Perspective. Addison-Wesley Professional, Boston (2015)
2. Shaw, J.: The four pillars of DevOps: agility for the enterprise (Agile Cambridge) (2014). https://www.slideshare.net/johnfcshaw/four-pillars-of-devops-john-shaw-agile-cambridge-2014. Accessed 01 Oct 2017
3. Mosser, S.: The Cookie Factory (J2E 7 reference implementation), version 2.2 (2017). https://github.com/polytechnice-si/4A_ISA_TheCookieFactory
4. Woodward, M.R.: Mutation testing-its origin and evolution. Inf. Softw. Technol. **35**(3), 163–169 (1993)
5. Evans, E.: Domain-Driven Design: Tacking Complexity In the Heart of Software. Addison-Wesley Longman Publishing Co., Inc., Boston (2003)
6. Benni, B., Mosser, S., Collet, P., Riveill, M.: Supporting micro-services deployment in a safer way: a static analysis and automated rewriting approach. In: Symposium on Applied Computing, Pau, France, April 2018

DevOps Round-Trip Engineering: Traceability from Dev to Ops and Back Again

Miguel Jiménez[1]([✉]), Lorena Castaneda[1], Norha M. Villegas[2],
Gabriel Tamura[2], Hausi A. Müller[1], and Joe Wigglesworth[3]

[1] University of Victoria, Victoria, BC, Canada
{miguel,lcastane,hausi}@uvic.ca
[2] Universidad Icesi, Cali, Valle del Cauca, Colombia
{nvillega,gtamura}@icesi.edu.co
[3] IBM Toronto Laboratory, Toronto, Canada
wiggles@ca.ibm.com

Abstract. DevOps engineers follow an iterative and incremental process to develop Deployment and Configuration (D&C) specifications. Such a process likely involves manual bug discovery, inspection, and modifications to the running environment. Failing to update the specifications appropriately leads to technical debt, including configuration drift, *snowflake* configurations, and erosion across environments. Despite the efforts that DevOps teams put into automating operations work, there is a lack of tools to support the development and maintenance of D&C specifications. In this paper, we propose TORNADO, a two-way Continuous Integration (CI) framework (*i.e.*, Dev $\xrightarrow{\text{CI}}$ Ops and Dev $\xleftarrow{\text{CI}}$ Ops) that automatically updates D&C specifications when the corresponding system changes, enabling bi-directional traceability of the modifications. TORNADO extends the concept of CI, integrating operations work into development by committing code corresponding to manual modifications. We evaluated TORNADO by implementing a proof of concept using Terraform templates, OpenStack and CircleCI, demonstrating its feasibility and soundness.

Keywords: DevOps · Round-Trip Engineering · Traceability · Software deployment · Continuous integration

1 Introduction

Changes in the artefacts used throughout software development and operations are inherently causally connected to one another. For example, modifying the deployment specifications will affect the corresponding system and the infrastructure it runs on. Analogously, updating the physical infrastructure will cause updates to the software and networking configuration. Traditionally, this relationship has been implicit and poorly supported by software development processes and tools. DevOps practices have increased its visibility in the context

© Springer Nature Switzerland AG 2019
J.-M. Bruel et al. (Eds.): DEVOPS 2018, LNCS 11350, pp. 73–88, 2019.
https://doi.org/10.1007/978-3-030-06019-0_6

of a continuous development process [1,2], impacting mostly the forward direction (*i.e.*, Dev → Ops). In contrast, there is a lack of standard and technology-supported processes to bridge explicitly and repeatedly in the backward direction (*i.e.*, Dev ← Ops) [3–6]. This inability hinders the process of keeping operation and development information consistent with the deployed system.

Many organisations adopt a forward-only development strategy to avoid configuration inconsistency. Any modification to the system or its infrastructure must be performed in the forward direction, using, for example, infrastructure as code (IaC). This approach ensures consistency between the running system and its D&C specifications, and at the same time allows tracing the changes. However, DevOps engineers and operators still follow a manual bug discovery and exploratory experimentation process that leads to fixing faults. D&C specifications are the result of an incremental process, in which each step is likely to involve manual actions and inspection. Therefore, it is still a task of the engineers to capture the drift between an experimental environment and the original setting, before updating the specifications. Failing to do so leads to configuration drift, *snowflake* configurations, erosion across environments, and other forms of technical debt [7–9]. There is a need to support keeping the D&C specifications in sync.

Automatically maintaining the consistency between D&C specifications and a running system is known as automatic Round-Trip Engineering (RTE) [10–12]. Our contributions are as follows. We introduce TORNADO, a framework for realizing. RTE in DevOps. We demonstrate how the concept of continuous integration [13] can be extended from its traditional use to integrate operations work into development. TORNADO is a two-way con**T**inu**O**us integ**R**atio**N** fr**A**mework for **D**ev**O**ps (*i.e.*, Dev $\xrightarrow{\text{CI}}$ Ops and Dev $\xleftarrow{\text{CI}}$ Ops) that enables bidirectional traceability [14] of changes and transformation between a running system and its D&C specifications. Our evaluation consists of a proof of concept implementation based on Terraform templates[1] and OpenStack.[2] This implementation allows us to demonstrate the feasibility and soundness of TORNADO.

This paper is structured as follows. Section 2 presents our motivation. Section 3 introduces fundamental concepts used in the description of our proposal and discusses related work. Section 4 presents TORNADO. Section 5 presents our evaluation. Finally, Sect. 6 concludes the paper and outlines future work.

2   Motivation

In this section, we describe the motivation for TORNADO, by highlighting relevant concerns about consistency and quality of D&C specifications.

Experimentation on production-like environments enables DevOps engineers and operators to develop new features and fix faults by performing ad-hoc modifications. There are D&C specifications, such as Terraform templates, that need

---

[1] https://www.terraform.io (accessed Oct, 2018).
[2] https://www.openstack.org (accessed Oct, 2018).

be updated accordingly. These updates range from low-level configurations, such as opening ports in a firewall, upgrading or downgrading software packages, to structural changes, such as duplicating services or modifying the scaling policies of virtual resources. Failing to propagate these changes to the specifications appropriately leads to configuration inconsistencies.

The state of the practice for D&C testing is based on static analysis and functional tests [7,15,16]. The former provides quick feedback on minor programming mistakes, such as syntax errors. The latter consists of deploying the infrastructure and execution of unit, integration and system tests to determine if the deployed resources and their configuration are adequate. Deploying and re-deploying the system and its infrastructure to sandbox environments is resource and time consuming. Furthermore, modifying a specification can adversely impact another. For example, modifying a `hostname` on a network configuration file without appropriately replicating the update to other specifications (*e.g.*, software deployment) will likely cause a connection timeout. This hinders the experimentation process and requires manual inspection and debugging. Bugs may not appear prior to deployment because specifications are not usually connected, unless they are input to a common compiler/interpreter. Run-time modelling[3] seems to be a feasible alternative to capture the notations' domain logic and validate them prior to deployment, reducing the cases in which the infrastructure must be deployed for testing purposes. It also reduces the developer's cognitive load, as feedback is provided in a timely fashion.

3   Fundamentals and Related Work

This section introduces fundamental concepts for describing our framework and presents related research.

3.1   Round-Trip Engineering

Round-Trip Engineering (RTE)[4] is the process of ensuring the consistency of multiple, changing and interconnected software artefacts [10–12,18]. These artefacts participate in a source-target relationship, in which a derivation process creates the target from the source artefact. Target artefacts are usually further altered due to maintenance work or changing requirements [12]. Therefore, these artefacts may no longer be the result of the derivation process and, thus, creating inconsistencies when source artefacts are modified and the derivation process is applied again. RTE ensures consistency between these artefacts by reflecting changes to the target artefact back to the source artefacts.

RTE is closely related to Forward and Reverse Engineering (FE and RE, respectively). FE is the process of deriving one or more target artefacts from one or more source artefacts. RE is the process of reconstructing these sources from the target artefacts, recovering any information lost in the derivation process [10,19].

---

[3] In the literature often referred to as models@run.time [17].

[4] Model synchronisation and RTE are often used interchangeably in the literature [12].

3.2   Continuous Integration

Continuous Integration (CI) is an agile software engineering practice that allows developers to frequently merge work to a shared mainline multiple times per day [13,20]. It includes frequent automated building and testing of the software in response to code modifications. A typical implementation of this practice includes a CI server that pulls code from a version control repository and executes interconnected steps to compile the code, run unit tests, check quality and build deployable artefacts. Even though automating the integration process is important for adoption, the relevance of CI lies in the frequency of integration. It has to be regular enough to provide quick feedback to developers, thereby improving their productivity and the software quality [20]. CI has the effect of producing shorter release cycles.

3.3   Infrastructure as Code

Infrastructure as Code (IaC) is an approach to provisioning and managing dynamic infrastructure resources through machine-readable configuration files [7,15,16]. It is also referred to as programmable infrastructure in reference to the adaptation and application of practices and tools from software engineering on IT infrastructure management. As a result, changes to the computing infrastructure and/or the execution environment are made in a structured way, by means of reliable and established processes [7]. The benefits of IaC include repeatability of creating and configuring execution environments, management automation, development agility and infrastructure scalability [16].

3.4   Related Work

Software deployment is specified using semi-formal graphical notations, informal diagrams, scripts, domain-specific languages (DSLs), and modelling languages.

The *UML deployment diagram* is a well-known notation that provides a graphical language to describe a static representation of a system's architecture. Though it has been refined in several versions of the UML standard, it continues to be one of the least adopted diagrams among UML users [21] and within the model-driven engineering (MDE) community [22]. This diagram allows to specify only a portion of the required system elements (*e.g.*, infrastructure provisioning, network configuration and elasticity requirements [23,24]). UML lacks the semantics for translating deployment diagrams into code, therefore existing transformation approaches limit the diagram semantics and the supported technologies.

Wettinger *et al.* [25] propose (i) a methodology to implement the DevOps paradigm in practice with a high degree of automation; and (ii) DevOpslang, a DSL to deploy cloud applications. The purpose of DevOpslang is to bridge the gap between developers and operators by supporting the proposed methodology. Nevertheless, the automation considered in its design seems incomplete with respect to its motivation: it only considers forward engineering, from development to operations, leaving out the continuous cycle as advocated in DevOps. Thus, offering no support at run-time.

Thiery *et al.* [26] address the problem of providing testers with an automated and provider-independent method to deploy and test cloud applications. They define a DSL that allows testers to describe how an application is deployed, and which cloud resources are required and available for the deployment. The DSL generates a set of provider-specific commands based on the providers' command-line applications. The authors claim to support a re-deployment scenario in their evaluation, however, it is rather a deployment to a new cloud platform (*i.e.*, a new deployment). The proposed DSL does not consider any kind of support once the application has been deployed.

Glaser [27] proposes a model-driven and topology-based framework that generates concrete deployment instances compliant with TOSCA. These instances are derived based on a domain model specification whose parameters change over time. The proposed framework updates the running infrastructure on user demand. To achieve this, Glaser proposes a DSL to map domain modelling parameters to parameters of the cloud infrastructure. The proposed DSL implements forward engineering only, providing no support on the operations side.

Holmes [28] proposes MING, a model and view based framework for describing and deploying cloud data centres. MING separates concerns into different views, namely, inventory, networking and configuration, allowing stakeholders to relate to concerns that are relevant to them. These views are realized by an OpenStack-tailored DSL. MING allows to adapt an already deployed data center, either adding new resources or providing software upgrades. As for the aforementioned works, MING realizes forward engineering only.

Significant work has been done in automating the processes to integrate development and operations better. IaC plays an important role in this effort, as it enables the application of software engineering practices to infrastructure design and management. However, there are still many opportunities to strengthen the linkage between both sides of the DevOps development cycle. Moreover, emerging practices, such as continuous experimentation and feedback, require standard and automated processes to integrate run-time data back into development.

4   TORNADO: A Framework for RTE in DevOps

The design-time artefacts supported by TORNADO are text-based, structured specifications. Our framework reconciles these specifications with their corresponding elements from the running environment. To do so, we introduce a run-time support layer that bridges D&C work from development and operations. This layer contains models at run-time (MARTs) that represent the elements from the running environment. These models are eventually transformed into text to keep the specifications updated. Figure 1 depicts a high-level overview of our framework. It shows how information flows between design- and run-time through the run-time support layer.

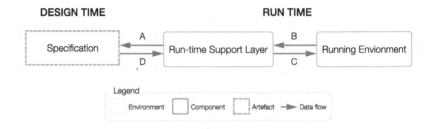

Fig. 1. High level overview of TORNADO

We adhere to the MART definition proposed by Bencomo *et al.* [29]:

An MART can be defined as an abstract representation of a system, including its structure, behaviour and goals, which exists in tandem with a given system during the actual execution time of that system [...]

TORNADO is based on Castañeda's operational framework [30]. This framework comprises four main components: a notation-model mapping, a catalogue of operations to update the model's instances, the run-time semantics from the application domain, and causal links. The latter are used to propagate changes among the models that are connected, as in the example presented in Sect. 2 about a software deployment specification associated with a network configuration file. The models associated with these specifications must be causally connected as follows: the software model references a host name defined in the network model; when the latter changes, the change is propagated to the former, so it is updated accordingly.

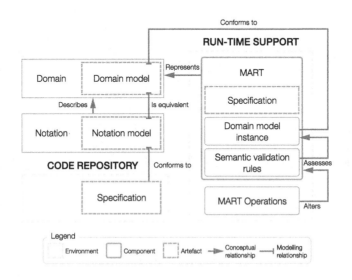

Fig. 2. TORNADO's concepts

Figure 2 depicts what an MART is in terms of its internal components. In TORNADO, an MART is not only a model instance but a 3-tuple containing a model instance, a specification instance (*i.e.*, one or more files) and a set of semantic validation rules. The model and specification instances are kept in sync automatically. The validation rules check the quality of the model to guarantee its integrity. For example, a computing resource may be given an IP address outside its subnet range. A simple validation rule can discover this mistake, avoiding the deployment of the whole infrastructure, offering quicker feedback and spending fewer resources. Furthermore, these validations can be delegated to other software components. In our example, the network configuration verification can be delegated to simulation engines or network virtualisation platforms, which can be run in memory without the need for deploying more resources.

As shown in Fig. 2, an MART is associated with a set of operations. Each operation contains the run-time semantics to alter the model instance. An operation is associated with a set of Pre- and Post-validation rules, which check the state of the model before and after altering it.

The relationship between a specification and an MART is detailed in Fig. 2. A MART conforms to a domain model, and must be equivalent to a notation. That is, TORNADO expects a one-to-one relationship between the specification notation and its corresponding model. However, achieving such a relationship is often difficult; it may be necessary to limit the facts that can be expressed with the notation to guarantee said equivalence. To map the concepts from one model to another, the pair model-specification is associated with a set of transformations. For example, an MART representing the networking domain can be set up to work with OpenStack HOT[5] and/or HCL[6] (*i.e.*, Terraform templates' notation). Each of these configurations knows how to update the model instance and the specification file, given a change in either of them.

Next, we describe the arrows A, B, C and D from Fig. 1. These arrows are later refined in Fig. 3.

A: Specification → MART

This interaction is initiated by a developer. Once she pushes changes to the version control repository, a CI server temporarily instantiates the corresponding MART based on the current version of the specification. If it passes the quality checks and the MART is already deployed to the run-time support layer, the existing MART is updated and the CI server proceeds to apply the changes to the running environment. In case the MART is being instantiated for the first time, a new instance is deployed.

B: MART → Running Environment

This interaction is not further explored in this paper, given our motivation to integrate operations work in the opposite direction. Nevertheless, an MART may update a running environment as part of the change propagation chain from a causal connection, as described above.

---

[5] https://docs.openstack.org/heat/latest/template_guide (accessed Oct, 2018).
[6] https://www.terraform.io/docs/configuration/syntax.html (accessed Oct, 2018).

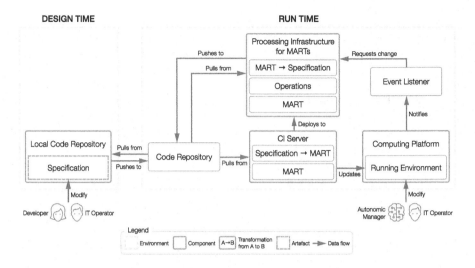

Fig. 3. Continuous integration loop in TORNADO

C: MART ← Running Environment

This interaction is initiated by a change in the running environment. A listener catches an event propagated by the supporting platform and initiates a procedure to update the MART instance accordingly.

D: Specification ← MART

This interaction is initiated when an MART instance is updated by the running environment it represents. A procedure is triggered to transform the instance to the corresponding specification notation. The resulting text is used to update the remote file in the version control repository.

Figure 3 depicts TORNADO's continuous integration loop. This loop extends the concept of CI to frequently integrate changes into a running environment into development. D&C specifications are usually treated in the same way as application code. This traditional use of CI only considers integrating work at the request of developers. It means that any kind of manual work would require an operator to remember and translate data from one tool to another, from one syntax to another, and possibly from one paradigm to another (*e.g.*, imperative to declarative). The continuous integration loop we propose automates that process. Furthermore, DevOps engineers and operators are not the only actors who modify a running environment. Autonomic managers have already assumed a significant role in understanding run-time operations. Dynamic scaling policies, for example, automatically scale computing resources in response to changing service demand. The actions of these autonomic managers are not generally reflected in the specifications.

In our proposal, the CI server deploys the model directly to the processing infrastructure instead of updating an already deployed model one event at a time.

4.1   CI Considerations

This subsection discusses three main CI considerations regarding the implementation and adoption of TORNADO. We outline concerns that could potentially affect the development workflow, and propose alternative solutions.

C1: Contribution Model. TORNADO enables the run-time support layer to make code contributions. Although CI provides mechanisms to guarantee quality, unsupervised changes can produce adverse effects. This can happen, for example, due to an operation mistake or a bug in the run-time semantics associated with a model. In addition to the *committer* model, in which the run-time support layer is added as a collaborator to the repository (*i.e.*, it is granted write access), we propose the *contributor* model, in which code modifications are proposed as pull requests rather than committed directly.

In the case of the committer model, there would be no delay in reflecting the changes in the specifications. For this reason, this model would likely produce fewer merge conflicts. However, it does not mitigate the risk of unwanted side-effects. In the case of the contributor model, the risk is completely avoided. Nevertheless, additional time must be allocated to review the pull requests, delaying the update and increasing the possibility of merge conflicts. While a pull request remains open, the MART instance is inconsistent with respect to the specification or the running environment.

It is common today that computing platforms and autonomic managers make decisions to affect a running system. Therefore, it is acceptable, at least in some cases, to grant commit access to the run-time support layer. We believe that providing both contribution alternatives is the best option.

C2: Conflict Resolution. Conflict resolution is not a trivial task. It requires spending time inspecting the code and making informed decisions about the merging conflict(s). Therefore, automating conflict resolution requires simplifying the problem. We suggest two strategies to do so. First, we propose to avoid conflicts related to formatting. The transformation from MART to specification must follow a standard process, which always generates statements in the same order, case and format (*e.g.*, spacing and indentation). To facilitate following these measures in development, we propose to use a formatting utility before committing changes. And second, we propose to give priority to one of the actors (*e.g.*, the run-time support layer). In case of merge conflicts, the run-time support layer can decide to either drop the local changes or replace the remote ones, according to its assigned priority level. The former requires to rollback the latest changes to keep the MART instance consistent with the remote specification.

C3: Quality Assurance. One of the most important parts of CI is the continuous application of quality control. TORNADO re-uses the concept of pre- and post-validation rules from Castañeda's operational framework [30] to ensure quality conditions before and after modifying the model. However, there may be concerns regarding the model itself, rather than its state with respect to a certain operation. For instance, referring to the example above about the IP address outside of range. The state itself is erroneous, making it necessary to check its quality before deployment. There are also other kinds of concerns related to business restrictions; validations on the model instance allows, for example, to limit what can be deployed by the tenant. These business restrictions can be implemented as semantic restrictions on the model, as the model itself represents entities from the rules' domain.

5   Evaluation

In this section, we present a proof of concept implementation of TORNADO. This implementation covers all the topics discussed in Sect. 4, including the CI considerations. The source code of this implementation is available in a Github repository.[7]

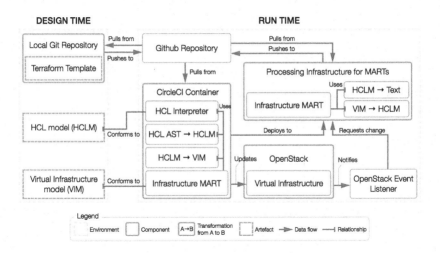

Fig. 4. Evaluation setup

Figure 4 depicts the evaluation setup. We chose the IaC tool Terraform and the OpenStack platform to realise this proof of concept. Consequently, the notation specification is HCL (*i.e.*, Terraform templates' notation) and the running environment is a virtual infrastructure. Figures 5 and 6 represent the HCL and virtual infrastructure models, respectively. Notice that these models are limited with respect to the entities they represent. However, they are complex enough to demonstrate the usefulness and soundness of this framework.

---

[7] https://github.com/RigiResearch/jachinte-DevOps2018-evaluation.

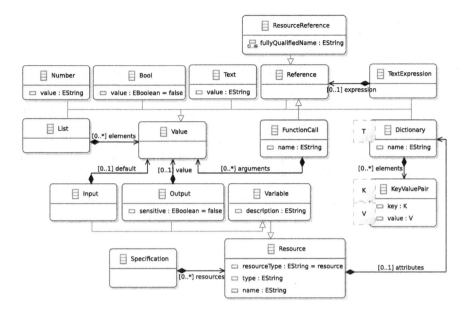

Fig. 5. HCL model

The HCL and infrastructure models were developed using the Eclipse Xcore project[8], and the model transformations using the Xtend language[9]. The HCL interpreter was developed using Eclipse Xtext[10].

Next we describe the main components of the evaluation setup and describe the development workflow associated with this implementation.

Infrastructure MART. This MART is composed of a Terraform specification, an instance of the Infrastructure model and a set of supported operations and validations on the model instance. The specific operations supported at the time of writing this paper are: adding a new resource and removing an existing one. Supporting more operations requires implementing the interface `Operation`. As an example, we added one semantic validation that constraints the RAM size of any virtual machine instance to be launched. Adding more validations is possible by implementing the interface `Rule`. The MART ensures that the model instance and the specification are always in sync, so any modification to one another causes a synchronization process and a commit if necessary. When the specification changes, the Terraform state is updated consequently. Before committing, the MART invokes the Terraform format command. Commit messages end with "[skip ci]" to avoid unnecessary CI builds. However, CI could be used to reinforce quality policies on operations (manual) work.

---

[8] https://wiki.eclipse.org/Xcore (accessed Oct 2018).
[9] http://www.eclipse.org/xtend (accessed Oct 2018).
[10] http://www.eclipse.org/Xtext (accessed Oct 2018).

Processing Infrastructure for MARTs. This component offers a service to register or update an MART and execute operations on it. Registering a new MART causes the corresponding code repository to be cloned. Updating an existing MART causes its corresponding repository to be updated accordingly.

CircleCI Container. This component uses the HCL interpreter to create an Abstract Syntax Tree (AST) out of a Terraform template. It uses the AST to instantiate the HCL model and then transforms it to an instance of the virtual infrastructure model. Then, it instantiates the Infrastructure MART and executes the semantic validations associated with it. If the MART passes the validations, it is deployed to the processing infrastructure for MARTs and the resources specified in the Terraform template are deployed. If the validations fail, the developer is notified. This workflow is specified in a YAML[11] configuration file containing three jobs: `validate_terraform`, `deploy_models` and `deploy_terraform`.

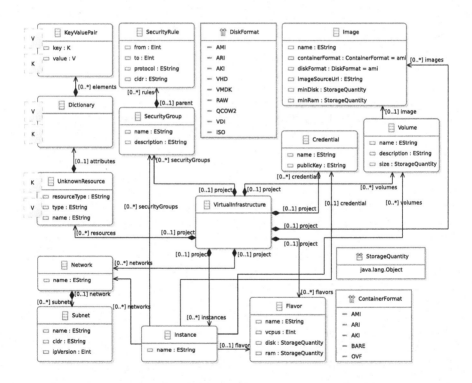

Fig. 6. Virtual infrastructure model

---

[11] http://yaml.org (accessed Oct 2018).

5.1 Development Workflow

The development workflow is as follows. An operator creates a Terraform template using OpenStack as cloud provider. When the template is pushed to the Github repository, the CI server pulls the template and creates a local instance of the Infrastructure MART based on the template. If the instance passes the semantic validations (*i.e.*, there are no instances violating the RAM constraint), the MART is deployed to the processing infrastructure for MARTs. Then, the CI server deploys the Terraform template, updating the OpenStack resources. The event listener consumes the events generated by OpenStack but ignores them, as these changes are authored by a known user name associated with the CI server and the changes have been already applied to the model. At this point, the template and the OpenStack resources are in sync. When the operator modifies the OpenStack resources (*i.e.*, creates or removes resources using the Horizon dashboard or the CLI client), the event listener gets a notification. It then executes the corresponding operation on the MART by means of the processing infrastructure for MARTs. The MART adapts accordingly, committing and pushing any modification to the template to the Github repository.

Fig. 7. Updates to the Terraform template on Github

Figure 7 depicts three screenshots taken from the test Github repository. The first one displays the initial state of the template, as created by the developer (*i.e.*, user *jachinte*). The second and third screenshots display the template after the processing infrastructure (*i.e.*, PrIMoR on behalf of user *miguel*) committed changes. In the last case, a new file is added and referenced from the template.

6 Conclusions and Future Work

There is a lack of standard processes and tools in DevOps to integrate operation information back into development readily. In this paper, we focused on the lack of automation support for updating D&C specifications from manual changes to experimental setups. DevOps engineers and operators are in charge of keeping these specifications consistent, remembering every change and translating them from one syntax and paradigm to another. We presented TORNADO, a two-way CI framework (*i.e.*, Dev $\xrightarrow{CI}$ Ops and Dev $\xleftarrow{CI}$ Ops) that keeps D&C specifications always in sync with the systems they configure and deploy. We evaluated TORNADO by implementing a proof of concept based on Terraform templates and the OpenStack platform, demonstrating its feasibility and soundness.

Although TORNADO focuses on RTE for D&C, it potentially enables further synchronisation between other design artefacts (*e.g.*, architecture design) and the D&C specifications, completing the continuous development loop. This would provide operators and autonomic managers with a standard mechanism to contribute to the evolution of the system. That is, their actions would directly affect the development artefacts too.

Acknowledgments. This work was funded in part by the National Sciences and Engineering Research Council (NSERC) of Canada, IBM Canada Ltd. and IBM Advanced Studies (CAS), the University of Victoria (Canada), and Universidad Icesi (Colombia).

References

1. Sharma, S., Coyne, B.: DevOps for Dummies. Limited IBM Edition (2013)
2. Zhu, L., Bass, L., Champlin-Scharff, G.: DevOps and its practices. IEEE Softw. **33**(3), 32–34 (2016)
3. Fagerholm, F., Guinea, A.S., Mäenpää, H., Münch, J.: Building blocks for continuous experimentation. In: Proceedings of the 1st International Workshop on Rapid Continuous Software Engineering, RCoSE 2014, pp. 26–35. ACM, New York (2014)
4. Shahin, M., Babar, M.A., Zhu, L.: The intersection of continuous deployment and architecting process: practitioners' perspectives. In: Proceedings of the 10th ACM/IEEE International Symposium on Empirical Software Engineering and Measurement, ESEM 2016, pp. 44:1–44:10. ACM, New York (2016)
5. Fabijan, A., Dmitriev, P., Olsson, H.H., Bosch, J.: The evolution of continuous experimentation in software product development: from data to a data-driven organization at scale. In: 2017 IEEE/ACM 39th International Conference on Software Engineering, ICSE 2017, pp. 770–780 (2017)
6. Schermann, G., Cito, J., Leitner, P.: Continuous experimentation: challenges, implementation techniques, and current research. IEEE Softw. **35**(2), 26–31 (2018)
7. Morris, K.: Infrastructure as Code: Managing Servers in the Cloud, 1st edn. O'Reilly Media Inc., Sebastopol (2016)
8. Spanoudakis, G., Zisman, A.: Inconsistency management in software engineering: survey and open research issues, pp. 329–380. World Scientific Publishing Company (2012)
9. Kruchten, P., Nord, R.L., Ozkaya, I.: Technical debt: from metaphor to theory and practice. IEEE Softw. **29**(6), 18–21 (2012)
10. Henriksson, A., Larsson, H.: A definition of round-trip engineering. Technical report (2003)
11. Sendall, S., Küster, J.: Taming model round-trip engineering. In: Proceedings of Workshop on Best Practices for Model-Driven Software Development, p. 1 (2004)

12. Hettel, T., Lawley, M., Raymond, K.: Model synchronisation: definitions for round-trip engineering. In: Vallecillo, A., Gray, J., Pierantonio, A. (eds.) ICMT 2008. LNCS, vol. 5063, pp. 31–45. Springer, Heidelberg (2008). https://doi.org/10.1007/978-3-540-69927-9_3

13. Shahin, M., Babar, M.A., Zhu, L.: Continuous integration, delivery and deployment: a systematic review on approaches, tools, challenges and practices. IEEE Access **5**, 3909–3943 (2017)

14. ISO/IEC/IEEE, International Standard - Systems and software engineering - Vocabulary. ISO/IEC/IEEE 24765:2010(E), pp. 1–418 (2010)

15. Hüttermann, M.: Infrastructure as Code, pp. 135–156. Apress (2012)

16. Nelson-Smith, S.: Test-Driven Infrastructure with Chef: Bring Behavior-Driven Development to Infrastructure as Code. O'Reilly Media Inc., Sebastopol (2013)

17. Blair, G., Bencomo, N., France, R.B.: Models@run.time. Computer **42**(10), 22–27 (2009)

18. Rahm, J., Graube, M., Urbas, L.: A proposal for an interactive roundtrip engineering system. In: 2017 22nd IEEE International Conference on Emerging Technologies and Factory Automation (ETFA), pp. 1–7, September 2017

19. Tilley, S.R., Wong, K., Storey, M.A.D., Müller, H.A.: Programmable reverse engineering. Int. J. Softw. Eng. Knowl. Eng. **04**(04), 501–520 (1994)

20. Fitzgerald, B., Stol, K.J.: Continuous software engineering: a roadmap and agenda. J. Syst. Softw. **123**, 176–189 (2017)

21. Petre, M.: UML in practice. In: Proceedings 35th International Conference on Software Engineering, ICSE 2013, pp. 722–731. IEEE Press, Piscataway (2013)

22. Hutchinson, J., Rouncefield, M., Whittle, J.: Model-driven engineering practices in industry. In: Proceedings 33rd International Conference on Software Engineering, ICSE 2011, pp. 633–642. ACM, New York (2011)

23. Inzinger, C., Nastic, S., Sehic, S., Vögler, M., Li, F., Dustdar, S.: MADCAT: a methodology for architecture and deployment of cloud application topologies. In: Proceedings 8th International Symposium on Service Oriented System Engineering, SOSE 2014, Oxford, UK, pp. 13–22 (2014)

24. Copil, G., Moldovan, D., Truong, H.L., Dustdar, S.: SYBL: an extensible language for controlling elasticity in cloud applications. In: Proceedings 13th IEEE/ACM International Symposium on Cluster, Cloud and Grid Computing, CCGrid 2013, pp. 112–119 (2013)

25. Wettinger, J., Breitenbücher, U., Leymann, F.: DevOpSlang – bridging the gap between development and operations. In: Villari, M., Zimmermann, W., Lau, K.K. (eds.) ESOCC 2014. LNCS, vol. 8745, pp. 108–122. Springer, Heidelberg (2014). https://doi.org/10.1007/978-3-662-44879-3_8

26. Thiery, A., Cerqueus, T., Thorpe, C., Sunyé, G., Murphy, J.: A DSL for deployment and testing in the cloud. In: Proceedings of the 2014 IEEE International Conference on Software Testing, Verification, and Validation Workshops, ICSTW 2014, pp. 376–382. IEEE Computer Society (2014)

27. Glaser, F.: Domain model optimized deployment and execution of cloud applications with TOSCA. In: Grabowski, J., Herbold, S. (eds.) SAM 2016. LNCS, vol. 9959, pp. 68–83. Springer, Cham (2016). https://doi.org/10.1007/978-3-319-46613-2_5

28. Holmes, T.: MING: model- and view-based deployment and adaptation of cloud datacenters. In: Helfert, M., Ferguson, D., Méndez Muñoz, V., Cardoso, J. (eds.) CLOSER 2016. CCIS, vol. 740, pp. 317–338. Springer, Cham (2017). https://doi.org/10.1007/978-3-319-62594-2_16

29. Bencomo, N., Bennaceur, A., Grace, P., Blair, G., Issarny, V.: The role of models@run.time in supporting on-the-fly interoperability. Computing **95**(3), 167–190 (2013)
30. Castaneda, L.: Runtime modelling for user-centric smart applications in cyber-physical-human systems. Ph.D. thesis, Department of Computer Science, University of Victoria (2017)

DevOps is Simply Interaction Between Development and Operations

Floris Erich[(✉)]

Robot Innovation Research Center,
National Institute of Advanced Industrial Science and Technology, Tsukuba, Japan
floris.erich@aist.go.jp

Abstract. Based on a systematic literature review and interviews with six organizations regarding their use of DevOps, we take a look at a number of differing perspectives on what DevOps entails. We argue for a definition of DevOps as simply being "interaction between development and operations". This simple definition implies that DevOps is not a new thing which only certain organizations practice, but rather a fundamental characteristic of software and systems engineering that every organization is confronted with and manages to a certain extent.

Keywords: DevOps · Development · Operations

1 Introduction

Various definitions of DevOps are encountered in the literature and in practice. DevOps has for example been defined as "a set of practices intended to reduce the time between committing a change to a system and the change being placed into normal production, while ensuring high quality" [1]. Meanwhile DevOps has also been identified as "an organizational approach aimed at creating empathy and cross-functional collaboration" [5]. Another definition of DevOps is "infrastructure being governed by the same processes that govern development" [9]. Based on a Systematic Mapping Study, DevOps has been defined as "A development methodology aimed at bridging the gap between Development and Operations, emphasizing communication and collaboration, continuous integration, quality assurance and delivery with automated deployment utilizing a set of development practices" [8]. And DevOps is seen as a "a cultural movement that changes how individuals think about their work, values the diversity of work done, supports intentional processes that accelerate the rate by which businesses realize value, and measures the effect of social and technical change" [3].

Some of these definitions were based on personal opinion, the perspective of a single organization or on reviews of academic and industrial literature. The goal of this paper is to study how various organizations practice DevOps and to synthesize a definition of DevOps that covers both the academic and industrial usage of the term, thus extending one of our earlier publications [6]. The organizations

© Springer Nature Switzerland AG 2019
J.-M. Bruel et al. (Eds.): DEVOPS 2018, LNCS 11350, pp. 89–99, 2019.
https://doi.org/10.1007/978-3-030-06019-0_7

that were interviewed have requested for their names not to be mentioned, hence in this paper we will be calling them FinCom1, FinCom2, SupportCom, Portal-Com, UtilCom and CommunitySoft. All of these organizations tried to adopt DevOps into their ways of working.

2   Interviews

The interviews took place in 2014 and 2015, in person, and typically on location at the organization which was the subject of the interview. In the case of PortalCom the interview took place over the phone. In the case of UtilCom a discussion was held at the institute of the first author at that time (University of Tsukuba, Japan). In case of CommunitySoft the interview took place via email.

2.1   FinCom1

FinCom1 is a Dutch bank with over 50000 employees, serving both private and corporate account holders. Before adopting DevOps, FinCom1 had already started to adopt Scrum, ITIL and CMMI. The interviewee was the manager of a DevOps team, and was recommended to be interviewed by its CTO.

FinCom1 defines DevOps as being an extension to the adoption of Scrum.

The goals which they wanted to accomplish by adopting DevOps were to (1) reduce lead time for new projects, (2) improve their problem solving capability, and (3) to improve the quality and amount of feedback received from users.

Their approach was to (1) introduce DevOps departments organized around major services, (2) introduce interdisciplinary DevOps teams for components which together form the services, and (3) create a role of DevOps engineer.

FinCom1 encountered various problems in their adoption of DevOps, such as (1) personnel not adjusting to the level of openness they considered DevOps to require, (2) software developers reacting negatively to being on-call and (3) friction arising from differences in the transformative workflow of development and the reactive workflow of operations personnel.

Adopting DevOps did have some positive results, at it (1) decreased the lead time required for new projects to start, from a couple of months to a couple of weeks, (2) improved communication between personnel, and (3) improved the software quality.

2.2   FinCom2

FinCom2 is a Dutch insurance firm which also serves both private and corporate account holders. At the time of the interview it had over 3000 employees and over 281 million euros net revenue. Similarly to FinCom1 it used Scrum, ITIL and CMMI before adopting DevOps. The interview was with two employees, a business analyst and a agile coach/lean business expert.

FinCom2 defines DevOps as "a way of collaboration in which processes are automated as much as possible" and claims DevOps "breaks down the silos, burns the walls down, makes everything one integrated whole".

The goals of the DevOps adoption by FinCom2 were to (1) increase agility and flexibility, and (2) increase the percentage of processes handled without human intervention (also called the Straight Through Processing grade).

The approach of FinCom2 was firstly to use CAMS (Culture, Automation, Measurement and Sharing) as a framework for measuring DevOps adoption. One of the interviewees gave the following description of how they applied CAMS: "Recently, in a meeting with management we looked at bottlenecks. For each bottleneck, we assigned a C, A, M or S. About 80% of the bottlenecks received a C, they are related to culture." Secondly, FinCom2 introduced DevOps teams. Thirdly, they adopted Continuous Deployment and Continuous Delivery, referring to Humble and Farley's book as inspiration [7]. One of the interviewees commented that implementing DevOps can often be "as simple as getting the right people together" and "literally bringing the people in a room and then sitting with each other for an hour".

Problems with adopting DevOps at FinCom2 where (1) developers forgetting to use feature switches, causing the wrong code to be made available in production, (2) difficulty in getting employees to spend time on process improvement, as employees were focusing too much on improving the product itself, and (3) skepticism from management personnel which were unconvinced about the merits of DevOps as they saw it as "yet another approach to creating software".

At the time of the interview FinCom2 had only accomplished minor results from adopting DevOps, with one team improving their testing capabilities according to a model from XebiaLabs [12].

2.3   SupportCom

SupportCom is a small/mid sized Dutch software company (300 employees) that creates a web application which can be used for providing customer support. Before adopting DevOps the company had adopted Scrum. The interview was with a project manager who was also managing a DevOps team.

The interviewee defined DevOps as simply getting development and operations personnel to work closely together, by sharing the same space and by being part of the same team.

Their goals of adopting DevOps were to reduce the release time of their software and to realize a cloud offering of their product. They had started their cloud offering five years ago, which went well at the start, however, as their customer base grew their product and development workforce started to face scaling issues. Another goal of DevOps was to eliminate silos, "not just between development and operations but also with support, sales and consultancy".

Their approach was to introduce a single DevOps team working in a single space. This team was replacing the traditional development team working on an "operations heavy service". The division of work of this team was basically 60% sprinting (implementing new features) and 30% fire-fighting (solving production issues) This way of dividing work is similar to as advocated by Google's site reliability engineering approach [2]. Additionally they adopted Continuous Deployment and Continuous Delivery.

The problems they encountered were (1) skepticism from both development and management personnel, and (2) that empowering teams to solve problems internally leads to less documentation of the problems occuring. According to the interviewee: 'It all becomes a little bit more ad hoc. If there is a fire which has to be put out then it becomes like a black box. "I'm not sure what they are doing, but they are solving it, or something." In how we deal with that I still see an challenge.'

SupportCom noticed an increase in speed and effectiveness of problem solving. The interviewee had this to say when asked what adopting DevOps has brought them: "Solve problems faster I think, that less escalating has to happen. [...] that there [used to be] escalation via five people or more. And before you know it you [were] two weeks further".

2.4   PortalCom

PortalCom is a Dutch subsidiary of a multinational organization which creates intranet portals. The Dutch subsidiary had around 100 employees, while the organization as a whole had around 5000 employees. They used Scrum before adopting DevOps, and the DevOps adoption was an effort local to the Dutch subsidiary. The interview was with an entrepreneur/DevOps team member.

PortalCom defines DevOps as a culture of understanding between development and operations personnel and a movement towards integration of all phases of the software process. Before adopting DevOps "Dev and Ops did not speak each other's language" and that "DevOps is about making the bridge smaller so that we understand each other", using the bridge as a metaphor of the divide between development and operations personnel. The interviewee also explicitly stated that "DevOps is not something you can be. It is not a function, it is not a title." and that DevOps "is a piece of culture, it's a piece of understanding".

The goals of adopting DevOps were (1) to support a switch to a cloud computing model of offering their software and (2) to increase software development capabilities.

As for how the organization implemented DevOps, the interviewee gave an explanation framed around the development and operations divide: "It is not just some piece of operations being added to a development department, but also testing is very important, so is quality assurance. Those are the parties which in the past, before DevOps was introduced, were separate departments, divisions or groups. If you introduce DevOps you would expect that those people would sit together more often, speak their expectations more often, about what they exactly need to do and what they have to test, what they need to bring live. So more understanding arises." Additionally the organization is adopting Continuous Deployment and Continuous Delivery.

A big problem with adopting DevOps was that it required highly skilled workers with cross-disciplinary skills. Those kind of people were hard to find due to many managers desiring them for their teams and a lack of good candidates for hire.

The results of adopting DevOps at PortalCom were an inceased development speed, faster release cycles and a higher amount of problems getting solved directly within the DevOps teams.

2.5   UtilCom

UtilCom is a cloud service provider that operates worldwide, with over a 1000 employees. The company did not adopt any formal software development method before adopting DevOps, instead allowing each team to pick their own way of working. This is also the case of DevOps at UtilCom, not every team in the organization practices, but various teams have decided to do so. The interview was with a senior software engineer at UtilCom.

UtilCom defines DevOps as "the principles and practices needed to create scalable service infrastructure".

While UtilCom leaves it upto the teams to decide to formally practice DevOps, according to the interview the organization actually saw the practices growing organically. Many principles and practices which are now considered to be part of DevOps were independently implemented by UtilCom.

Some of the DevOps practices at UtilCom are:

1. Explicitly recognizing the unique skill set required from server script engineers performing operations, countering the derogatory term "script junkies".
2. Teaching software engineering techniques to operations personnel.
3. Having one subteam within a larger team (the larger having around 100 team members) acting as a DevOps team and specializing in problems spanning the disciplines of development and operations.
4. Using distributed teams to increase redundancy.
5. Adopting various technical practices: Continuous Deployment, Continuous Delivery, feature switches, staging areas, upgrade/downgrade testing, Infrastructure as Code and Infrastructure as a Service.
6. Differentiating between three kinds of deployments: Deployments with only production code, deployments with only configuration, and deployments with a mix of both production code and configuration.

UtilCom encountered that development and operations personnel have conflicting ways of measuring progress. The interviewee believes that new performance measurements are needed to deal with this.

The adoptation of DevOps principles and practices at UtilCom has resulted in (1) reduced on-call rotations thanks to infrastructure automation, (2) less false and duplicate alarms and (3) a decrease in escalations as shown by historical escalation patterns.

2.6   CommunitySoft

CommunitySoft is an online open source community with around 1800 members from all over the world, which is registered as a charity in the United Kingdom.

Project teams are free to choose the way they want to work, though the use of agile software development techniques is typical. The interview was with a co-founder of the organization who also acts as a project manager.

Their definition of DevOps is simply "getting development done and into operations".

The goal of adopting DevOps is to get direct feedback from stakeholders by continuously giving them access to a working version of the system under development. Note that this goes a step further than typical agile software development projects, in which simply giving a presentation of a product under development was often considered a delivery.

CommunitySoft has adopted Continuous Deployment and Continuous Delivery, as well as adopting a GitHub workflow, automated testing, cloud hosting (Heroku) as well as having different environments to which their software gets deployed (development, staging and production).

Problems which CommunitySoft encountered with adopting DevOps are (1) that it is hard to automate every check and hence still requiring a person to perform some verification steps, (2) that there are a lot of different opinions of what DevOps is, and that sometimes teams were spending too much time discussing this, and (3) that it was hard to find a good balance between feature development and process improvements.

Thanks to adopting DevOps, the organization is capable of continuously delivering working software to its stakeholders.

3   Types of Implementation

Our main findings are that DevOps implementations exist at a spectrum ranging from business-driven top-down implementations and technology-driven bottom-up implementations. The organizations that we interviewed were located at various positions in this spectrum.

Both type of implementations have similar goals, such as reducing lead time, improving problem solving ability, increasing feedback, reducing system downtime, reducing the workforce size, reducing miscommunication and more frequent software releases.

In terms of implementation however both type of implementations differ significantly.

Business-driven top-down implementations will typically focus on how the organization is structured. We can consider FinCom1 and FinCom2 to be of this kind. The decision to adopt DevOps in these organizations came from management, and the types of changes made is related to the way the organization is structured. Organizations might merge seperate departments doing development and operations into single departments organized by product or service. They will try to put both development and operations personnel in the same team. Some organizations go as far as introducing the special title of DevOps engineer to replace traditional titles such as software engineer and system administrator. They might adopt frameworks and process models such as the Scaled Agile Framework (SAFe) and Disciplined Agile Delivery (DAD).

Technology-driven bottom-up implementations will instead focus on the tools used by the development and operations personnel. We can consider UtilCom and CommunitySoft to be of this kind. Traditional tools such as version control (such as SVN and Git) play a central role in the DevOps tool stack. Developers write code and commit it to a repository. A continuous integration pipeline (stored in systems such as Jenkins and Travis) will then take the source code and perform transformations on it to create derived artifacts such as executables and documentation. Where DevOps differs from traditional software engineering is that the artifacts are not only created but also made available to stakeholders who can evaluate the artifacts. Tangentially various DevOps tools focus on the way these environments are configured, evolving from a collection of ad-hoc scripts to declarative configuration-as-code approaches using tools such as CFEngine and Terraform, as well as hosting artifacts in virtualized environments and containers.

PortalCom and SupportCom fall between these two categories. It seems like both organizations are experimenting with DevOps at a smaller scale, in each case for a single product.

Supporting the move the cloud based software is a major goal in many cases of DevOps adoption. It seems like "traditional" software engineering approaches such as Agile are ill suited for offering cloud based software, as they do not formally define how to deal with problems occuring in operations.

In the cases that we studied, DevOps is typically implemented in concert with Continuous Deployment and Continuous Delivery.

4   DevOps as Interaction Between Development and Operations

The concept of DevOps first appeared in practice, before empirical software engineering researchers started to look at it. Because of this, there is no clear widely agreed upon definition of what DevOps actually means. While Bass, Weber and Zhu give an operational definition of DevOps [1], this definition does not match how our interviewees see DevOps, and it also begs the question which practices are part of DevOps. This definition of Dyck matches the spirit of DevOps [5], however it does not match the more extreme perspectives of DevOps that we encountered in some organizations, for example DevOps as simply putting development and operations personnel in the same room. Meanwhile, the definition of Loukides is in line with the technology-driven perspective of DevOps [9], but seems to ignore the business-driven perspective. The definition of Jabbari et al. [8] gives a definition that seems the match that of most of our interviewees, but by calling DevOps a methodology and by naming specific practices the definition becomes too specialized. Daniels and Davis define DevOps to be a cultural movement [3], which is in line with the definition of a few of our interviewees, but at the same time does not seem to be an implementable artifact such as other interviewees see DevOps.

One way to solve the problems with defining DevOps is to consider it from a wider perspective. By considering DevOps to be the interaction between development and operations, we can accomodate the multiple perspectives of DevOps simply as different approaches to improve this interaction. At the same time, we see the terms development and operations as abstract definitions which need to be further defined in actual discussions. Development and operations might for example refer to departments, teams, skills, roles and jobs.

It also implies that DevOps is not an artifact but rather a fundamental characteristic of software and systems engineering. And it implies that in the future we should not study DevOps as something which can be obtained, like a process or tool. Instead we can ask more qualitative questions that try to measure the satisfaction of the interaction and approaches to improve this interaction.

In the remainder of this discussion we will look at ways in which using the definition of DevOps being interaction between development and operations can be applied to existing terminology in practical and academic discussions. Some of the applications are inspired by the literature, some by the interviews which we performed, and some will be hypothetical.

4.1   DevOps Departments

A term used by some of our interviewees, but not typically in the literature, is that of a DevOps department. In the case of the DevOps department, let us consider three ways of applying the DevOps term. Firstly, a DevOps department can be a department in which development and operations *teams* interact with each other regularly. In practice, for large organizations such as FinCom1 and FinCom2, the first step of a DevOps transformation is moving from having separate development and operations departments to having DevOps departments. Secondly, a DevOps department can be a department in which multiple *DevOps teams* interact with each other while working on related parts of a product or service. In practice, for large organizations such as FinCom1 and FinCom2, this is often the second step in a DevOps transformation. Thirdly, a DevOps department can be a department which takes the place of an operations department, in which case operations personnel gets trained to use software engineering techniques to solve operational problems. This can actually be considered an antipattern to DevOps as interaction between development and operations, as the interaction decreases by assigning more responsibilities to a single discipline.

4.2   DevOps Teams

The DevOps team is a term found more commonly than that of a DevOps department. Let us again consider three ways of applying the DevOps term. Firstly, a DevOps team can be a team in which development and operations *personnel* interact with each other as members of a single team. This was for example the case at SupportCom, in which a specialized team was created to work on the cloud offering of their product. Secondly, a DevOps team can be a team in which multiple *DevOps engineers* interact with each other as members of a single team. This is the case at FinCom1 and FinCom2, which both introduced the job title DevOps engineer. Thirdly, a DevOps team can be a team which acts as a support unit for a DevOps transformation. One of the interviewees at FinCom2 described himself and the other interviewee as being such a team.

4.3 DevOps Engineers

The job title DevOps engineer is quite controversial. Even though there are actually many organizations hiring DevOps engineers and there are many people indentifying themselves as such, some consider the job description to be against the spirit of DevOps. Let us consider various ways of applying the DevOps term in the case of the DevOps engineer. Firstly, a DevOps engineer can be an engineer who realizes the interaction between development and operations, in which case the DevOps engineer would be similar to a process engineer. This is a hypothetical definition, however it could be argued that the interviewees at FinCom2 could describe themselves as this. Secondly, a DevOps engineer can be an engineer who has a skill set spanning development and operations, in which case the DevOps engineer is like a hybrid between a software engineer and an operations engineer. This is how FinCom1 and FinCom2 use the term. Thirdly, a DevOps engineer can be an engineer specialized in using DevOps tools, in which case the DevOps engineer is similar to a built or release engineer. This was the case at UtilCom, in which the DevOps team primarily supported the development teams by creating and maintaining tools.

4.4 DevOps Tools

Many tools predating the rise of DevOps have relabled themselves as DevOps tools, and many new tools categorized by their creators as DevOps tools have been developed. Let us consider some ways in how the DevOps term can be applied to DevOps tools. Firstly, DevOps tools could be tools which allow development and operations personnel to interact. Examples of this are project management systems such as Jira and bug trackers such as Bugzilla. Secondly, DevOps tools could be tools that bridge the disciplines of development and operations. Examples of this are CI systems such as Jenkins and Travis, especially if more advanced pipelines are used to chain different steps in the deployment and delivery process together. Thirdly, DevOps tools could be tools that automate the interaction between development and operations personnel. Examples of this are release automation tools such as Ansible and cloud orchestration engines such as Kubernetes.

4.5 CA(L)MS

Various categorizations for DevOps principles and practices have been proposed. Damon Edwards and John Willis proposed CAMS [11]: Culture, Automation, Measurement and Sharing. Jez Humble proposed CALMS [10]: Culture,

Automation, Lean, Measurement and Sharing. Chris Jackson proposed CALMS as [10]: Culture, Automation, Lean, Metrics and Sharing. Other variations on the acronym exist, such as CALMSS (Culture, Automation, Measurement and management, Sharing, Sourcing) as proposed by Forrester [4], but we will ignore these as they are not widely used.

Let us take a quick look at how DevOps as interaction between development and operations could fit with these categorizations.

Culture DevOps is about creating a culture in which development and operations personnel interact regularly.

Automation DevOps is about automating steps which typically require interaction between development and operations personnel.

Measurement/Metrics DevOps is about implementing measurements that span the disciplines of development and operations, or DevOps is about measuring the interaction between development and operations personnel, or DevOps is about giving development personnel access to measurements typically used by operations personnel and vice versa.

Lean DevOps is about optimizing the interaction between development and operations personnel.

Sharing DevOps is about having a shared space in which development and operations personnel interact, or DevOps is about maintaining the systems used by development and operations personnel to interact, or DevOps is about development and operations personel sharing about their involvement on different parts of the same system.

5   Conclusion

Software has always needed to be both developed and operated in order to provide value, however a move from mainframe computers to personal computers moved most of the operational burden to the consumer of software. With a shift to a cloud computing model of offering software also the operational burden has shifted back to the organizations developing the software.

What we hoped to convey in this paper is that DevOps is a simple thing with major implications on each of the aforementioned levels. In fact, we consider the interaction between development and operations to be the supporting factor behind many principles and practices which can be considered modern software engineering. In the cases which we discussed, this interaction took place on various levels, such as the individual level (the skillset of employees), the team level (how a team is composed, for example only development personnel, only operations personnel, a mix of both, or having only multi-disciplinary DevOps engineers), the tool level (many companies offer tools that can allegedly be used to implement DevOps), the department level (many organizations reorganized to have departments in which both development and operations personnel are located).

What we hope the reader takes away from this paper is that when discussing DevOps there is a high likelihood that different definitions of DevOps will exist in the mind of the participants of the discussion. Even so, at the core of each definition of DevOps will be the interaction between development and operations. Anything added on top of this interaction should be considered to be implementation details.

Acknowledgements. I would like to thank my master thesis supervisors Maya Daneva and Chintan Amrit, my PhD supervisor Kenji Suzuki, and my current employer Japan's Institute of Advanced Industrial Science and Technology for their continued support.

References

1. Bass, L., Weber, I., Zhu, L.: DevOps: A Software Architect's Perspective. Addison-Wesley Professional, Boston (2015). ISBN 978-0-13-404984-7
2. Beyer, B., et al.: Site Reliability Engineering. O'Reilly, Sebastopol (2016)
3. Daniels, R., Davis, J.: Effective DevOps. O'Reilly Media, Sebastopol (2016)
4. DeMartine, A., Oehrlich, E., Doerr, M.: CALMSS: a model for assessing modern service delivery. Research report, Forrester Research (2015)
5. Dyck, A., Penners, R., Lichter, H.: Towards definitions for release engineering and DevOps. In: Proceedings of the Third International Workshop on Release Engineering, p. 3. IEEE Press (2015)
6. Erich, F., Amrit, C., Daneva, M.: A qualitative study of DevOps usage in practice. J. Softw.: Evol. Process **29**(6) (2017). https://doi.org/10.1002/smr.1885
7. Humble, J., Farley, D.: Continuous Delivery: Reliable Software Releases Through Build, Test, and Deployment Automation, 1st edn. Addison-Wesley Professional, Boston (2010). ISBN 0321601912, 9780321601919
8. Jabbari, R., et al.: What is DevOps?: A systematic mapping study on definitions and practices. In: Scientific Workshop Proceedings of XP2016, Edinburgh, UK, pp. 12:1–12:11. ACM (2016). https://doi.org/10.1145/2962695.2962707, ISBN 978-1-4503-4134-9
9. Loukides, M.: What is DevOps? O'Reilly Media, Sebastopol (2012). http://radar.oreilly.com/2012/06/what-is-devops.html
10. Rackspace: Quantifying DevOps capability: it's important to keep CALMS, August 2014. https://blog.rackspace.com/quantifying-devops-capability-its-important-to-keep-calms
11. Willis, J.: What DevOps means to me, July 2010. https://blog.chef.io/2010/07/16/what-devops-means-to-me/
12. XebiaLabs: Whitepaper: introducing continuous delivery in the enterprise (2013). http://go.xebialabs.com/rs/xebialabs/images/WP_2013-01-XebiaLabs-Continuous-Delivery.pdf

Teaching DevOps in Corporate Environments
An Experience Report

Manuel Mazzara, Alexandr Naumchev[✉], Larisa Safina, Alberto Sillitti, and Konstantin Urysov

Innopolis University, Innopolis, Russian Federation
{m.mazzara,a.naumchev,l.safina,a.sillitti,k.urysov}@innopolis.ru

Abstract. This paper describes our experience of training a team of developers of an East-European phone service provider. The training experience was structured in two sessions of two days each conducted in different weeks with a gap of about fifteen days. The first session was dedicated to the Continuous Integration Delivery Pipeline, and the second on Agile methods. We summarize the activity, its preparation and delivery and draw some conclusions out of it on our mistakes and how future session should be addressed.

1 Introduction

Our society is observing a trend of rapid technological development and a global process of automation. The public often identifies as *technological progress* a new release of a telephone or of a new kind of digital device. However, technological progress is not only about "hard" technologies – tangible products that can be touched and ultimately purchased. Instead, it is a balanced mixture of both technical and business innovation, including process innovation. To survive, companies must fight for every single customer, propose competitive prices, and optimize their operations [5]. Innovative business models appear everywhere from the game industry to the mobile application domain, and the borders of Information Technology become blurred. For example, is Uber a taxi or an IT company? Is Airbnb a realtor? The separation between Information Technology and other businesses is not so neat anymore, so that software development techniques and operations need to catch up with this trend.

It is obvious when the next release of Windows come, but what about a web service (e.g., Google, Yandex search)? Agile Methods deal with this problem only from the software development point of view focusing on customer value, managing volatile requirements, etc. However, the current needs require much more than that and involve the entire life cycle of a software system, including its operation. The DevOps approach [4,11] and microservices architectural style [8,9] with its domains of interests [5,14,20,21] have the potential of changing how companies run their systems as Agile have changed how they develop their software. DevOps is a natural evolution of the Agile approaches from the software

J.-M. Bruel et al. (Eds.): DEVOPS 2018, LNCS 11350, pp. 100–111, 2019.
https://doi.org/10.1007/978-3-030-06019-0_8

itself to the overall infrastructure and operations that is made possible by the spread of cloud-based technologies and the everything-as-a-service approaches. In this context, even the infrastructure is becoming code with all the advantages and complexity that is well-known in common software development.

However, embracing DevOps is more complex than embracing just Agile [1]. It requires changes at organization level and the development of a new skill set and approaches that need to be adopted by different teams which could be (almost) autonomous [6]. Therefore, training is of paramount importance to establish a common background for all the different groups, including the management.

Our team is specialized in delivering corporate training for management and developers. This study describes our experience of training a team of developers of an East-European phone service provider for several days. The training experience was structured in two sessions of two days each conducted in different weeks with a gap of about fifteen days in the middle in order not to disrupt for too long the working schedule. The first session was dedicated mostly to the Continuous Integration Delivery Pipeline while the second on Agile methods in general.

2   Session I: DevOps

The first session was conducted over two full days at the office of our customer. The training was conducted following a schedule shared in advance. Out target group was a team of developers reporting to a line manager located in a different city reachable only by flight. Previous communication with this specific team was not possible, the only information we had was partial and communicated by the remote line manager. Therefore, the original agenda had to be adjusted on site.

2.1   Training Process

The training covered the following topics and it was organized in four major parts, including the discussion of the survey, which appeared in several moments, although here it is for simplicity reported only at the end. Here we report the agenda and the key points of each session.

Introduction. The narrative was built as follows:

- Trends in IT and impact on software architectures and development.
- Requirements volatility and Agile development.
- Challenges of distributed development.
- Microservices.

Key Points. The session emphasized the difference between *hard technologies* and *soft technologies*. On one side there is industrial production of commercial item of technological nature, on the other there is continuous improvement and "agilization" of development process. Issue of Requirements volatility and how this led to agile methods were discussed. Relevance of distributed team development in the modern setting was described in detail to conclude the session with a survey on *microservices*, which are considered the privilege architecture for DevOps with their scalability features [9]. The key difference between monolithic service updates (Fig. 1) and microservice deployment (Fig. 2) was presented to motivate the need of migration to microservices and why this topic is so closely related to DevOps. Figure 1 shows that the approach works well with a few developers and a single language, and that the need for microservices emerges for large teams and diverse platform components.

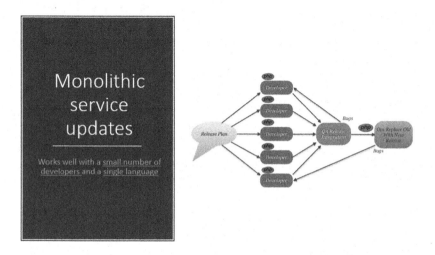

Fig. 1. Monolithic service updates

Continuous Integration Delivery Pipeline. Here the full delivery pipeline was discussed:

- Source code control.
- Build automation.
- Automated testing.
- Static code analysis.
- Integration testing.
- Deployment automation.
- Monitoring.

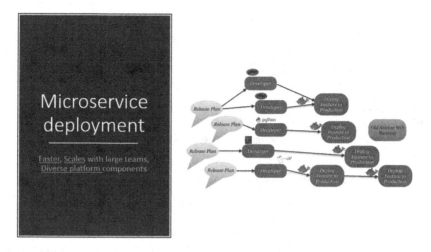

Fig. 2. Microservice deployment

Key Points. The overall session worked on the idea that it is desirable that software in mainline can be rapidly built and deployed to production at any point. The declared benefits of this approach are:

- Reduction of manual effort.
- Acceleration of release cycles.
- Improvement of release quality.
- Increased collaboration between development, QA, support and operations teams.
- Reduction in costs for deployment and support.

The fundamental principles of DevOps as generally agreed upon by the most influential early members of the DevOps community, were summed up in the acronym "CAMS": **C**ulture, **A**utomation, **M**easurement, **S**haring.

Tools. We analyzed tools for the following purposes:

- Version control.
- Build automation.
- Testing (including mutation testing [18]).
- Continuous integration.
- Configuration management.
- Continuous monitoring.
- Seamless development ([12, 13, 15–17, 23]).

Key-Points. This part emphasized on the practical aspects showing tools to support the idea of continuous delivery. During the discussion with teams, we were asked to speak about the mutation testing, which was out of scope of our main topic. However, we found it interesting enough to adapt our initial agenda and cover it. We have also decided on a little experiment and included the topic on seamless development, to see how well ideas born in academia can be spread among the industry.

Discussion of the Survey. The survey data collected before the training was analyzed question by question to give focused and specific advice to the team, apart from the generalities discusses in the previous parts.

2.2   Objectives of the Training

The idea of the training was not just to lecture the theory behind DevOps, but also to address specific software process-related issues preventing the client to benefit from applying DevOps as much as possible. To figure out these issues, we had to collect some data about the audience. Due to the high level of corporate privacy, we could not use internal data of the company. The schedule was tight, which is why we could not afford negotiating possible non-disclosure agreement that would let us gain the insights we needed. We decided to develop of a questionnaire that, in our opinion, would uncover some insights about the team. The questionnaire consisted of 17 questions related to DevOps practices, and in the end, coincidentally, we have received 17 responses.

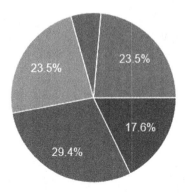

Fig. 3. How much time does it typically take to deploy changes? (Blue for "less than one hour", light blue for "don't know", red for "less than one day", yellow for "one day to one week", green for "one week to one month".) (Color figure online)

2.3   Analysis of the Results

Although we were expecting to understand something about the current level of DevOps practices in the team, the responses to the questionnaire made us think about communications inside the team. Running the questionnaire and analyzing the results revealed the following anomalies in the structure of the responses:

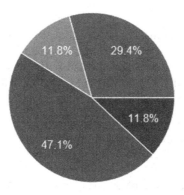

Fig. 4. Do you automate application testing? (Blue for "yes", red for "mostly yes", yellow for "no", green for "don't know".) (Color figure online)

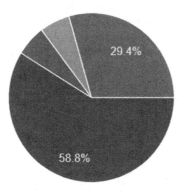

Fig. 5. Does your team practice retrospective and postmortem meetings? (Blue for "yes", red for "only retrospectives", yellow for "only postmortems", green for "no".) (Color figure online)

– High diversity of opinions for some questions (Fig. 3).
– A lot of "don't know" replies for some straightforward questions (Fig. 4).
– Contradicting responses for some questions (Fig. 5).

These anomalies raised the following questions to address during the training:

– Does the team consist, in fact, of several sub-teams?
– To what extent are the teams distributed?
– How does the level of DevOps practices' maturity vary among the teams?
– How should we adjust the contents of the training to meet the identified variability?
– How should we adjust the questionnaire itself, so that we minimize the likelihood of the mentioned anomalies in the future?

An ideal solution would be to create another questionnaire targeting these questions. The schedule, however, did not allow us to do so. The only solution was to figure out the missing information on site, and then adjust the training on the go, between the two training days. By the end of the first day of the training, we have revealed the following information, with respect to the above questions:

- The team consists of 4 sub-teams. Each sub-team has their own goals, problems, and concerns about the software process.
- The smallest team, consisting of 4 members, is from another city. Some teams are distributed.
- The smallest team is not even considering applying DevOps because of its size. One of the sub-teams possesses good understanding of DevOps and applies it in their daily practices.
- One team's customer is the head branch of the company.
- Every day the customer tells the team what to deploy during the day.
- Fridays have the largest number of deployments requested.
- Around 80% of releases are tested after deployment.
- Sometimes they work on weekends, which is a natural consequence of the previous two points.
- The customer does not want the team to use automatic deployments, because they lack trust to the team.

These important pieces of information have little to do with the questionnaire that we sent to the trainees. We will use this information when it comes to composing a questionnaire for another training.

After having the above points figured out during the first day of the training, we have spent a half of the night before the second day to completely rework the contents.

3 Session II: Agile

The second session was held for two full days in the same office. At the beginning, the main topic was "Agile software development" and Scrum in particular. However, the requirements were changed at the last moment, as the customer asked to pay more attention on Kanban, since they were thinking to use it in the future. Overall, it was clear that development team was in doubt which process they need to follow.

3.1 Training Objectives and Process

Gathering More Data. Due to changing requirements from the company it was clear that one of the most important demand for this training will be identification of suitable methodology for development teams. To achieve this goal, we decided to use a framework described in *"Choose your weapon wisely"* [19]. It provides information about different trade-offs for popular development processes:

- Rational Unified Process (RUP) [3]
- Microsoft's Sync-and-Stabilize Process (MSS) [7]
- Team Software Process (TSP) [10]
- Extreme Programming (XP) [2]
- Scrum [22]

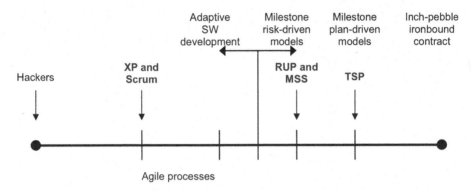

Fig. 6. Spectrum of processes (from Rookwood [19])

Information about processes was divided in four parts:

1. Overview (short description of the process).
2. Roles (information about positions for the process).
3. Artifacts to produce (including documentation).
4. Tool support (overview of tools available on the market for using the process).

Picking the Right Process. After a brief introduction of all processes, the development teams were asked to fill out the forms with a set of questions (see Fig. 7). All the questions were divided on four main groups:

- Team and product size (number of engineers involved in a single development team and product size in terms of LOC and complexity).
- Developers and organization (number of competent and experienced engineers).
- Product and its types (life critical, embedded, ERP system, etc.).
- Requirements and their stability.

Three teams participated in a survey, as a result it was identified that Agile methodologies (XP and Scrum) fit better than others for 90% of respondents. Thus, it was decided to focus on Agile development processes – Scrum, XP and Kanban.

Question	RUP	MSS	TSP	XP	Scrum
Team Size					
Total Developers					
Product Size and Complexity					
Competent and Experienced Developers					
Level of Hacker Sentiment					
Management Style					
Organization-Wide Processes					
New Process Adoption					
Type of Product					
Requirements Stability					
Requirements Traceability					
Totals					

Fig. 7. Question tally sheet (from Rookwood [19])

3.2 Analysis of the Results

There is a huge difference in teaching students and mature engineers. The last ones already have prior knowledge and their own opinion on how things should be done. There is a common pattern in how teams are changing their development processes.

Phase One: Waterfall. One of the biggest problems of waterfall, besides those problems of working with emerging requirements, are *"walls"* between different departments inside the organization. The Waterfall model typically does not imply cross-functional teams, meaning that different teams work independently from each other on different parts of the project. In such organizations it is typical to see parts of a deliverable moving between this institutional *"walls"*, from department to department. For example, the analytics team collects the requirements, provide the specification and then pass it over to developers; developers code it as fast as possible and pass it to testers, who have most of the problems. The most obvious drawbacks of this approach is that testers receive one large piece of functionality without having any strong support from developers.

Phase Two: Water-Scrum-Fall. After a while the team will identify obvious problems of waterfall model and will try to change development processes, as agile methodologies very popular nowadays there is a big chance that the team will choose it. However, changing the process in big organization is complicated, and as a first result of that changes we can get water-scrum-fall model, where the whole team will be split on three parts: managers, development and QA teams and customer(s). This separation breaks several important rules of agile approach. For example, estimations quite always produced by managers based on value and money without interaction with development team, development team do not have access to the customer, which eventually adds more bugs and change requests.

Phase Three: Tailored Scrum with Practices from XP and Kanban. The hardest part of changing development process is a move from second to the third phase, and the key of success here is a strong leader of development team, who will manage these changes and will be able to convince all team members to follow picked processes.

4   Lesson Learned and Conclusions

Our experience thought us a few relevant lessons:

- It is important to get in advance as much information as possible about the audience the training meant to.
- Talking directly to the relevant people, possibly technical and on-site.
- Be clear on the outcome of the training, be sure that what the audience need and expect corresponds to what we want to present.

In our case we had limited access to the development team prior to the training. Previous Skype calls only happened with management residing in a different city. We were only able to collect information via a generic questionnaire on development practices. We realized that the questionnaire may have been ambiguous in some parts, and possibly too generic. For example, we were not prepared for the fact that more than one heterogeneous team would be participating, which made some questions irrelevant and did not target all the participants.

Therefore, we had to spend considerable amount of time collecting missing information on-site about the teams participating and technologies they used. At the end of the first day we decided to refocus our program, and the second day was mostly related to QA practices which targeted the investigated problems better.

This case was a reminder for us of utterly importance of collecting requirements and how things can be easily misunderstood or slow down if there are any obstacles during this process. Both refocusing the topic during the DevOps session and changing the topic for the following Agile session led us to the conclusion that it is not always easy to collect all required information beforehand, especially with limited ways and amount of time, and this information may not always show the real problems teams are struggling with. So, the trainers themselves should be ready to step aside from the main topic.

References

1. Agile and DevOps: Friends or foes? https://www.atlassian.com/agile/devops. Accessed 01 July 2018
2. Extreme programming: a gentle introduction. http://www.extremeprogramming.org/. Accessed 01 July 2018
3. Rational unified process: overview. http://sce.uhcl.edu/helm/rationalunifiedpro cess/. Accessed 01 July 2018
4. Bass, L., Weber, I., Zhu, L.: DevOps: A Software Architect's Perspective, 1st edn. Addison-Wesley Professional, Boston (2015)
5. Bucchiarone, A., Dragoni, N., Dustdar, S., Larsen, S.T., Mazzara, M.: From mono-lithic to microservices: an experience report from the banking domain. IEEE Softw. **35**(3), 50–55 (2018)
6. Bucena, I., Kirikova, M.: Simplifying the DevOps adoption process. In: Joint Pro-ceedings of the BIR 2017 pre-BIR Forum, Workshops and Doctoral Consortium co-located with 16th International Conference on Perspectives in Business Infor-matics Research (BIR 2017), Copenhagen, Denmark, 28–30 August 2017 (2017)
7. Cusumano, M.A., Selby, R.W.: How microsoft builds software. Commun. ACM **40**(6), 53–61 (1997)
8. Dragoni, N., et al.: Microservices: yesterday, today, and tomorrow. In: Mazzara, M., Meyer, B. (eds.) Present and Ulterior Software Engineering, pp. 195–216. Springer, Cham (2017). https://doi.org/10.1007/978-3-319-67425-4_12
9. Dragoni, N., Lanese, I., Larsen, S.T., Mazzara, M., Mustafin, R., Safina, L.: Microservices: how to make your application scale. In: Petrenko, A.K., Voronkov, A. (eds.) PSI 2017. LNCS, vol. 10742, pp. 95–104. Springer, Cham (2018). https://doi.org/10.1007/978-3-319-74313-4_8
10. Humphrey, W., Over, J.: Introduction to the Team Software Process (SM), 1st edn. Addison-Wesley Professional, Boston (1999)
11. Jabbari, R., bin Ali, N., Petersen, K., Tanveer, B.: What is DevOps?: A system-atic mapping study on definitions and practices. In: Proceedings of the Scientific Workshop Proceedings of XP2016, XP 2016 Workshops, pp. 12:1–12:11. ACM, New York (2016)
12. Meyer, B.: Object-Oriented Software Construction, 2nd edn. Prentice-Hall, Inc., Upper Saddle River (1997)
13. Meyer, B.: Multirequirements. In: Seyff, N., Koziolek, A. (eds.) Modelling and Quality in Requirements Engineering (Martin Glinz Festscrhift). MV Wissenschaft (2013)
14. Nalin, M., Baroni, I., Mazzara, M.: A holistic infrastructure to support elderlies' independent living. In: Encyclopedia of E-Health and Telemedicine. IGI Global (2016)
15. Naumchev, A., Meyer, B.: Complete contracts through specification drivers. In: Proceedings - 10th International Symposium on Theoretical Aspects of Software Engineering, TASE 2016 (2016)
16. Naumchev, A., Meyer, B.: Seamless requirements. Comput. Lang. Syst. Struct. **49**, 119–132 (2017)

17. Naumchev, A., Meyer, B., Rivera, V.: Unifying requirements and code: an example. In: Mazzara, M., Voronkov, A. (eds.) PSI 2015. LNCS, vol. 9609, pp. 233–244. Springer, Cham (2016). https://doi.org/10.1007/978-3-319-41579-6_18

18. Reales Mateo, P., Polo, M., Fernández-Alemán, J., Toval, A., Piattini, M.: Mutation testing. IEEE Softw. **31**, 30–35 (2014)

19. Rockwood, J.: Choose your weapon wisely. Carnegie Mellon University. http://gsl. mit.edu/media/programs/mexico-summer-2014/materials/j._rockwood_choose_ your_weapon_wisely.pdf

20. Salikhov, D., Khanda, K., Gusmanov, K., Mazzara, M., Mavridis, N.: Jolie good buildings: internet of things for smart building infrastructure supporting concurrent apps utilizing distributed microservices. In: Proceedings of the 1st International Conference on Convergent Cognitive Information Technologies, pp. 48–53 (2016)

21. Salikhov, D., Khanda, K., Gusmanov, K., Mazzara, M., Mavridis, N.: Microservice-based IoT for smart buildings. In: Proceedings of the 31st International Conference on Advanced Information Networking and Applications Workshops (WAINA) (2017)

22. Schwaber, K., Sutherland, J.: The Scrum guide (2001)

23. Waldén, K., Nerson, J.M.: Seamless Object-Oriented Software Architecture. Prentice-Hall, Upper Saddle River (1995)

ENACT: Development, Operation, and Quality Assurance of Trustworthy Smart IoT Systems

Nicolas Ferry[1]([✉]), Arnor Solberg[1], Hui Song[1], Stéphane Lavirotte[2],
Jean-Yves Tigli[2], Thierry Winter[3], Victor Muntés-Mulero[4], Andreas Metzger[5],
Erkuden Rios Velasco[6], and Amaia Castelruiz Aguirre[6]

[1] SINTEF Digital, Oslo, Norway
{nicolas.ferry,arnor.solberg,hui.song}@sintef.no
[2] Université Côte d'Azur, CNRS, I3S, Sophia Antipolis, France
{stephane.lavirotte,jean-yves.tigli}@unice.fr
[3] EVIDIAN, Les Clayes-sous-Bois, France
thierry.winter@evidian.com
[4] Beawre, Barcelona, Spain
victor.muntes@beawre.com
[5] paluno (The Ruhr Institute for Software Technology),
University of Duisburg-Essen, Essen, Germany
andreas.metzger@paluno.uni-due.de
[6] Fundación Tecnalia Research & Innovation, Derio, Spain
{erkuden.riosvelasco,amaia.castelruizaguirre}@tecnalia.com

Abstract. To unleash the full potential of IoT and flourishing innovations in application domains such as eHealth or smart city, it is critical to facilitate the creation and operation of trustworthy Smart IoT Systems (SIS). Since SIS typically operate in a changing and often unpredictable environment, the ability of these systems to continuously evolve and adapt to their new environment is decisive to ensure and increase their trustworthiness, quality and user experience. The DevOps movement advocates a set of software engineering best practices and tools, to ensure Quality of Service whilst continuously evolving complex systems. However, there is no complete DevOps support for trustworthy SIS today. In this paper we present a research roadmap to enable DevOps in such systems and introduce the ENACT DevOps concepts and Framework.

Keywords: Internet of Things · DevOps · Trustworthiness

1 Introduction

By 2020, Gartner envisions that 21 billion Internet-of-Things (IoT) endpoints will be in use[1], representing great business opportunities. However, complex challenges remain to be solved to efficiently exploit the full potential of the rapidly

---

[1] http://www.gartner.com/newsroom/id/3598917.

© Springer Nature Switzerland AG 2019
J.-M. Bruel et al. (Eds.): DEVOPS 2018, LNCS 11350, pp. 112–127, 2019.
https://doi.org/10.1007/978-3-030-06019-0_9

growing IoT infrastructure. Until now, IoT system innovations have been mainly concerned with sensors, device management and connectivity, with the mission to gather data for processing and analysis in the cloud in order to aggregate information and knowledge [1]. This approach has conveyed significant added value in many application domains, however, it does not unleash the full potential of the IoT[2]. The next generation IoT systems need to perform distributed processing and coordinated behaviour across IoT, edge and cloud infrastructures [2], manage the closed loop from sensing to actuation, and cope with vast heterogeneity, scalability and dynamicity of IoT systems and their environments. Moreover, the functioning and correctness of such systems will be critical, ranging from business critical to safety critical. Thus, aspects related to trustworthiness such as security, privacy, resilience and robustness, are challenging aspects of paramount importance [1]. Therefore, the next generation of IoT systems needs to be trustworthy. In this paper, we will call them trustworthy smart IoT systems, or for short; trustworthy SIS.

To realize the digital society and to flourish innovations, it is critical to facilitate the creation and operation of trustworthy SIS. However, developing and managing the next generation trustworthy SIS that operates in the midst of the unpredictable physical world represents daunting challenges. For example, to ensure that such systems always work within safe operational boundaries [3] (e.g., controlling the impact that actuators have on the physical world) and to manage conflicting actuation requests. Moreover, the ability of these systems to continuously evolve and adapt to their changing environments is decisive to ensure and increase their trustworthiness, quality and user experience.

This is at the core of the DevOps movement, which advocates a set of software engineering best practices and tools, to ensure Quality of Service whilst continuously evolving complex systems and foster agility, rapid innovation cycles, and ease of use [4]. Therefore, DevOps has been widely adopted in the software industry. However, there is no complete DevOps support for trustworthy smart IoT systems today [3,5]. According to [5], a key reason is *because of the extremely dynamic nature of IoT systems, it poses additional challenges, for instance, continuous debugging and testing of IoT systems can be very challenging because of the large number of devices, dynamic topologies, unreliable connectivity, and heterogeneous and sometimes invisible nature of the devices*. Current DevOps solutions also lack mechanisms for continuous quality assurance [3], for example, mechanisms to ensure end-to-end security and privacy as well as mechanisms able to take into consideration open context and actuation conflicts (e.g., allowing continuous testing of IoT systems within emulated and simulated infrastructures). It also remains challenging to perform continuous deployment and evolution of IoT systems across, IoT, edge, and cloud spaces [3]. These are key features to provide DevOps for trustworthy SIS.

In this paper we first provide a research roadmap that identifies the critical challenges to enable DevOps in the realm of trustworthy SIS. We discuss the related contribution of the ENACT DevOps Framework and introduce an evo-

---

[2] https://ec.europa.eu/digital-single-market/en/internet-of-things.

lution of the DevOps methods and tools to address these challenges. Finally, we present the initial ENACT DevOps Framework as our current realization of these methods and tools. The proposed framework will be explored and further developed in the newly founded ENACT H2020 project that started in January 2018.

The remainder of the paper is organized as follows. Section 2 presents the research roadmap in terms of technical challenges and state-of-the-art. Section 3 details the overall ENACT approach and illustrates how it will help addressing these research challenges. Section 4 describes the set of enablers that forms the core of the ENACT DevOps Framework and Sect. 5 concludes.

2   ENACT Research Roadmap

The key research question is the following: *how can we tame the complexity of developing and operating smart IoT systems, which (i) involve sensors and **actuators** and (ii) need to be **trustworthy**?*. Our approach is largely to evolve DevOps methods and techniques as baseline to address this issue. We thus refine the research question as follows: *how can we apply and evolve the DevOps tools and methods to facilitate the development and operation of trustworthy smart IoT systems?*. The answer to these questions form the core of the ENACT research roadmap presented below.

Research Challenge 1: Support Continuous Delivery of Trustworthy SIS

Context: Very little effort has been spent on providing solutions for the delivery and deployment of application across the whole IoT, edge and cloud space. In particular, there is a lack of languages and abstractions that can be used to support the orchestration of software services and their deployment on heterogeneous devices [6].

State-of-the-Art: In the past years, multiple tools have emerged to support the building as well as the automated and continuous deployment of software systems with a specific focus on cloud infrastructures (*e.g.*, Puppet[3], Chef[4], Brooklyn[5], TOSCA[6], CloudMF [7], etc.). Model-Driven Engineering techniques have also been investigated to design and reconfigure a network of resource-constrained devices. One trend is to provide an architecture-based approach to design and build flexible embedded systems, (*e.g.*, the Koala model [8] and Think [9]). Kevoree [10] relies on models at run-time to support the dynamic adaptation of distributed cloud and cyber physical systems supporting hot deployment of component types. The HEADS FP7 EU project proposes ThingML [6], a language that provides a set of compilers to derive source code (*e.g.*, Java, C/C++) optimised for various IoT platforms.

---

[3] https://puppet.com.

[4] https://www.chef.io/.

[5] https://brooklyn.apache.org/.

[6] https://www.oasis-open.org/committees/tosca.

Research Challenge 2: Support the Agile Operation of Trustworthy SIS

Context: The operation of large-scale and highly distributed IoT systems can easily overwhelm operation teams. Major challenges are then to improve their efficiency and the collaboration with developer teams for rapid and agile evolution of the systems. However, there is a lack of mechanisms dedicated to smart IoT systems able to *(i)* monitor their status, *(ii)* indicate when their behaviour is not as expected, *(iii)* identify the origin of the problem, and *(iv)* automate typical operation activities (See footnote 5). Furthermore, because it is impossible to anticipate all the adaptations a system may face when operating in an open context, there is an urgent need for mechanisms that will automatically maintain the adaptation rules of a smart IoT system.

State-of-the-Art: A self-adaptive system modifies its own structure and behaviour at run-time to respond to its perception of its environment, of itself and of its requirements [11]. Software developers face two important challenges when building self-adaptive systems [12]. On the one hand, it is difficult or may even be infeasible for software developers to exhaustively explore, anticipate or resolve all possible situations that an adaptive system may encounter during its operation. On the other hand, it is difficult for software developers to determine how a modification of the system's structure or behaviour impacts on the satisfaction of the system's requirements. These two challenges make it hard to determine the required set of system configurations a self-adaptive system needs to implement. In addition, these challenges make it hard to define which configurations to choose in response to the anticipated situations. A self-adaptive system thus may encounter situations that have not been fully understood or anticipated in the software development process [13]. Should an unanticipated situation occur at run-time, a self-adaptive system thus may wrongly reconfigure itself, (*e.g.*, the self-adaptive system may choose a configuration that is not able to address the situation). To attack the aforementioned problems, researchers have started applying online learning techniques to improve the way that a self-adaptive system adapts [14,15]. Online learning means that learning is performed at run-time, taking into account observations about the actual system execution and system environment. Online learning incrementally updates the self-adaptive system's knowledge base; *e.g.*, its adaptation rules or the models based on which adaptation decisions are made. However, so far, techniques and methodologies for self-adaptive systems have focused on the system as the entity that may be adapted only. In the presence of IoT actuation, a new avenue for adaptive behaviour becomes possible that has not yet been addressed. In addition, existing online learning techniques for self-adaptive systems do not take into account the impact of system evolution (*i.e.*, the manual modification of the system by humans [16]). During evolution, software developers may modify the system, for instance, to correct bugs, to remove seldom used features, or to introduce new features, thereby also changing the possible adaptations of the system.

Identifying the root causes of faults or problems is also of major importance. However, performing root-cause analysis in complex and dynamic IoT environments is not deeply studied in the literature. Several IoT-related problems have been detected. For instance, Aggarwal [17] discusses challenges related to incomplete data transmission from sensors for Big Data analytics. Failures in fog computing can be localized at sensor, network, service platform or web application levels [18]. Some other efforts focus on the convergence of Big Data analysis techniques and Cyber Physical Systems [19], describing a data-driven approach to building fault tolerant control systems. However, they use highly accurate mathematical models that do not comply with usual scalability and computational complexity in large IoT structures. Finally, recent work [20] proposes some initial techniques to manage scalability issues for root-cause analysis in IoT and fog environments.

Research Challenge 3: Support Continuous Quality Assurance Strengthening Trustworthiness of SIS

Context: Ensuring quality of service is a complex task that needs to be considered throughout the whole life-cycle of a system. This is all the more exacerbated in the smart IoT system context where it is infeasible for developers and operators to exhaustively explore, anticipate or resolve all possible context situations that a system may encounter during its operation. This is due to the open context in which these systems operate and as a result can hinder their trustworthiness. This is particularly important when the system can have an impact on the physical world through actuators. In addition, testing, ensuring end-to-end security as well as the robustness of such systems is challenging [5]. A major limitation of classical quality assurance tools when applied in IoT is the lack of mechanisms to include, as part of the tests, constraints related to the distribution and infrastructure of IoT and edge computing[7].

State-of-the-Art: An important aspect of trustworthiness is security and privacy. Different works identify the diverse security and privacy threats of IoT. One of the most prominent is the work of Open Web Application Security Project (OWASP) that identifies the top ten most common vulnerabilities of IoT systems [21] covering the whole IoT architecture layers (from Insecure Web Interface to Poor physical security flaws). Authors in [22] exemplify hands on the "most severe, yet easy to abuse" IoT threats, namely: leakage of the personally identifiable information (PII), leakage of sensitive user information and unauthorized execution of functions. Cvitic et al. [23] analysed the security aspects for each layer of the IoT architecture: the biggest security risk is at perception layer of the IoT architecture due to the specific limitations of devices and the transmission technology used at this layer, followed by the middleware layer based on cloud computing and inherited vulnerabilities of that concept.

Test and validation is also an important aspect of trustworthiness. Testing of IoT Services is currently limited to service functionality by using existing

---

[7] http://events.windriver.com/wrcd01/wrcm/2016/08/WP-devops-in-the-internet-of-things.pdf.

software testing tools (*e.g.*, Katalon Studio[8], HP Unified Functional Testing[9] or CA Technologies Application Test[10]), which are prepared to verify automatically that the service provides an expected answer for a set of specified and known scenarios as well as testing the communication integrity between different devices. Nevertheless, IoT deployment is heavily impacted by the underlying hardware specification, capabilities, availability and changes in the physical environment, typically not considered by current testing tools. The lack of tools for systematically testing IoT services in different large-scale, heterogeneous, physical environments is a research challenge [24]. Real-Time Operating Systems (RTOS) provide a virtual environment in which developers can test their solutions and deploy the software to the physical device which has the same RTOS installed. Several RTOS are available in the market[11], selecting RTOS is largely based on the set of supported devices. Current combination of RTOS and other IoT middleware are not capable of scaling up to large-scale deployments due to the limited computation resources of centralized emulations. In the literature, there are simulation strategies to approximate IoT behaviour thanks to parallel and distributed computation [25] and multi-level simulation [26]. Several companies started offering their own infrastructure of IoT devices to test applications within a predefined set of popular IoT devices[12]. Although this partially solves the issue of obtaining data from the physical world and provides testing on real devices, availability of these testing services is significantly impacted by the demand for these services and tests are limited to the currently deployed devices and their location with no option to scale or make changes on the devices. Recent efforts focus on producing self-learning IoT virtualizers to facilitate testing in IoT environments[13].

Research Challenge 4: Leverage the Capabilities of Existing IoT Platforms and Fully Exploit Legacy, Proprietary and Off-the-Shelf Software Components and Devices

Context: Real IoT systems are never developed from scratch: they build upon off-the-shelf components as well as legacy sub-systems and they can rely on the wide range of IoT platforms that have been developed over the past decade. The large number of IoT platforms available today is not only accidental, it reflects that different IoT systems or even different parts of a single IoT system have different requirements in terms of device management, integration, security, protocols, analytics, visualisation, etc.

---

[8] https://www.katalon.com.

[9] https://saas.hpe.com/en-us/software/uft.

[10] https://www.ca.com/us/products/ca-application-test.html.

[11] FreeRTOS: http://www.freertos.org/index.html, RIoT OS: https://www.riot-os.org/, ERIKA Enterprise: http://erika.tuxfamily.org/drupal/.

[12] FIT IoT-lab: https://www.iot-lab.info/, IoT lab: http://www.iotinnovationlab.com/, JOSE: https://www.nict.go.jp/en/nrh/nwgn/jose.html, FIESTA-IoT: http://fiesta-iot.eu/.

[13] https://knowthings.io.

State-of-the-Art: There are hundreds of IoT platforms available[14] among which a vast majority are proprietary and closed solutions. There are also more open solutions such as the European SOFIA[15], FIWARE[16] and CRYSTAL[17] platforms. The SOFIA open source IoT platform was designed to facilitate systems interoperability aiming at promoting new services and applications, specially focusing on smart scenarios. SOFIA is a platform providing physical world information to intelligent services, thus, enabling interoperability among distinct sectors, systems and devices. SOFIA is open-source, multi-platform, multi-language and communication-agnostic. The FIWARE middleware IoT platform is a cloud-based infrastructure that aims at providing a cost-effective creation and delivery of Future Internet applications and services using public APIs to facilitate the application development in many sectors, along with public reference implementations for each component. FIWARE has a dynamic ecosystem providing assets such as a public sandbox for testing purposes or a network of hubs. CRYSTAL defines a Reference Technology Platform that provides a common ground for integrating lifecycle and engineering tools across different engineering disciplines and from multiple stakeholders involved in the development of large scale safety-critical systems. Crystal bases its entire strategy on the use of the emerging open standard OSLC (Open Services for Lifecycle Collaboration) as a standard for the Interoperability Specifications (IOS) in order to achieve common tool and data interoperability in heterogeneous systems engineering development environments.

In the following section we details the overall ENACT approach and contributions to support the DevOps for trustworthy SIS.

3   ENACT Approach

The overall ENACT approach is to deliver novel IoT platform enablers to:

1. Enable DevOps in the realm of trustworthy smart IoT systems, and enrich it with novel concepts for end-to-end security and privacy, resilience and robustness strengthening trustworthiness, taking into account the challenges related to "collaborative" actuation and actuation conflicts identification and management.
2. Facilitate the smooth integration of these to leverage DevOps for existing and new IoT platforms and approaches. The ENACT enablers represent novel concepts realised as open software engineering methods and tools.

In the following we summarize the key contribution of the ENACT Framework to the research challenges introduced in Sect. 2.

---

[14] https://iot-analytics.com/current-state-of-iot-platforms-2016/.

[15] https://about.sofia2.com/category/idiomas/en/page/3/.

[16] https://www.fiware.org/about-us/.

[17] http://www.crystal-artemis.eu.

Contribution to Research Challenge 1: To reduce delivery time and to foster continuous evolution of trustworthy SIS, the ENACT DevOps Framework will provide automation to close the gap between development and operation activities following the philosophy of DevOps [4], and foster the continuous creation, evolution, and deployment of trustworthy SIS. In particular, the ENACT DevOps Framework will deliver enablers to accomplish orchestration of sensors, actuators, software services and topology configurations, and support the automatic testing and deployment of this orchestration across the IoT, edge and cloud space.

Contribution to Research Challenge 2: The ENACT DevOps Framework will facilitate the operations of SIS in a trustworthy and agile fashion. To efficiently maintain and evolve the system according to system requirements, the ENACT DevOps Framework will provide and exploit online learning mechanisms (e.g., extending the ones proposed in [15]). This will allow dynamic self-improvement of the adaptation mechanisms of the SIS, thereby taking into account itselfcontext changes and behavioural drift. To ensure the trustworthy operation of smart applications and in particular the proper actuation on the physical environment, the ENACT DevOps Framework will provide enablers to analyse which actions are permissible in the given run-time context, thereby avoiding potential conflicting actuations and adaptations. Moreover, the ENACT DevOps Framework will enable root cause analysis and prediction in smart IoT systems with respect to trustworthiness, QoS requirements and SLAs.

Contribution to Research Challenge 3: To strengthen trustworthiness, the ENACT DevOps Framework will provide a set of coherent enablers to: *(i)* continuously validate and test the proper system design and operation; *(ii)* control and adapt the system structure, behavior and infrastructure including operation-time monitoring of the system and its underlying infrastructure (*i.e.*, nodes, devices, virtual machines, software stack, location and ownership of nodes, etc.); *(iii)* enhance robustness and resilience of smart IoT applications; *(iv)* provide new context-aware security and privacy mechanisms for end-to-end security and privacy across IoT, fog, and cloud infrastructures, integrating not only smart preventive security mechanisms but also reactive security measures; and *(v)* a novel risk-driven management support system that allow identifying threats and supports humans in the selection of device and service features that are important to adhere to specific security, location and QoS requirements. Because smart applications may involve actuators that can have direct impact on the physical world, special attention will be given to ensure the consistency of the different actuation behaviours and the management of intelligent behaviour also at the edge and IoT end.

Contribution to Research Challenge 4: The ENACT DevOps Framework will provide the missing links to implement a DevOps software process for IoT systems. The core of the ENACT enabler will be kept independent from the underlying implementation choices (*i.e.*, programming languages, libraries, IoT plat-

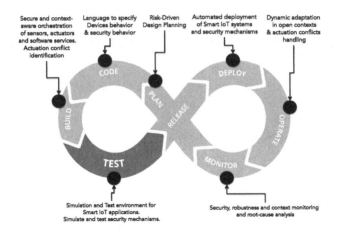

Fig. 1. ENACT support of DevOps for trustworthy smart IoT systems

form, protocols, devices, etc.). A documented plug-in mechanism will allow to specialize the ENACT enablers to exploit the underlying platform for the implementation of continuous integration, deployment, dynamic adaptation, testing, usage analytics, etc. In the ENACT Framework, plugins for various IoT platforms such as SOFIA, FIWARE and TelluCloud will be developed. Targeting SOFIA and FIWARE ensures the broad applicability of ENACT. TelluCloud allow for the validation of the plug-in mechanism on a proprietary platform. The ENACT approach and enablers have to take advantage of existing components as well as allow choosing the best suited IoT platforms for the task. That includes both platforms available today and future ones.

3.1 DevOps Life-Cycle of SIS

The ENACT DevOps approach is to evolve DevOps methods and techniques to support the development and operation of smart IoT systems, which *(i)* involve sensors and actuators and *(ii)* need to be trustworthy.

DevOps practices aim to ensure a rapid and efficient value delivery to market. DevOps ideas promote a tight collaboration between the developers (Dev) and the teams that deploy and operate the software systems (Ops). DevOps seeks to decrease the gap between a product design and its operation by introducing software design and development practices and approaches to the operation domain and vice versa. In the core of DevOps there is automation and continuous processes supported by different tools at various stages of the product life-cycle. In particular, the ENACT DevOps Framework will support the DevOps practices during the development and operation of trustworthy smart IoT systems and provide innovations and enablers that will feature trustworthy IoT systems related to seven stages of the process as depicted in Fig. 1.

Plan: The ENACT approach is to support the planning of IoT systems development cycles as well as the smooth transition towards the code stage, introducing a new enabler for risk-driven and context-aware selection of the most relevant and trustworthy devices and services to be used in the future stages. *(Research Challenge 1)*

Code: The ENACT approach is to leverage the model-driven engineering approach and in particular evolve recent advances of the ThingML [6] language and generators to support modelling of system behaviours and automatic derivation across vastly heterogeneous and distributed devices at the IoT and edge end. *(Research Challenge 1)*

Build and Deploy: The ENACT approach is to provide a new deployment modelling language to specify trustworthy and secure orchestrations of sensors, actuators and software components, along with the mechanisms to identify and handle potential actuation conflicts at the model level. The deployment engine will automatically collect the required software components and integrate the evolution of the system into the run-time environment across the whole IoT, edge and cloud space. *(Research Challenge 1 & 2)*

Test: Targeting the constraints related to the distribution and infrastructure of IoT systems, ENACT enablers will allow continuous testing of smart IoT systems in an environment capable of emulating and simulating IoT and edge infrastructures. This system will also be able to simulate some basic attacks or security threats. *(Research Challenges 1 & 3)*

Operate: The ENACT approach is to provide enablers for the automatic adaptation of IoT systems based on their run-time context, reinforced by online learning. Such automatic adaptation will address the issue that the management complexity of open-context IoT systems exceeds the capacity of human operation teams, and by this, improve the trustworthiness of the smart IoT system execution. *(Research Challenge 2)*

Monitor: The ENACT approach is to deliver innovative mechanisms to observe the status and behaviour of the running IoT systems for quality assurance and root cause analysis, and support the testing of these systems at run-time. *(Research Challenge 2)*

In addition to the DevOps related contributions identified above, the ENACT DevOps Framework will provide specific cross-cutting innovations related to trustworthiness, which can be seamlessly applied, in particular based on the following ENACT concepts:

Resilience and Robustness: The ENACT approach is to provide novel solutions to make the smart IoT systems resilient by providing enablers for diversifying IoT service implementations, and deployment topologies (*e.g.*, implying that instance of a service can have a different implementation and operate differently, still ensuring consistent and predictable global behavior). This will lower the risk for privacy and security breaches and significantly reduced impact in case of cyber-attack infringes. *(Research Challenge 3)*

Security, Privacy and Identity Management: The ENACT approach is to provide support to ensure end-to-end security of trustworthy SIS. This does

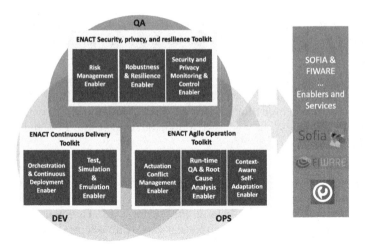

Fig. 2. The ENACT Framework architecture

not only include smart preventive security mechanisms but also the continuous monitoring of *(i)* security metrics and *(ii)* the context with the objective to trigger reactive security measures. *(Research Challenge 3)*

In the following section we present the design of the ENACT DevOps Framework that will support the DevOps life-cycle of trustworthy smart IoT systems.

4   The ENACT DevOps Framework

The current initial ENACT DevOps Framework is designed as depicted in Fig. 2 and consists of some experimental prototypes of the enablers. This section describes the design of the ENACT DevOps Framework.

The ENACT DevOps Framework is designed as a set of loosely coupled enablers that can be easily integrated with existing IoT platforms via a plug in mechanism. The ENACT enablers are categorized in three groups as follows: *(i)* the toolkit for the continuous delivery of smart IoT systems, *(ii)* the toolkit for the agile operation of smart IoT systems, and *(iii)* the ENACT facilities for trustworthiness. The set of enablers can be seamlessly combined and they can easily integrate with existing IoT platform services and enablers.

4.1   ENACT Continuous Delivery Toolkit

The designed ENACT DevOps Framework includes two enablers that improve the continuous delivery of smart IoT systems, with a specific focus on *(i)* agile and continuous evolution and *(ii)* early-detection of issues in the software development process. A particular concern is to support the testing of smart IoT systems and the gradual migration from the test to the operation environment.

Orchestration and Continuous Deployment Enabler: This ENACT enabler aims to facilitate the engineering and continuous deployment of smart IoT systems, allowing decentralized processing across the heterogeneous IoT, edge and cloud space. Specifically, a domain-specific modelling language facilitates the design of smart IoT systems by supporting the modelling derivation and orchestration of trustworthy IoT, edge and cloud services that are enabled for context-aware and risk-driven assimilation of the most proper mechanisms for trustworthy execution. The language is designed to come with an execution engine that will support the automatic deployment of software components over IoT, edge and cloud resources, building on work providing a multicloud deployment engine [7]. The enabler is designed to leverage recent techniques for ensuring the proper isolation of each individual service (*i.e.*, containerization using technologies such as Docker[18], rkt[19], or Triton[20]). In addition, it embeds mechanisms to identify actuation conflicts (*i.e.*, conflicts related to concurrent access to a same actuator or due to conflicting modifications of the environment - *e.g.*, opening the windows may conflict with the action of turning off the heating system in order to regulate the temperature) and to generate and deploy the respective controller (*i.e.*, software components whose role is to manage access to the actuators).

Test, Emulation and Simulation Enabler: IoT systems need to cope with the uncertainty related to the physical world (*e.g.*, communication links may fail, nodes may run out of battery, etc.). The delivery model advocated to manage this uncertainty should provide proper support to assess the system's behaviour and trustworthiness early in the life cycle. ENACT will deliver an enabler to test smart IoT systems that includes simulation and emulation of IoT services and devices. In particular, a hardware abstraction layer (HAL) will be in charge of offering physical resources and sensors as software services. In addition, this enabler may be based on self-learning IoT virtualizers to automatically model IoT elements and facilitate testing. Finally, this system will also be able to simulate some basic attacks or security threats.

4.2   ENACT Agile Operation Toolkit

We have designed three innovative enablers to significantly reduce the burden of managing and maintaining smart IoT systems. Key requirements are *(i)* to ensure the trustworthiness of such systems under operation and *(ii)* to automate operation activities as much as possible.

Context-Aware Self-adaptation Enabler: Because anticipating all possible context situations that smart IoT systems may encounter during its operation is not possible, it is difficult for software developers to determine how a run-time adaptation of the system may impact the satisfaction of the system behaviour and

---

[18] https://www.docker.com.

[19] https://coreos.com/rkt.

[20] https://docs.joyent.com/public-cloud.

of the interactions with the environment. To address this challenge, this enabler is designed to apply online learning techniques to improve the way a smart IoT system adapts during its operation. Online learning means that learning is performed at run-time, taking into account observations about the actual system execution and system context. Online learning incrementally updates the smart IoT system's knowledge base; *e.g.*, its adaptation rules or the models based on which adaptation decisions are made.

Root Cause Analysis Enabler: This enabler offers a resilient root cause analysis system, which is designed to leverage edge infrastructures to perform diagnostics on a segregated part of the system without connectivity to a centralized diagnostic module or service. With the system behaviour models created for this analysis, this enabler is able to predict future states of the system and provide warnings and recommendations.

Context Monitoring and Actuation Conflict Management Enabler: Because of the uncertain, dynamic, and partially known nature of the physical environment, it is very difficult or even illusory to assess at run- time the conformity of the effects of actions in this environment with deterministic models. This enabler is designed to provide a set of observers to monitor the behavioural drift of smart IoT systems that may arise when operating in such open context. In addition, it is designed to exploit the computed drift measure to dynamically adjust the behaviour of the system. This enabler relies on the finite state machines composition theory and model checking tools. By means of deterministic models of the devices, their physical context along with some predefined constraints, a set of device controllers (*i.e.*, software components whose role is to manage access to the actuators) will be generated at design-time and deployed to prevent conflicting and antagonist actions that may occur at run-time.

4.3   ENACT Trustworthiness Toolkit

The ENACT DevOps Framework will deliver a set of enablers addressing specific crosscutting trustworthiness concerns such as ensuring proper robustness, security and privacy of smart IoT systems.

Robustness and Resilience Enabler: Recent multidisciplinary research on software engineering and ecology suggests that a promising way to approach resilience in software systems is to diversify software, and system topology [27], implying that each instance of a service has a different implementation and operates differently, still ensuring that its global behaviour is consistent and predictable. Thus, instead of exposing the very same code and topology in millions of instances, each individual instance can be unique, making the overall system more resilient. Currently, the digitalisation is typically based on commonalities and replications, which can have some severe implications. For example, if a system can break into one "keyless" car, it allows to steal any car that uses the same "keyless" system [28]. This ENACT enabler is inspired from nature where diversity has been a key mechanism for resilience for all forms of life, by enabling them to adapt to changes in the environmental conditions and evolve immunity to perturbations. This enabler is designed to automate the introduction and management of diversity in smart IoT systems and builds on recent research developed in particular [29].

Risk Management Enabler: This enabler is designed to provide a risk-driven guidance to architects, developers, feasibility study engineers and other potential stakeholders to design the architecture of their IoT systems and thus support them in the selection of devices, IoT services and mechanisms to ensure trustworthy execution of IoT systems. This is achieved by detecting potential vulnerabilities affecting one or more devices and analyzing trade-off between security and trustworthiness level offered by the devices and services, risk and quality impact. This service can be integrated with the ENACT Continuous Delivery Toolkit, to allow its exploitation in an iterative design process for rapid software evolution. The MODAClouds[21] and MUSA[22] Decision Support Systems will serve as baseline and be extended in ENACT with specific focus on *(i)* the IoT domain and *(ii)* trustworthiness mechanisms. We will also study the potential impact that the late detection of these risks may have in the software development process planning.

Security and Privacy Monitoring and Control Enabler: This enabler will provide mechanisms to monitor end-to-end the security, privacy of a smart IoT system. A set of relevant metrics will be defined and notifications will be raised when the monitored metrics deviated from the normal (*i.e.*, risk under control) behaviour. This enabler will include mechanisms and tools to support the user data awareness and control in the form of intelligent notification able to provide insights on what is actually the security issue in the IoT environment. We will leverage open source solutions, particularly for network and system levels monitoring, while new innovative solutions will be developed for the application level security and privacy assessment. Finally, this enabler will provide mechanisms for controlling the security, privacy and trustworthiness behaviour of smart IoT systems. This includes the early reaction models and mechanisms that address the adaptation and recovery of the IoT application operation in case the monitored metrics deviated from the expected behaviour. A specific focus will be given to the confidentiality and integrity of data and services via end-to-end Context-based Access control and authorization mechanisms for smart IoT systems. This includes the early reaction models and mechanisms that address the adaptation and recovery of the IoT application operation on the basis of the application context. Today, no protocol can deliver dynamic authorization based on context for both IT and OT (operational technologies) domains. This work will advance state-of-the art mechanisms and leverage on Evidian's IoT access control solutions.

---

[21] http://www.modaclouds.eu.
[22] http://www.musa-project.eu.

5   Conclusion

We presented a set of challenges related to the development, operation, and quality assurance of trustworthy smart IoT systems that need to be distributed across IoT, edge and cloud infrastructures and involve both sensors and actuators. The ENACT DevOps Framework will offer a set of novel solutions to address these challenges. Most of these enablers will be delivered as open source artefacts.

References

1. IEC: IoT 2020: Smart and secure IoT platform. IEC white paper (2016)
2. NESSI: Cyber physical systems: Opportunities and challenges for software, services, cloud and data. NESSI white paper (2015)
3. NESSI: SOFTWARE CONTINUUM: Recommendations for ICT Work Programme 2018+. NESSI report (2016)
4. Humble, J., Farley, D.: Continuous Delivery: Reliable Software Releases through Build, Test, and Deployment Automation. Addison-Wesley Professional, Boston (2010)
5. Taivalsaari, A., Mikkonen, T.: A roadmap to the programmable world: software challenges in the IoT era. IEEE Softw. **34**(1), 72–80 (2017)
6. Morin, B., Fleurey, F., Husa, K.E., Barais, O.: A generative middleware for heterogeneous and distributed services. In: 19th International ACM SIGSOFT Symposium on Component-Based Software Engineering (CBSE), pp. 107–116. IEEE (2016)
7. Ferry, N., Song, H., Rossini, A., Chauvel, F., Solberg, A.: CloudMF: applying MDE to tame the complexity of managing multi-cloud applications. In: IEEE/ACM 7th International Conference on Utility and Cloud Computing (UCC), pp. 269–277. IEEE (2014)
8. Van Ommering, R., Van Der Linden, F., Kramer, J., Magee, J.: The koala component model for consumer electronics software. Computer **33**(3), 78–85 (2000)
9. Fassino, J.P., Stefani, J.B., Lawall, J.L., Muller, G.: Think: a software framework for component-based operating system kernels. In: USENIX Annual Technical Conference, General Track, pp. 73–86 (2002)
10. Fouquet, F., Morin, B., Fleurey, F., Barais, O., Plouzeau, N., Jezequel, J.M.: A dynamic component model for cyber physical systems. In: Proceedings of the 15th ACM SIGSOFT Symposium on Component Based Software Engineering, pp. 135–144. ACM (2012)
11. De Lemos, R., et al.: Software engineering for self-adaptive systems: a second research roadmap. In: de Lemos, R., Giese, H., Müller, H.A., Shaw, M. (eds.) Software Engineering for Self-Adaptive Systems II. LNCS, vol. 7475, pp. 1–32. Springer, Heidelberg (2013). https://doi.org/10.1007/978-3-642-35813-5_1
12. Esfahani, N., Kouroshfar, E., Malek, S.: Taming uncertainty in self-adaptive software. In: Proceedings of the 19th ACM SIGSOFT Symposium and the 13th European Conference on Foundations of Software Engineering, pp. 234–244. ACM (2011)
13. Fredericks, E.M., DeVries, B., Cheng, B.H.: AutoRELAX: automatically RELAXing a goal model to address uncertainty. Empirical Softw. Eng. **19**(5), 1466–1501 (2014)

14. Esfahani, N., Elkhodary, A., Malek, S.: A learning-based framework for engineering feature-oriented self-adaptive software systems. IEEE Trans. Softw. Eng. **39**(11), 1467–1493 (2013)
15. Sharifloo, A.M., Metzger, A., Quinton, C., Baresi, L., Pohl, K.: Learning and evolution in dynamic software product lines. In: Proceedings of the 11th International Symposium on Software Engineering for Adaptive and Self-Managing Systems, pp. 158–164. ACM (2016)
16. Metzger, A., Di Nitto, E.: Addressing highly dynamic changes in service-oriented systems: towards agile evolution and adaptation. In: Software Design and Development: Concepts, Methodologies, Tools, and Applications, p. 164 (2013)
17. Aggarwal, C.C.: Managing and Mining Sensor Data. Springer, New York (2013). https://doi.org/10.1007/978-1-4614-6309-2
18. Dastjerdi, A.V., Gupta, H., Calheiros, R.N., Ghosh, S.K., Buyya, R.: Fog computing: principles, architectures, and applications. arXiv preprint arXiv:1601.02752 (2016)
19. Niggemann, O., Biswas, G., Kinnebrew, J.S., Khorasgani, H., Volgmann, S., Bunte, A.: Data-driven monitoring of cyber-physical systems leveraging on big data and the internet-of-things for diagnosis and control. In: DX@ Safeprocess, pp. 185–192 (2015)
20. Zasadziński, M., Muntés-Mulero, V., Solé, M., Carrera, D.: Fast root cause analysis on distributed systems by composing precompiled Bayesian networks. In: Proceedings of World Congress on Engineering and Computer Science, vol. 1, pp. 464–469 (2016)
21. OWASP: Internet of Things Top Ten. Technical report (2014)
22. Kolias, C., Stavrou, A., Voas, J., Bojanova, I., Kuhn, R.: Learning internet-of-things security "hands-on". IEEE Secur. Priv. **14**(1), 37–46 (2016)
23. Cvitić, I., Vujić, M., Husnjak, S.: Classification of security risks in the IoT environment. In: 26th International DAAAM Symposium on Intelligent Manufacturing and Automation, pp. 731–740 (2016)
24. Kecskemeti, G., Casale, G., Jha, D.N., Lyon, J., Ranjan, R.: Modelling and simulation challenges in internet of things. IEEE Cloud Comput. **4**(1), 62–69 (2017)
25. D'Angelo, G., Ferretti, S., Ghini, V.: Simulation of the internet of things. In: 2016 International Conference on High Performance Computing & Simulation (HPCS), pp. 1–8. IEEE (2016)
26. D'Angelo, G., Ferretti, S., Ghini, V.: Multi-level simulation of internet of things on smart territories. Simul. Model. Pract. Theory **73**, 3–21 (2017)
27. Allier, S., et al.: Multitier diversification in web-based software applications. IEEE Softw. **32**(1), 83–90 (2015)
28. Verdult, R., Garcia, F.D., Ege, B.: Dismantling megamos crypto: wirelessly lock-picking a vehicle immobilizer. In: USENIX Security Symposium, pp. 703–718 (2013)
29. Baudry, B., Monperrus, M., Mony, C., Chauvel, F., Fleurey, F., Clarke, S.: DIVERSIFY: ecology-inspired software evolution for diversity emergence. In: Proceedings of the International Conference on Software Maintenance and Reengineering (CSMR), Belgium, pp. 444–447 (2014)

From Monolith to Microservices:
A Classification of Refactoring Approaches

Jonas Fritzsch[1($\boxtimes$)], Justus Bogner[2], Alfred Zimmermann[2],
and Stefan Wagner[1]

[1] Institute of Software Technology, University of Stuttgart, Stuttgart, Germany
{jonas.fritzsch,
stefan.wagner}@informatik.uni-stuttgart.de
[2] Reutlingen University of Applied Sciences, Reutlingen, Germany
{justus.bogner,
alfred.zimmermann}@reutlingen-university.de

Abstract. While the recently emerged Microservices architectural style is widely discussed in literature, it is difficult to find clear guidance on the process of refactoring legacy applications. The importance of the topic is underpinned by high costs and effort of a refactoring process which has several other implications, e.g. overall processes (DevOps) and team structure. Software architects facing this challenge are in need of selecting an appropriate strategy and refactoring technique. One of the most discussed aspects in this context is finding the right service granularity to fully leverage the advantages of a Microservices architecture. This study first discusses the notion of architectural refactoring and subsequently compares 10 existing refactoring approaches recently proposed in academic literature. The approaches are classified by the underlying decomposition technique and visually presented in the form of a decision guide for quick reference. The review yielded a variety of strategies to break down a monolithic application into independent services. With one exception, most approaches are only applicable under certain conditions. Further concerns are the significant amount of input data some approaches require as well as limited or prototypical tool support.

Keywords: Microservices · Monolith · Modernization · Refactoring ·
Cloud · Decomposition · Transformation · Modularization ·
Software architecture

1 Introduction

An increased tendency by organizations to move existing enterprise-scale applications to the cloud can be observed. The reasons to do so are manifold: high availability and redundancy, automatic scaling, easier infrastructure management and compliance with latest security standards ensure a more agile and combined flow of development and operation, also referred to as DevOps [5]. Driven by this new paradigm, the design, build, deployment and maintenance of business applications has fundamentally changed. To overcome this gap and make existing monolithic applications "cloud-ready",

© Springer Nature Switzerland AG 2019
J.-M. Bruel et al. (Eds.): DEVOPS 2018, LNCS 11350, pp. 128–141, 2019.
https://doi.org/10.1007/978-3-030-06019-0_10

they need to run as flexible, loosely-coupled compositions of specialized services, which lately emerged as the Microservices architecture style.

Monolithic applications that have grown over years can become large, complex and in later stages even fossilize [39], meaning the accumulated technical debt results in obscure structures that make the product unmaintainable with a reasonable effort. Even in earlier stages, a single developer or even architect is unable to keep detailed insight into all components and their interfaces. This makes the monolith hard to maintain and cumbersome with regards to adapting newer and better technologies. Furthermore, the effort for changing initial design choices later on requires immense effort. Besides, monolithic applications are often incapable to scale on the module level, but rather per duplicating instances of the whole application. This is in most cases an inefficient approach in responding to quickly changing workloads while maintaining optimal resource utilization.

A new architectural style, referred to as Microservices, promises to address these issues. It started as a trend in software engineering industry practice which was first described in detail by Lewis and Fowler [25]. Contextually related modules have to be identified and encapsulated into a service, providing high cohesion inwards and loose coupling outwards. To leverage most from the design, functionality has to be split up with appropriate granularity. However, building a new application from scratch based on a Microservices architecture can be a very expensive and time-consuming task. On the other hand, the process of refactoring a mature monolithic application into Microservices can be a long-lasting endeavor too, depending on the condition of the system in place.

This study aims to fill the gap in scientific research by comparing and classifying refactoring approaches proposed in academic literature. The results can help architects and developers to gain an overview of currently available refactoring approaches and hereby facilitate their specific transformation process. Researchers may profit from the findings through quickly understanding the current state of the field. The key objective of the study design is formulated as a research question:

RQ: What are existing architectural refactoring approaches in the context of decomposing a monolithic application architecture into Microservices and how can they be classified with regards to the techniques and strategies used?

2 Architectural Refactoring and Decomposition

Refactoring as an activity to extend the lifetime of existing software products is a behavior preserving code transformation to improve the source code that structurally deteriorated over time [30] or accumulated technical debt [39]. According to Pirkelbauer [33], agile software development methodologies benefit in particular due to frequent changes. Plenty of research has been conducted in this area already, which mainly targets refactoring at source code level. Fowler et al. consolidated the field in their well-known book "Improving the design of Existing Code, more than 70 Patterns explained" [15]. Dietrich distinguishes code-level from architectural refactoring by referring to the latter ones as high-impact refactorings [11]. They can be seen as architectural activities that remove a particular architectural smell while improving one or more quality attributes, without changing the system's scope and functionality [41]. Moreover, it may result in an altered organizational structure [35], which is an interesting aspect: According to Conway's Law [10], organizations tend to produce system designs that reflect the organization's communication structures [23, 38]. Consequently, architecture and organization are interdependent to some degree, which furthermore distinguishes the process from pure code refactoring. Drivers for a refactoring are feature extensions and design changes [33], but also anti-patterns [8] and code smells [15], whereas such high-impact refactorings are rather driven by requirements to run software in the cloud (platform changes, deployment and release cycle changes) as well as interconnected organizational changes. In contrast to code-level refactoring, architectural refactoring is common in the context of adopting Microservices.

From a software architects' perspective, a proper decomposition into services with the appropriate granularity can be seen as the main challenge in a refactoring process: In general, one could imagine various ways to split a system into smaller parts. Amundsen [2] outlines a few of them, e.g. based on *implementation technology* (computationally heavy services written in C may be separated from chatty components using Node.js) or based on *geography* (also specific legal, commercial or cultural aspects). Besides them, one could think of even other viewpoints, like the architectural style, certain non-functional requirements, personal experiences or education. The characteristics of Microservices promote following the functional decomposition perspective [37]. In this context it is referred to as decomposition around business capabilities. Dependencies throughout the technical layers are hereby greatly reduced, whereas a rather lightweight integration layer on top is a common solution to integrate the resulting Microservices [26].

So, what are the means to identify business capabilities in a monolith? Lewis and Fowler [25] bring the notion of a *bounded context* into effect. It originates from Evans book Domain-Driven Design [13], which provides the means to identify such contexts within a complex domain [25]. According to Richardson, bounded contexts can be separated through decomposing by verbs (use cases) or by nouns (resources) [36]. Newman stresses the term *seam* from Michael Feathers book "Working Effectively with Legacy Code" [14]. It similarly describes a way to separate portions of code that can be treated independently from other parts and hereby obtain "loosely coupled and strongly cohesive" [29] Microservices. In practice, the lack of a universally valid algorithm that guides the decomposition process makes it to "somewhat of an art", as Richardson points out [74]. Extracting a domain model from an application's code base can be a significant challenge. If incorrectly applied, it can lead to architectures that combine the drawbacks of both styles, Monolith and Microservices.

3 Related Work

Our literature review has revealed a lack of systematic guidance on the refactoring process for existing monolithic applications. Several publications discussing Microservices also cover the aspect of migrating monoliths to Microservice-based architectures to some extent [22, 25, 29, 36], but the topic is still evolving.

A systematic mapping study conducted in 2016 identified 3 out of 21 studies dealing with migration topics [31], while Di Francesco et al. found 16 out of 71 migration-related studies during their review in 2017 [16]. The papers found were mainly solution proposals, followed by experience reports and opinion papers. The field is not mature yet, Microservices migration and architectural refactoring are still referred to as future trends [31]. The very recent and comprehensive study by Balalaie et al. compiles a set of empirically identified design patterns for Microservices migration and rearchitecting [3]. The patterns originate from observations of medium to large-scale industrial projects. Compared to our work, the concepts are presented on a higher level of abstraction and do not cover specifics of concrete approaches proposed in literature. Still, the study complements our work in terms of empirical values. Widening the scope to Service-based Systems in general, there is a mature state of research regarding Service-Oriented Architecture (SOA). According to Bogner et al. [6], Microservices and SOA "share a large set of design-related commonalities". Klose et al. for instance discuss the identification of services for SOA development from a business point of view [21]. Although the suitability for Microservices may be limited due to the differences of the architectural styles, the included comparison of approaches regarding service identification mark a decent overview at that time. To the best of our knowledge, there is currently no holistic literature review of refactoring approaches and decomposition techniques available that facilitates this process. Our study attempts to fill this research gap.

4   Research Method and Search Strategy

By means of a literature review, existing refactoring techniques in the Microservices context are identified, investigated, classified and presented in textual and visual form. Brereton et al. propose a three-step review process that serves as a basic structure for this review: planning, conducting, and documenting [7]. Fundamental constraints of a literature review are the databases to query and the search strings to use. For the used queries, three of the most frequented scientific libraries and indexing systems in computer science have been selected: ACM Digital Library, IEEE Xplore and Google Scholar. The choice of these databases and indexing systems is guided by the fact that they have been proven most relevant for conducting systematic literature reviews in the software engineering field [32]. Other aspects are their high accessibility and ability to export search results conveniently. Figure 1 illustrates the basic steps for our literature search.

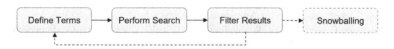

Fig. 1. Search strategy used for the review.

The following search string(s) have been used for querying the databases:

```
("microservice" OR "micro-service") [AND "monolith*"]
[AND ("refactor" OR "transform" OR "migrat*" OR
"decompos*" OR "partition*" OR "granular*")]
```

The obtained studies have been filtered according to a set of selection criteria: Only peer reviewed articles published in English have been included, the abstract had to clearly show a contribution towards the research question and we expected a documented validation of proposed approach. Guidelines recommend to use a snowballing activity applied on the list resulting from the initial selection [40]. The initial search results yielded by the queries have been enlarged by such a snowballing activity. Finally, a qualitative assessment of the studies has been performed by focusing on technical depth, recency and relevance of the content presented.

5 Results

The performed literature review identified a variety of studies with different orientation, coverage and level of detail. Many of them were tailored to specific scenarios, focusing on specific requirements or aspects while not discussing the theoretical background.

Table 1. Reviewed publications.

	List of Authors and Publications
1	Escobar, D. et al.: Towards the understanding and evolution of monolithic applications as microservices. In: Proceedings of 42nd Latin American Computing Conference, CLEI. (2016) [12]
2	Levcovitz, A. et al.: Towards a Technique for Extracting Microservices from Monolithic Enterprise Systems. In: 3rd Brazilian Workshop on Software Visualization, Evolution and Maintenance (VEM). pp. 97–104 (2015) [24]
3	Ahmadvand, M., Ibrahim, A.: Requirements reconciliation for scalable and secure microservice (de)composition. In: Proceedings - 2016 IEEE 24th International Requirements Engineering Conference Workshops, REW 2016. pp. 68–73 (2016) [1]
4	Baresi, L. et al.: Microservices Identification Through Interface Analysis. In: ESOCC 2017: Service-Oriented and Cloud Computing. pp. 19–33 (2017) [4]
5	Gysel, M. et al.: Service cutter: A systematic approach to service decomposition. In: Lecture Notes in Computer Science. pp. 185–200 (2016) [17]
6	Mazlami, G. et al.: Extraction of Microservices from Monolithic Software Architectures. In: 2017 IEEE International Conference on Web Services (ICWS). pp. 524–531 (2017) [27]
7	Mustafa, O., Gómez, J.M.: Optimizing economics of microservices by planning for granularity level Experience Report. (2017) [28]
8	Hassan, S. et al.: Microservice Ambients: An Architectural Meta-Modelling Approach for Microservice Granularity. In: Proceedings - 2017 IEEE International Conference on Software Architecture, ICSA. pp. 1–10 (2017) [18]
9	Klock, S. et al.: Workload-Based Clustering of Coherent Feature Sets in Microservice Architectures. Proc. - 2017 IEEE Int. Conf. Softw. Archit. ICSA. 11–20 (2017) [20]
10	Procaccianti, G. et al.: Towards a MicroServices Architecture for Clouds. VU University Amsterdam (2016) [34]

Ten approaches provided an adequate level of abstraction and potential for generalization according to the underlying strategy used to steers the decomposition (see Table 1). The work by Chen et al. [9] was published after completion of the review and thus did not go into the list of selected publications.

5.1 Classification

While analyzing the selected approaches, we identified distinct decomposition strategies. They determine the required artefacts (besides source code) as an input, the granularity of the resulting services and if the approach can be applied to greenfield-developments in addition. Out of the reviewed studies, the following categories have been defined by grouping similar strategies:

- *Static Code Analysis aided* approaches require the application's source code and derive a decomposition from it (through possible intermediate stages).
- *Meta-Data aided* approaches require more abstract input data, like architectural descriptions in form of UML diagrams, use cases, interfaces or historical VCS data.
- *Workload-Data aided* approaches aim to find suitable service cuts by measuring the application's operational data (e.g. communication, performance) on module or function level and use this data to determine a fitting decomposition and granularity.
- *Dynamic Microservice Composition* approaches try to solve the problem more holistically by describing a Microservices runtime environment. Other than the above categories, the resulting set of services is permanently changing in each iteration of re-calculating the best-fitting composition (based on e.g. workload).

Tables 2 and 3 give an overview of the reviewed approaches. The classification defined above can be found in the *Type* column. The *Applicability* column distinguishes between approaches that support Microservices greenfield developments and others that focus on existing monolithic applications. Other constraints like technology-restrictions are listed in this column as well. *Strategy* points out the utilized decomposition strategy. *Atomic Unit, Granularity* indicates the smallest unit that the approach is able to handle, which in the end determines the possible range of granularity. Some approaches automatically calculate the granularity, i.e. number of resulting services, whereas others leave it up to the user. *Input* and *Output* list artefacts needed and produced by the approach. Some approaches describe metrics for a result evaluation, which can be found under *Result Evaluation*. Four of the approaches offer tool-support, as the respective column shows. Our review revealed a general lack in this area, which is mandatory to achieve a certain degree of automation. It hinders an empirical evaluation and thorough assessment of the approaches. Lastly, the column *Validation* shows the kind of method used to validate the approach like experiments, case studies or proof-of-concepts (Table 4).

Table 2. Overview of decomposition approaches, part 1.

#	Approach	Authors (Year)	Type	Applicability	Strategy	Atomic unit, granularity
1	Towards the understanding and evolution of monolithic applications as microservices	Escobar, et al. (2016) [12]	SCA, based on static code analysis from Java annotations	MO, JEE multi-tier applications	Calculate clusters of EJBs that form a microservice, identify data types through Java annotations	Atomic unit: EJB, adjustable granularity during clustering threshold provided by user
2	Towards a Technique for extracting micro-services from monolithic enterprise systems	Levcovitz, et al. (2016) [24]	SCA, focusing on multi-tier applications	MO, multi-tier applications consisting of at least 3 tiers	Construct microservice candidates based on dependencies between facades and database tables, bridged by business functions	Atomic unit: set of facades, business functions, database table, granularity as result
3	Requirements reconciliation for scalable and secure microservice (de) composition	Ahmadvand, et al. (2016) [1]	MDA, focusing on security and scalability	GR + MO, application defined by use cases and requirements	Calculate microservice decomposition based on security and scalability requirements	Atomic unit as defined in use case diagrams
4	Microservices identification through interface analysis	Baresi, et al. (2017) [4]	MDA, based on semantic similarity of (Open) API specification	GR + MO	Calculate suitable service cuts through clustering of interface specifications according to their semantic similarity	Single operation as provided by OpenAPI spec., granularity parameterizable
5	Service cutter: a systematic approach to service decomposition	Gysel, et al. (2016) [17]	MDA, extracts coupling information from software engineering artifacts (ERM, use cases)	GR + MO	Calculate clustering of nanoentities to form microservices based on number of weighted properties, clustering algorithm exchangeable	Nanoentity (data, operation or artifact), granularity as result or input param, depending on algorithm
6	Extraction of microservices from monolithic software architectures	Mazlami, et al. (2017) [27]	MDA, based on version control meta data	MO, applications having meaningful VCS meta data	Calculate decomposition via graph-based clustering out of version history by either: logical, Semantic or Contributor Coupling	Class as atomic unit, granularity as result

(*continued*)

Table 2. (*continued*)

#	Approach	Authors (Year)	Type	Applicability	Strategy	Atomic unit, granularity
7	GranMicro: a black-box based approach for optimizing microservices based app's	Mustafa, et al. (2017) [28]	WDA, black box-based approach, considering non-functional requirements	MO, web-applications generating expressive access logs	Utilize web usage mining techniques to optimize service decomposition based on non-functional requirements	Functional units that can be identified through web access logs
8	Microservice Ambients: an architectural meta-modelling approach for microservice granularity	Hassan, et al. (2017) [18]	DMC, dynamic composition, model granularity at runtime	GR + MO	Define architectural elements (Ambients) with adaptable boundaries, use workload data for adaptation of granularity at runtime	"Unit of mobility" as abstract definition of an atomic unit
9	Workload-based clustering of coherent feature sets in microservice architectures	Klock, et al. (2017) [20]	DMC, dynamic composition approach for workload-optimized deployment	GR + MO	Calculate optimal deployment and granularity based on workload using a genetic algorithm	Feature as atomic unit (chunk of functionality that delivers business value)
10	Towards a microservices architecture for clouds	Procaccianti, et al. (2016) [34]	DMC, MDA, data-driven, bottom-up approach	GR + MO	Bottom-up, data-driven, process-mining algorithm	Functional property, granularity adapts dynamically

5.2 Decision Guide

Figure 2 illustrates the essentials of the presented approaches in form of a decision guide. The architect planning to migrate a monolithic application to Microservices can use this flow chart to quickly find the appropriate approach for a specific scenario. Starting on top, a set of alternatives will lead to the most appropriate approach first, symbolized by the number. Should this option not fulfill the architect's requirements, the dashed line will lead back to the main thread and propose the next best alternative. Each approach is labeled with its associated type (symbolized by the orange ellipse), according to its classification (column *Type*). Should all approaches be discarded, the last one proposed will be "Service Cutter" with No. 5, at the bottom right of the flow chart. It can be seen as a general-purpose approach offering the most mature tool support as of date of this review. However, the approach requires a comprehensive specification of the system including coupling criteria, which may not always be available to such extent [4].

Table 3. Overview of decomposition approaches, part 2.

#	Input	Output	Result evaluation	Tool support	Validation
1	Source code (Java)	Visualization in four different diagrams: EJB data, EJB shared types, MS, MS invocation	Metrics based on source code	n/a	JEE application with 74.566 LoC, 624 classes and 35993 methods
2	Source code	Candidate list of microservices	n/a	n/a	Case study on a 750 KLOC banking application
3	Use cases (UML) with assessment of security and scalability requirements	Candidate list of microservices	n/a, announced for future research	n/a	Sample application
4	OpenAPI specification of interface; reference vocabulary (as fitness function)	Candidate list of microservices	Qualitative, no metrics	Experimental prototype of decomposition tool and sample datasets, https://github.com/mgarriga/decomposer	452 OpenAPI specifications, comparison of samples with results from 5 SW-engineers, comparison with service cutter (#4)
5	Domain Model (ERM) and User representations (use cases, characteristics of nano-entities and roles) in JSON	Candidate list of microservices, export to JSON, graphical representation of service and dependencies	Qualitative service design checklist assessing service cut (excellent, expected, acceptable, unreasonable)	Service Cutter, open source prototype implementing the approach, https://github.com/ServiceCutter/ServiceCutter	Case studies: fictitious trading system and DDD sample application "Cargo Tracking", performance tests
6	Source code and VCS meta data	Candidate list of microservices	Quality of service cut using custom metrics: Team size reduction (tsr), average domain redundancy (adr)	POC available as open source Java project, https://github.com/gmazlami/microserviceExtraction-backend(and-frontend)	Experiment using a set of sample code bases from open-source projects (200 to 25000 commits, 1.000 to 500.000 LOC, 5 to 200 contributors)
7	Web access logs	Diagram of service model	Performance metrics (response time, CPU utilization)	n/a	Sample e-bookshop web application

(continued)

Table 3. (*continued*)

#	Input	Output	Result evaluation	Tool support	Validation
8	Aspect-oriented description of the software architecture using the ambient-PRISMA textual language	Microservice composition with dynamic granularity adaptation at runtime, based on predefined parameters indicating QoS	Qualitative evaluation on effectiveness/expressiveness of modelling and facilitating design time and runtime analysis	n/a	Experiment using a hypothetical application for an online movie subscription-based system
9	Representation of the architecture by a set of features, workload model	Descriptive and visual output of suggested model, resulting in concrete MS architectures at runtime	Performance metrics measuring the quality of a deployment	MicADO (Microservice Architecture Deployment Optimizer) URL: see publication	Case study using ERP software "AFAS" (27 features with a total of 238 properties and 72 dependency relations between features)
10	Properties or blocks extracted from source code, capabilities (non-functional)	Microservice composition	n/a	n/a	Proof of concept: sample application for "synthetic video processing"

Table 4. Legend to Tables 2 and 3.

Type	
SCA	Static code analysis aided (either source code or more abstract artefacts like architectural UML diagrams or APIs of the applications architecture)
MDA	Meta-data aided (version control history data, non-functional requirements)
WDA	Workload-data aided (gathered during runtime, like performance data or web-access logs)
DMC	Dynamic microservice composition (approach to model or adapt service composition/granularity at runtime based on workload data)
Applicability	
GR	Microservices-greenfield development
MO	Monolith-migrations
GR + MO	Applicable for both scenarios

Approaches treating granularity as a dynamically changing factor are grouped in a single box and not further differentiated. These approaches describe a Microservices runtime environment in contrast to a fixed partitioning determined at design-time. As such environments are not discussed in necessary detail here, the condensed depiction will account for their complexity.

Decision Guide

for Decomposition Approaches of Monolithic Applications

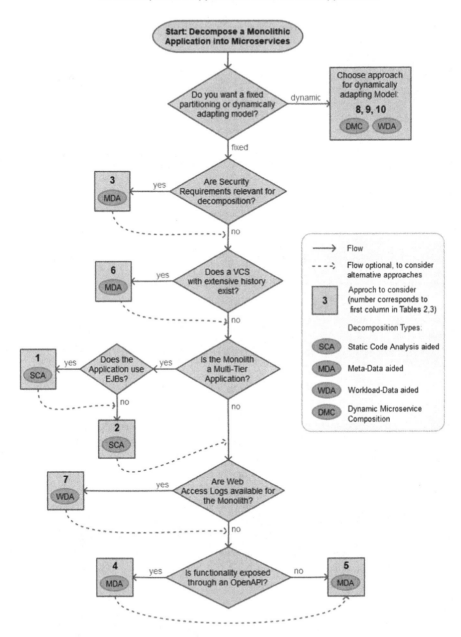

Fig. 2. Decision guide for decomposition approaches.

6 Conclusion

By means of a literature review we identified and categorized 10 recently proposed architectural refactoring approaches for transforming monolithic applications into Microservices. The approaches have been categorized into four groups by the underlying strategy used for the decomposition, which can be seen as the most challenging step from a software architect's perspective. Thereby we answer our initially phrased research question.

In general, the findings reveal a shortage of practically applicable approaches that offer adequate tool support and metrics to verify the results. Almost all of the reviewed approaches are not universally applicable and require different sets of input data. Thus, an accompanying decision guide in form of a flow chart has been created to help readers in quickly identifying the appropriate approach for a certain scenario. The most structured and universal method has been proposed by Gysel et al. [17], which can be seen as a solid basis for further research. However, the practical applicability is limited due to its dependence on a "detailed and exhaustive specification of the system" [4]. Microservices architecture as a field "rooted in practice" [16] is widely discussed in industry. It can be expected that further research will very likely reveal new approaches that can be incorporated and thus extend the findings of this study. Potential future research could focus on testing different approaches using an adequate example or real-world application. To do so, quality attributes and related metrics to assess the quality of a decomposition should be defined in a first step.

Several threats to validity have to be mentioned for this research. The conducted review did not follow the guidelines of a systematic literature review as proposed by e.g. Kitchenham and Charters [19], which would improve repeatability and reproducibility of the results and thus guarantee appropriate scientific rigor. For the systematic classification and presentation of the results Petersen et al. [32] provide a set of guidelines accordingly. The candidates for this review were obtained from only three academic search engines. Furthermore, the selected refactoring techniques have been investigated only theoretically. Thus, all results stem from assertions of the authors or other publications. A thorough investigation and assessment would require to exercise and test the approaches on the basis of one or more sample applications, better yet, real world systems. The decision guide has been created to suggest or rule out certain approaches for specific environments or indicate the limited applicability in this respect. However, it has neither been systematically constructed nor validated by architects. Future research on the topic of Microservices migration may consider these points to achieve more precise results.

Our future work in this field will focus on (1) novel approaches that combine static code analysis with operations data generated during runtime to achieve an optimally tailored partitioning, (2) quality attributes and related metrics to quantitatively assess the result of a decomposition in advance and (3) other means to automate and facilitate the transformation of monolithic architectures out of large, heterogeneous code bases.

References

1. Ahmadvand, M., Ibrahim, A.: Requirements reconciliation for scalable and secure microservice (de)composition. In: Proceedings - 2016 IEEE 24th International Requirements Engineering Conference Workshops, REW 2016, pp. 68–73 (2016)
2. Amundsen, M., et al.: Microservice Architecture. O'Reilly, California (2016)
3. Balalaie, A., et al.: Microservices migration patterns. Softw. Pract. Exp. **48**(11), 2019–2042 (2018)
4. Baresi, L., Garriga, M., De Renzis, A.: Microservices identification through interface analysis. In: De Paoli, F., Schulte, S., Broch Johnsen, E. (eds.) ESOCC 2017. LNCS, vol. 10465, pp. 19–33. Springer, Cham (2017). https://doi.org/10.1007/978-3-319-67262-5_2
5. Bass, L., et al.: DevOps: A Software Architect's Perspective. Addison-Wesley, Boston (2015)
6. Bogner, J., et al.: Analyzing the relevance of SOA patterns for microservice-based systems. In: Proceedings 10th Central European Workshop on Services and their Composition, March (2018)
7. Brereton, P., et al.: Lessons from applying the systematic literature review process within the software engineering domain. J. Syst. Softw. **80**(4), 571–583 (2007)
8. Brown, W., et al.: AntiPatterns: Refactoring Software, Architectures, and Projects in Crisis. Wiley, Hoboken (1998)
9. Chen, R., et al.: From monolith to microservices: a dataflow-driven approach. In: Proceedings Asia-Pacific Software Engineering Conference APSEC, December 2017, pp. 466–475 (2018)
10. Conway, M.: Conway's Law. http://melconway.com/Home/Conways_Law.html. Accessed 01 Oct 2018
11. Dietrich, J., et al.: On the detection of high-impact refactoring opportunities in programs. In: Proceedings of the Thirty-Fifth Australasian Computer Science Conference (ACSC), Melbourne (2012)
12. Escobar, D., et al.: Towards the understanding and evolution of monolithic applications as microservices. In: Proceedings of the 2016 42nd Latin American Computing Conference, CLEI (2016)
13. Evans, E.J.: Domain-Driven Design: Tackling Complexity in the Heart of Software. Addison Wesley, Boston (2003)
14. Feathers, M.: Working Effectively with Legacy Code. Prentice Hall, New Jersey (2004)
15. Fowler, M., et al.: Refactoring: Improving the Design of Existing Code. Addison-Wesley Professional, Boston (1999)
16. Di Francesco, P., et al.: Research on architecting microservices: trends, focus, and potential for industrial adoption. In: Proceedings - 2017 IEEE International Conference on Software Architecture, ICSA 2017, pp. 21–30 (2017)
17. Gysel, M., Kölbener, L., Giersche, W., Zimmermann, O.: Service cutter: a systematic approach to service decomposition. In: Aiello, M., Johnsen, E.B., Dustdar, S., Georgievski, I. (eds.) ESOCC 2016. LNCS, vol. 9846, pp. 185–200. Springer, Cham (2016). https://doi.org/10.1007/978-3-319-44482-6_12
18. Hassan, S., et al.: Microservice ambients: an architectural meta-modelling approach for microservice granularity. In: Proceedings - 2017 IEEE International Conference on Software Architecture, ICSA, pp. 1–10 (2017)
19. Kitchenham, B., Charters, S.: Performing systematic literature reviews in software engineering (2007)

20. Klock, S., et al.: Workload-based clustering of coherent feature sets in microservice architectures. In: Proceedings - 2017 IEEE International Conference on Software Architecture, ICSA, pp. 11–20 (2017)
21. Klose, K., et al.: Identification of services - a stakeholder-based approach to SOA development and its application in the area of production planning. In: ECIS 2007, pp. 1802–1814 (2007)
22. Krause, L.: Microservices: Patterns and Applications (2015)
23. Kwan, I., et al.: Conway's Law Revisited: The Evidence For a Task-based Perspective. IEEE Softw. **29**, 1 (2011)
24. Levcovitz, A., et al.: Towards a technique for extracting microservices from monolithic enterprise systems. In: 3rd Brazilian Workshop on Software Visualization, Evolution and Maintenance (VEM), pp. 97–104 (2015)
25. Lewis, J., Fowler, M.: Microservices - a definition of this new architectural term. http://martinfowler.com/articles/microservices.html. Accessed 01 Oct 2018
26. Lilienthal, C.: Langlebige Software-Architekturen: Technische Schulden Analysieren, begrenzen und abbauen. dpunkt.verlag (2017)
27. Mazlami, G., et al.: Extraction of microservices from monolithic software architectures. In: 2017 IEEE International Conference on Web Services (ICWS), pp. 524–531 (2017)
28. Mustafa, O., Gómez, J.M.: Optimizing economics of microservices by planning for granularity level. Experience Report (2017)
29. Newman, S.: Building Microservices. O'Reilly, California (2015)
30. Opdyke, W.F., Johnson, R.E.: Creating abstract superclasses by refactoring of stract classes finding matrix, February, pp. 66–73 (1993)
31. Pahl, C., Jamshidi, P.: Microservices: a systematic mapping study. In: Proceedings of the 6th International Conference on Cloud Computing and Services Science, pp. 137–146 (2016)
32. Petersen, K., et al.: Guidelines for conducting systematic mapping studies in software engineering: an update. Inf. Softw. Technol. **64**, 1–18 (2015)
33. Pirkelbauer, P., Dechev, D., Stroustrup, B.: Source code rejuvenation is not refactoring. In: van Leeuwen, J., Muscholl, A., Peleg, D., Pokorný, J., Rumpe, B. (eds.) SOFSEM 2010. LNCS, vol. 5901, pp. 639–650. Springer, Heidelberg (2010). https://doi.org/10.1007/978-3-642-11266-9_53
34. Procaccianti, G., et al.: Towards a MicroServices Architecture for Clouds. VU University Amsterdam (2016)
35. Rademacher, F., et al.: Differences between model-driven development of service-oriented and microservice architecture (SOA vs. MSA). In: 2017 IEEE International Conference on Software Architecture Workshops (ICSAW), pp. 38–45 (2017)
36. Richardson, C.: Microservice architecture. http://microservices.io/patterns. Accessed 01 Oct 2018
37. Richardson, C.: Microservice Patterns. Manning, New York (2017)
38. De Santana, A.M., et al.: Relationships between communication structure and software architecture: an empirical investigation of the Conway's Law at the Federal University of Pernambuco. In: Proceedings - 2013 3rd International Work. Replication Empirical Software Engineering Research, pp. 34–42 (2013)
39. Sneed, H.M., Seidl, R.: Softwareevolution - Erhaltung und Fortschreibung bestehender Softwaresysteme. dpunkt.verlag (2013)
40. Wohlin, C.: Guidelines for snowballing in systematic literature studies and a replication in software engineering. In: Proceedings 18th International Conference Evaluation and Assessment in Software Engineering - EASE 2014, pp. 1–10 (2014)
41. Zimmermann, O.: Architectural refactoring: a task-centric view on software evolution. IEEE Softw. **32**(2), 26–29 (2015)

DevOps Meets Dynamic Orchestration

Kiyana Bahadori(⊠) and Tullio Vardanega(⊠)

University of Padua, Padua, Italy
{bahadori,tullio.vardanega}@math.unipd.it

Abstract. Responding to the rising wave of demands brought forward by the digital economy requires injecting accelerated agility and speed into the software development life cycle. To build a technology stack that helps meet this demand, the DevOps methodology bridges the gap between software developers and the IT maintenance and operation professionals, by combining them into a unified team aligned around shared business goals, based on automation solutions that support rapid response to user demand while preserving stability and reliability. The concept of DevOps with its high pressure on automation, extended from application development to the maintenance and operation infrastructure, fosters more in-depth attention to the performance of infrastructure management.

This paper discusses how dynamic orchestration of infrastructure delivery in Cloud environment accelerates agility in the DevOps process, by enabling rapid deployment of dynamic workload.

Keywords: DevOps · Infrastructure agility · Dynamic orchestration

1 Introduction

Over the last few years, as innovation accelerates and customer needs rapidly evolve, agile software evolution has started to place increasing attention on IT operation, under the heading of DevOps [23], a professional movement that promotes collaborative interplay among people, process and products [9,18].

In the conventional sense, DevOps is the integration of the process practices and associated tooling that drive continuous integration and delivery of business software applications [13]. At its core, DevOps fosters deeper orientation toward performance and results, to decrease IT operational costs while improving software quality, reliability and time to market [6,9].

The DevOps concept rests on the adoption of automation solutions to create and manage tasks ("items" in the Agile TODO list) as dynamic assets in terms of *Infrastructure as Code* (IaC) [25,33]. The fundamental shift towards IaC, which exceeds mere infrastructure automation, placing emphasis on applying quality-centered software development practices in their production, verification, and deployment, requires a unified framework concept to assure stability and performance.

© Springer Nature Switzerland AG 2019
J.-M. Bruel et al. (Eds.): DEVOPS 2018, LNCS 11350, pp. 142–154, 2019.
https://doi.org/10.1007/978-3-030-06019-0_11

IaC seeks to afford maximum velocity to the continuous integration and delivery pipeline, enabling the user to treat the infrastructure management as an agile discipline, thus helping balance time, resource and quality, which are the critical assets in any business environment [33]. In fact, adhering to the IaC principles has rewarded those who practised them with the ability to create consistent, cleanly disposable, and reproduceable systems even in the most demanding circumstances of large-stage high-reliability IT infrastructures, such as Netflix, Facebook, Google, etc. [25].

Interestingly, adopting the IaC principle for better management of the infrastructure marries with the move towards microservices-based architectures [4,35], especially for more effective design of infrastructure assets.

In the meanwhile, the advent of container-based application deployment has delineated an attractive solution that improves scalability, and positions the microservices-architecture as the privileged choice for DevOps [4].

Designing applications as a collection of container-based microservices implies having multiple independent units, all individual products of autonomous development lines, collaborate in performing the actions that respond to a user request, presents coordination and management and optimization challenges on the infrastructure, which are best captured by the notion of *dynamic orchestration* [32].

Dynamic orchestration helps treat the automated tasks entailed by agile development as orderly chains of actions that begin with a request for virtual resource provisioning and culminate with continuous integration and delivery.

Realizing software releases in terms of as-a-service offerings, which is natural for web and Cloud service development, naturally positions their providers as the early adopters of DevOps principles after the agility and speed that they promise. In this context, DevOps embraces the operational aspects of defining a service as a product item that needs to be deployed, scaled, maintained, monitored and supported through it life cycle.

Not surprisingly, therefore, players such as Amazon [8] provide a DevOps-focused way of creating and maintaining their infrastructure.

Furthermore, the ability to draw intelligence from the life-cycle behavior of the system and use it to improve its performance, creates a most attractive, and still unexplored, link between DevOps and Machine Learning.

This work presents our re-interpretation of the relation between DevOps and infrastructure management, attended by dynamic orchestration, and illustrates the experimental results that we have achieved placing focus on infrastructure management at technology level.

The remainder of this paper is organized as follows: Sect. 2 briefly recaps the essence of DevOps; Sect. 3 discusses why software development requires infrastructure agility; Sect. 4 outlines our solution to catering for dynamic orchestration as part of an agile infrastructure; Sect. 5 presents some early experimental results that back our proposal; Sect. 6 concludes the paper drawing some conclusions and outlining future work.

2   DevOps: An Essential Brief

2.1   Origin and Motivation

Traditionally, software development has followed a linear Software Development Life Cycle (SDLC) that traverses planning, analysis, design, coding, and testing before enabling application deployment onto the production environment. In the traditional style, post-deployment maintenance of the application was in charge of the IT/Operation professionals (IT/Ops), whose organization tile had separate objectives (and distinct key performance indicators) from developers. However, the dominant focus of agile frameworks such as Scrum leans on development, less so on the operational aspects of software delivery.

In particular, the development objective is to release application service augmented with new features using agile development practices, whereas the operation objective during maintenance is to ensure continuous stability and reliability to the production environment. Over the years, these two teams siloed by their respective separation of concerns, has created barriers of practices and solutions to the problem of deploying service updates with new features quickly and frequently, without undermining the reliability and stability [14,21].

Over time, this hiatus broadened to encompass negative effects on the efficiency of the delivery cycle, as well as on the quality of the products and services provided.

DevOps originated as a natural evolution of the Agile methodology for Software Development, integrating traditional SDLC with Operational support into one single methodology centered on the notion of continuous action [15,23].

Kim et al. [23] articulate five major points to describe the fundamental principles of DevOps framewok, summed up in the acronym "CALMS": Culture, Automation, Lean, Measurement, Sharing. The core of these authors' idea rests on building a culture of collaboration that bridges the gap between Development (Dev) and Operations (Ops) to design, deliver, manage and improve operational features (operability) as on the way IT is used within the organization.

DevOps embodies those principles into a continual-improvement process called *Continuous Integration and Continuous Delivery pipeline* (CICD) in the intent to improve stability and performance of the organization's development and operation assets [28].

Figure 1 illustrates how the CICD workflow is designed to ensure deployable and scalable product delivery that can be updated in real time in response to monitored evidence collected throughout the entire software life cycle.

The Continuous Integration (CI) part of the CICD pipeline with more Dev focus has as its prime benefit to keep the developers synchronized with each other frequently. In fact, CI much reduces the delays related to integration issues as each step of integration involves highly automated test sessions aimed to detect latent errors as quickly as possible. In that respect, therefore, CI allows the rapid building of new features in the application while reducing the associated risks [17].

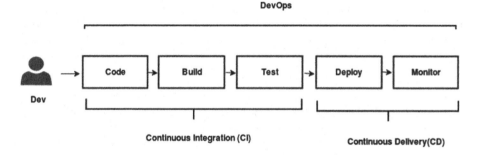

Fig. 1. CI/CD pipeline for software development

The main focus of the DevOps culture is commonly associated with Continuous Delivery (CD) with a more holistic view, originated from the goal of acquiring the ability that uses smart automation to create a repeatable and reliable process for delivering software [19].

The CD practices (cf. the right part of Fig. 1) subject the changes applied a software part to automated verification tests performed on the so-called deployment pipeline, in a fashion that gets the application increasingly close to the eventual production environment [16].

In effect, Continuous Delivery expands the concepts behind Continuous integration. CI started as a development strategy and expanded to encompass production deployments, which meant bringing the operations team closer to development. When the principles of DevOps came into play, they placed emphasis on the operational issues such as deployability, scalability and monitoring.

2.2   Seeking Infrastructure Agility

The DevOps culture required the CICD pipeline to be maximally agile, which can only be achieved through the assurance of readily available IT infrastructure as needed to run and test the developed code [25].

For this to truly happen, an automated workflow is needed. In fact, automation is central to the CICD pipeline [13]. The automation moves the adopting organization to abandoning error-prone and difficult-to-reproduce manual procedures, which are also intrinsically unable to scale, with a set of automated tasks that add velocity, scalability, consistency, and feedback to the workflow [23].

Automation is a critical element that relies on the IaC principle, which mandates the avoidance of manual configuration, and the adoption of code-based tools and software development technique to meet the need for dynamic provisioning of infrastructure at scale in response to demand [13,18].

The IaC principle postulates highly customized, machine-readable code that generates quality service components within a short turn-around time, which improves the perception and reputation of the IT in an organization, via automated configuration management or infrastructure provisioning [5].

Owing to this trait, IaC is often described as a programmable infrastructure that helps IT operations for provisioning and management automatically through code assets and resources that support the outcome delivery of the software development process.

Fig. 2. Infrastructure as code workflow

As shown in Fig. 2, the automation of IaC results in a workflow process that assures that all software assets are portable, reusable, and subject to version control.

3   Evolution Toward Accelerate Infrastructure Agility

3.1   The Cloud as the Natural Context of Application for DevOps

Cloud computing with its essential traits (on-demand self-service, broad network access, resource pooling, rapid elasticity, measured service), service models (IaaS, PaaS, and SaaS), and different deployment models (private, community, public and hybrid) offers the most natural context to exploit DevOps and enjoy its benefits [1].

Continuous delivery places strong demands on the automation of deployment. With the growth in size of the development team and of the product itself, the (automated) management of the underlying infrastructure became an increasingly central part of CICD [9, 25].

Accordingly, as the primary goal of DevOps is to improve the delivery of value, Cloud offers DevOps an advantageous infrastructure, which enables an effective team structure (topology) to be put in place between Dev and Ops personnel using Infrastructure-as-a-Service as its platform [24]. Figure 3 evokes this concept pictorially.

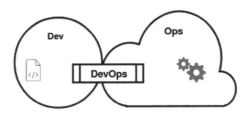

Fig. 3. Dev and Ops united in an Infrastructure-as-a-Service (platform) topology

In this topology, appropriate IaaS settings provide an elastic infrastructure to operation, to deploy and run applications on, assuring the low latency required to meet desired service level agreement (SLA), and facilitating the release of new software versions.

3.2 Containers and Microservices as Drivers to DevOps Collaboration

The adoption of Container technology as a lightweight and scalable solution to deployment challenges, which isolates the application and its dependencies within self-contained units agnostic of programming language and execution platforms, removes the need for runtime collaboration between Dev and Ops [27]. Docker [20], an open-source project supported by the most significant vendors in the IT ecosystem, has become the de-facto technology for automating the deployment of applications within containers.

Precise allocation of resources for individual containers enables efficient usage of the underlying infrastructure. However, this practice also adds one level of abstraction (the container layer itself) to the problem of managing the deployment infrastructure of applications.

Enjoying the native isolation capabilities of containers, with their lesser overhead and greater flexibility, has given rise to a novel style of application architecture constituted by a collection of containerized service residing on a container-centric infrastructure. This organization however requires novel management solutions.

DevOps encouragement for rapid integration and cross-team communication motivates abandoning siloed application architectures, and therefore favors the adoption of microservices, which break down the application into a granular set of independent units of discrete functions that are built and deployed independently and communicate via APIs external to their code base and therefore accessible with technology-neutral solutions [4, 11].

Embracing microservice-based applications the developers may build more robust software and implement the extent of scalability and performance features that operations personnel much desire [12, 31].

The rapid provisioning, isolation, and low overhead typical of containers make them an ideal compute vehicle to run microservices, while also increasing software portability [22]. Taken as part of the automated system, applications realized in terms of containerized microservices increase the agility and scalability dotation that serves the speed of deployment.

4 Dynamic Orchestration

Aside from the constant demand for infrastructure scaling in the face of ever larger software applications, the hardest part of the problem is the need to keep everything (all individual parts, all of their build recipes, and the overall deployment requirements) under control, topped with the unpredictability of operational demands and the risk of crossing project boundaries while sharing operational resources [10].

To get the most value out of the Cloud, containers, and microservices combined, requires innovative solutions for the coordination and management of infrastructure optimization. As noted in Sect. 1, the umbrella terms that encompasses those challenges is *dynamic orchestration* [32].

Figure 4 shows how dynamic orchestration evolves the concept of organizing applications and accommodating the need of (automated) coordination and management of the life cycle of their individual parts and of the whole.

Kubernetes [2], OpenShift [3], and Amazon [8] are the most commonly technology solutions that provide dynamic orchestration platforms for container-centric infrastructures.

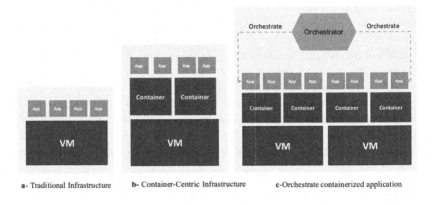

Fig. 4. Dynamic orchestration

Our contention here is that orchestrating containerized applications dynamically using automation in the faces of the continuous changes in the dynamics of service workloads, requires Artificial Intelligence techniques to learn, model and predict changes in system behavior in near-real time.

To explore the viability of this contention we looked at Auto-Regressive Integrated Moving Average (ARIMA) model [7] for forecasting a time series and Long-Short Term Memory (LSTM) as a special kind of Recurrent Neural Networks (RNNs), which is capable of learning features and long-term dependencies in the modeling of dynamic systems.

The objective of RNNs is to map an input sequence, one step at a time, into a corresponding output sequence, using integration of information captured in the hidden layer (recurrent unit) to predict the input sequence ahead, while optimizing the weight parameters of the network.

RNNs have been widely and successfully applied to many sequential tasks and time-series analysis [30]. The structure of RNNs is inspired on the biological neural network that is the brain. RNNs consist of multiple cascading layers (input, hidden, output) of non-linear artificial neurons that operate as basic cognitive units, and a feedback loop called a recurrent unit that provides persistent memory over time (through the input sequence) [30]. Most uses of RNNs to model long-term sequential dependencies in the state of the art report exposure to vanishing or exploding gradient during training [30]. Long-Short Term Memory (LSTM) [34] has been proposed to overcome those problems.

To this end, the LSTM modifies the layers of the RNN adding an internal state variable, which keeps track of the already processed inputs and therefore eases the modeling of long-term sequential time-series data sets without requiring massive and costly updates to the recurrent unit.

The effectiveness of the prediction algorithm is evaluated by the *Root Mean Squared Error* (RMSE) and *Mean Absolute Error* (MAE) metrics, which are defined as follows:

$$RMSE = \sqrt{MSE}$$

$$MSE = \frac{1}{n} \sum_{i=1}^{n} (Y_{i_{ground}} - Y_{i_{pred}})^2$$

$$MAE = \frac{\sum_{i=1}^{n} |Y_{i_{ground}} - Y_{i_{pred}}|}{n}$$

(1)

where $Y_{i_{ground}}$ is the actual output at time i, $Y_{i_{pred}}$ is the predicted output and n is the number of observations in the dataset. The smaller the RMSE or MAE values, the better the predictive quality of the model.

5   Experimental Environment

Having explained the context of interest to our work, we can now illustrate the strategy that we have adopted to embed our proposed method for orchestration of single-tier web application deployed on Amazon's Elastic Container Service.

The Elastic Container Service (ECS) of AWS provides a highly scalable container management that monitors, schedule and deploys containers across cluster of nodes corresponding to EC2 instance.

To create a simple, yet representative scenario for our experiments, we employed a cluster comprised of two EC2 instances of type t2.medium to run a container service composed of single tier web application (web tier) deployed on an Apache web server (see Fig. 5).

The implementation uses five parts:

1. Elastic Load Balancer, ELB,
2. Elastic Container Service, ECS,
3. Auto-scaling Group, ASG,
4. CloudWatch, CW, and
5. A Scheduler Module that bridges the ECS cluster with its associated CloudWatch.

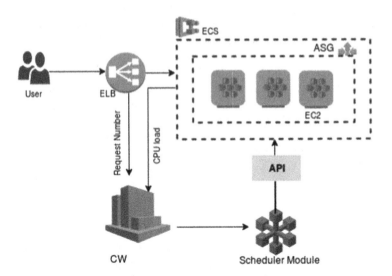

Fig. 5. Experimental framework for orchestrated container on AWS

The ELB, ECS, ASG and CW components are standard components of the AWS offering. The Scheduler Model was our own.

To generate the historical data to train and test the LSTM forecasting model, we used the AWS server metrics (request per second, CPU utilization) as collected by the AmazonCloudWatch service available with the Numenta Anomaly Benchmark (NAB) [26].

Subsequently, we generated live workload using Hey (rakyll) [29] with the same probability distribution as used in the production of the training dataset, which we jittered with random noise.

During the experiment, we used the CloudWatch service to monitor CPU utilization of ECS in the two dimensions of service level and cluster level, as well as the number of requests enqueued at the LB, to feed a prediction model and translate the output into the required number of containers. As part of that, we used the AWS API to access the provided key-value store to acquire the current state on each cluster node and integrated the resulting value in our custom scheduler.

In that setting, we compared the behavior of our custom model with that of the default ECS.

Overall, our experiments consisted of the following steps:

1. Designing and implementing automated scaling API for containers, which observes selected and configurable metrics from ECS;
2. Constructing an application performance model machine learning that predicts the number of container unit required to handle demand;
3. Periodically predicting future demand using time series and determining the application resource requirements using the performance model;
4. Automatically allocating resources using the predicted resource requirements;

5. Running experiments on real data to determine how fast the system can respond to emerging application needs.

5.1   Experimental Results

The first goal of our experiment was to compare the prediction of required number of containers obtained with the ECS default method against ours. Figure 6 shows the results that we obtained, which shows a lower error rate corresponding

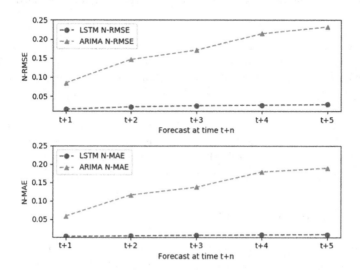

Fig. 6. Prediction error.

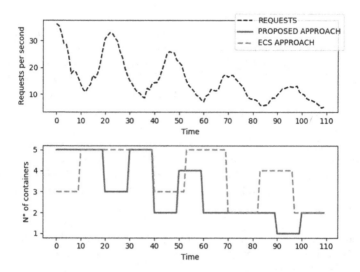

Fig. 7. Container allocation in response to varying load.

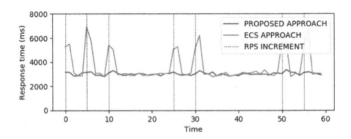

Fig. 8. Variation of service response time under variable user load.

to prediction time in applying the LSTM in comparison to the ARIMA model to proceed with the next step of the experiment.

Figure 7 plots the results we obtained, which show better performance of our model, where the service time provided to the user stays quite stable throughout significant changes in the intensity of user requests.

In the second part of our experiment as shown on Fig. 8, we used response time as a performance indicator, that is, the time to serve a user request to completion. Once again, the compared the default auto-scaling mechanism, threshold based on CPU utilization per node, against our predictive model.

6   Conclusion and Future Work

In this work, we have presented and discussed our view of how the dynamic orchestration capabilities required for containerized microserviced-based applications responds to the DevOps demand for increased agility in the whole development cycle. We have argued that Machine Learning is a necessary ingredient to enable the realization of sound and effective automation rules. To prove our point we presented the results from an experimental implementation of an Elastic Container Service (ECS) hosted on AWS, augmented with our machine learning implements, to increase the agility in deployment of containerized application. We evaluated that prototype against a few experimental scenarios, which showed the lower latency achieved by our method for application deployment.

In future work, we plan to extend this line of work looking into combined auto-scaling policies that operate at both container and node level, integrating business-level and service-level objectives (e.g., performance, cost, etc.) by converting them to utility functions that can be fed as additional input parameters such as online learning method into our models, so as to facilitate dynamic rule generation for a container orchestration platform for optimal resource provisioning in the Cloud.

Acknowledgments. The authors are grateful to Alessandro Menti and Giacomo Tirabassi of Kiratech, Italy, for the precious comments they provided on the intent and contents of this paper.

References

1. Armbrust, M., et al.: A view of cloud computing. Commun. ACM **53**(4), 50–58 (2010)
2. The Kubernetes Authors: Automated container deployment, scaling, and management (2018). https://kubernetes.io/
3. Red Hat OpenShift: Automated container deployment, scaling, and management (2018). https://www.openshift.com/
4. Balalaie, A., Heydarnoori, A., Jamshidi, P.: Microservices architecture enables devops: migration to a cloud-native architecture. IEEE Softw. **33**(3), 42–52 (2016)
5. Bang, S.K., Chung, S., Choh, Y., Dupuis, M.: A grounded theory analysis of modern web applications: knowledge, skills, and abilities for DevOps. In: Proceedings of the 2nd Annual Conference on Research in Information Technology, pp. 61–62. ACM (2013)
6. de Bayser, M., Azevedo, L.G., Cerqueira, R.: Researchops: the case for DevOps in scientific applications. In: 2015 IFIP/IEEE International Symposium on Integrated Network Management (IM), pp. 1398–1404. IEEE (2015)
7. Calheiros, R.N., Masoumi, E., Ranjan, R., Buyya, R.: Workload prediction using ARIMA model and its impact on cloud applications QoS. IEEE Trans. Cloud Comput. **3**(4), 449–458 (2015)
8. Chapman, D.: Introduction to DevOps on AWS (2014). https://aws.amazon.com/whitepapers/introduction-to-devops-on-aws/
9. Davis, J., Daniels, R.: Effective DevOps: Building a Culture of Collaboration, Affinity, and Tooling at Scale. O'Reilly Media Inc., Sebastopol (2016)
10. Debois, P.: Agile infrastructure and operations: how infra-gile are you? In: Agile 2008 Conference, pp. 202–207. IEEE (2008)
11. Dragoni, N., et al.: Microservices: yesterday, today, and tomorrow. In: Mazzara, M., Meyer, B. (eds.) Present and Ulterior Software Engineering, pp. 195–216. Springer, Cham (2017). https://doi.org/10.1007/978-3-319-67425-4_12
12. Dragoni, N., Lanese, I., Larsen, S.T., Mazzara, M., Mustafin, R., Safina, L.: Microservices: how to make your application scale. In: Petrenko, A.K., Voronkov, A. (eds.) PSI 2017. LNCS, vol. 10742, pp. 95–104. Springer, Cham (2018). https://doi.org/10.1007/978-3-319-74313-4_8
13. Ebert, C., Gallardo, G., Hernantes, J., Serrano, N.: DevOps. IEEE Softw. **33**(3), 94–100 (2016)
14. Erich, F., Amrit, C., Daneva, M.: A mapping study on cooperation between information system development and operations. In: Jedlitschka, A., Kuvaja, P., Kuhrmann, M., Männistö, T., Münch, J., Raatikainen, M. (eds.) PROFES 2014. LNCS, vol. 8892, pp. 277–280. Springer, Cham (2014). https://doi.org/10.1007/978-3-319-13835-0_21
15. Fitzgerald, B., Stol, K.J.: Continuous software engineering and beyond: trends and challenges. In: Proceedings of the 1st International Workshop on Rapid Continuous Software Engineering, pp. 1–9. ACM (2014)
16. Fowler, M.: Continuous delivery (2006). https://martinfowler.com/books/continuousDelivery.html
17. Fowler, M.: Continuous integration (2006). https://www.martinfowler.com/articles/continuousIntegration.html
18. Ho, V.: Bringing DevOps to the masses with Microsoft's Donovan Brown (2016). https://blogs.microsoft.com/firehose/2016/11/29/bringing-devops-to-the-masses-with-microsofts-donovan-brown/

19. Humble, J., Farley, D.: Continuous Delivery: Reliable Software Releases Through Build, Test, and Deployment Automation. Pearson Education, London (2010)
20. Docker Inc.: Docker datacenter enables DevOps (2018). https://www.docker.com/use-cases/devops
21. Jabbari, R., bin Ali, N., Petersen, K., Tanveer, B.: What is DevOps?: A systematic mapping study on definitions and practices. In: Proceedings of the Scientific Workshop Proceedings of XP2016, p. 12. ACM (2016)
22. Khan, A.: Key characteristics of a container orchestration platform to enable a modern application. IEEE Cloud Comput. **4**(5), 42–48 (2017)
23. Kim, G., Debois, P., Willis, J., Humble, J.: The DevOps Handbook: How to Create World-Class Agility, Reliability, and Security in Technology Organizations. IT Revolution, Portland (2016)
24. Matthew Skelton, M.P.: Devops topologies. https://web.devopstopologies.com/anti-types
25. Morris, K.: Infrastructure as Code: Managing Servers in the Cloud. O'Reilly Media Inc., Sebastopol (2016)
26. Numenta: The numenta anomaly benchmark (2018). https://github.com/numenta/NAB
27. Pahl, C.: Containerization and the PaaS cloud. IEEE Cloud Comput. **2**(3), 24–31 (2015)
28. Radcliffe, R.: DevOps today: what does it mean to you (2018). http://schedule.interop.com/session/devops-today-what-does-it-mean-to-you-/852618
29. rakyll/hey: rakyll/hey (2018). https://github.com/rakyll/hey
30. Salehinejad, H., Baarbe, J., Sankar, S., Barfett, J., Colak, E., Valaee, S.: Recent advances in recurrent neural networks. arXiv preprint arXiv:1801.01078 (2017)
31. Thönes, J.: Microservices. IEEE Softw. **32**(1), 116 (2015)
32. Venugopal, S.: Cloud orchestration technologies, IBM (2016). https://www.ibm.com/developerworks/cloud/library/cl-cloud-orchestration-technologies-trs/index.html
33. Virmani, M.: Understanding DevOps & bridging the gap from continuous integration to continuous delivery. In: 2015 Fifth International Conference on Innovative Computing Technology (INTECH), pp. 78–82. IEEE (2015)
34. Zhao, Z., Chen, W., Wu, X., Chen, P.C., Liu, J.: LSTM network: a deep learning approach for short-term traffic forecast. IET Intell. Transport Syst. **11**(2), 68–75 (2017)
35. Zhu, L., Bass, L., Champlin-Scharff, G.: DevOps and its practices. IEEE Softw. **33**(3), 32–34 (2016)

Using Code Generation to Enforce Uniformity in Software Delivery Pipelines

Christopher Jones[(✉)]

School of Computing, DePaul University, 243 S. Wabash Avenue,
Chicago, IL, USA
`christopher.jones@depaul.edu`

Abstract. Common approaches to implementing software delivery pipelines include hand-written scripts, domain-specific languages (DSLs), and the integration of specialized tools, each of which has been developed to automate one or more stages of these pipelines. However, each application is often treated as a proverbial snowflake – different from all other applications, even those within the same organization, or those using the same technology stack. Such pipelines are often technology-specific, making them time-consuming to change should the need arise. This paper describes *SPaaS*, an extensible DSL- and template-based pipeline generator, capable of producing software delivery pipelines for Jenkins. This paper examines how such generated pipelines can embody, facilitate, and enforce an organization's technical and governance policies, while also enabling product teams to inject specialized activities during pipeline execution. A preliminary proof-of-concept called *SPaaS*, is described and the advantages, disadvantages, and some inherent technical challenges of the overall approach are discussed.

1 Introduction

A software *pipeline* [1,2] is the process by which code moves from source code control to deployment and execution in a production environment. It is a technology-neutral term that encompasses other devops practices including continuous integration, continuous delivery, and infrastructure-as-code. Approaches for their implementation range from hand-written scripts to domain-specific languages (DSLs). Myriad tools exist for the purpose of assisting with the key activities that need to be performed by the pipeline[1]. Many organizations cannot or will not invest in all of the tools required to completely automate an entire pipeline, leading to pipelines that stitch together the tools that are in place and provide custom, hand-written scripts to address the activities for which no such tool is available. Such pipelines can be problematic for several reasons. First, while the implementation and maintenance of pipelines is important it is arguably not valuable; the effort would likely be better spent developing solutions

---

[1] For some of the available tools, see the "Periodic Table of DevOps Tools" from XebiaLabs at https://xebialabs.com/periodic-table-of-devops-tools/.

© Springer Nature Switzerland AG 2019
J.-M. Bruel et al. (Eds.): DEVOPS 2018, LNCS 11350, pp. 155–168, 2019.
https://doi.org/10.1007/978-3-030-06019-0_12

that deliver business value to customers rather than in getting the software built and deployed. Second, manually written software delivery pipelines encourage "snowflake" solutions, where each pipeline does things in a different way even if they are based on identical technical platforms. Third, custom pipeline scripts are difficult to manage and maintain in the face of shared concerns such as auditing, compliance, security, reporting, and governance.

There are also operational and financial considerations. Tool sprawl is a common issue when each team is responsible for its own technology stack. This is not economical, especially when considering vendor management and overall tool pricing. As with pipeline development, reducing the number of developers required to operate and maintain a suite of tools may prove to be an effective use of an organization's limited resources. Finally, such approaches can result in vendor lock-in, something that many organizations are sensitive to, especially as they migrate their applications to one or more cloud providers, an effort that often requires invasive changes to their software delivery pipelines.

The author's employer is in the process of migrating 300 applications to Amazon Web Services (AWS). While some applications are being "forklifted", others involve changes to make them more "cloudy". Their on-premise software delivery pipelines use a variety of tools including CloudBees Enterprise Jenkins Server [3] and IBM UrbanCode Deploy (uDeploy) [4]. As they migrate to AWS, they are considering replacing their existing tool chain with the AWS Code* suite [5], thereby permitting teams to implement their pipelines almost entirely within AWS. The mixture of on-premise and cloud-based tools, combined with a wide variety of build and deployment approaches across teams and products, and advised by differing levels of devops experience across their 1,200 technologists, has resulted in many non-portable pipelines. Furthermore, for historical compliance reasons, these pipelines often require hand-offs between multiple teams, an anti-pattern to devops adoption. For example, changes to deployment processes are always handled by the release engineering team, even though the product team knows precisely what those changes should be.

As they began migrating into AWS, each product team devised new pipelines to deploy their code, persisting the current snowflake-based model. In an attempt to gain some economies of scale, and in an effort to avoid snowflake solutions, the organization decided on a more centralized approach, where the knowledge gained in deploying one application could easily be applied to others. A small project was initiated in mid-2017 to provide a proof-of-concept to make this vision a reality, and the author was selected as the technical and project lead. The project had several goals. First, to enable product teams to focus only on the aspects of their software pipeline that were truly unique, delivering any "boilerplate" pipeline elements as a service. Second, to use as few tools as practical and to pull those tools from the organization's existing tool chain. Third, to encourage the teams to increase their devops capabilities. Fourth, to enable upgrades to the various pipelines to be as painless as possible.

The initial effort was only partially successful. The team was able to develop proofs-of-concept and some standardized templates for common product deployment models including server-based, container-based, and serverless. However, the team was often viewed as providing additional staff for the product teams to get them started with the templates, thus failing in the third goal. Finally, the overall approach did not lend itself to simple upgrades and improvements, a failure to address the fourth goal. The partial success of the project was significant enough that the organization chose to continue the effort and in mid-2018 a new team was formed within the organization. Named, "cloud services", the new team has the responsibility to propose, define, and evangelize solutions around cloud security, operations, and release engineering. The author was chosen to be the product owner. In an effort to address the same goals as the 2017 initiative, the team turned to code generation as an alternative to the original template-based approach. The approach was called "Software Pipeline as a Service (SPaaS)".[2]

2   Generalized Pipeline Development Approach

The approach to pipeline development underwent several evolutions, but each had to satisfy several goals including:

- Support for a variety of pipeline structures.
- Adherence to the "pipeline-as-code" model, where the code for the pipeline can be managed by the existing source code management software.
- Enable product teams to easily and rapidly evolve their pipelines to reflect new industry practices and technologies.
- Enable product teams to focus on the pipeline and not on any of the technologies required to execute the pipelines.

Initial ideas focused on providing a Center of Excellent (CoE) that could effectively act as in-house consultants to the product teams to accelerate their ability to implement their own pipelines. While this idea had merit, it was eventually dismissed as insufficient for several reasons. First, there were simply not enough people available to meet the demand. Second, the product teams wanted their own pipelines, but they did not want to spend the time required to develop them especially since that would have required spending time to learn even more new technologies besides what they were already absorbing by moving to a public cloud in the first place.

2.1   Pipeline Structure

Because of the number of pipelines within the organization, it would be difficult if not impossible to provide a single pipeline definition that would meet the needs of all of the organization's product teams. Nevertheless, such an effort was undertaken. A pipeline was produced similar to that described by Humble, et al. [1]. The stages and activities of that pipeline are shown in Fig. 1.

---

[2] SPaaS is used throughout this paper since that is the product name, even though it is no longer implemented as a hosted service.

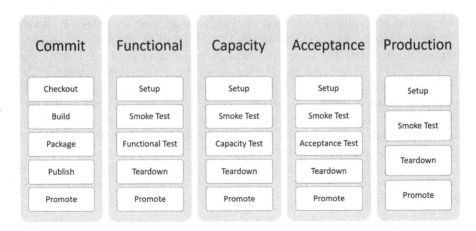

Fig. 1. Generalized pipeline process

Each pipeline is comprised of the five phases: *commit, functional, capacity, acceptance,* and *production.* Each stage is comprised of a series of activities. For example, the *commit* stage includes the *build* activity, whereas all stages except *commit* include the *setup, smoke test,* and *teardown* activities.

The most important aspects of this general pipeline process are that: it is technology neutral; it does not reference physical or virtual environments; and the stages and their activities are optional, which allows each product team to customize the pipeline's behavior to support their own needs, while still maintaining the overall pipeline structure.

2.2   Pipeline Generation

SPaaS' current approach involves a custom pipeline DSL, consumed and parsed by an open-source framework, with template-driven code generation, orchestrated using a Gradle [6] plugin. The structure of SPaaS is shown in Fig. 2. It consumes a pipeline definition language and produces the code for one or more physical pipeline languages. The pipeline definition language can be extended by updating the grammar and the various visitors invoked by Antlr-generated [7] lexing and parsing classes. The generated pipeline code can be changed by manipulating Freemarker [8] templates.

3   A Generalized Pipeline Generator

SPaaS requires five major activities:

1. **Pipeline definition**. The developers produce a pipeline definition describing their desired pipeline and a set of scripts implementing their custom logic. SPaaS' own pipeline definition is written in this way.

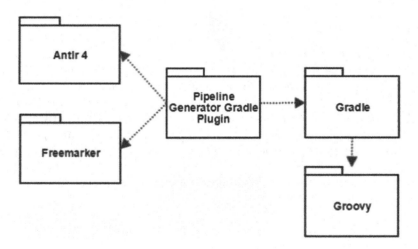

Fig. 2. Pipeline generator architecture

2. **Plugin configuration.** The plugin reads its configuration from a Gradle build file and configures the pipeline generation process.
3. **Definition parsing.** The plugin delegates to the Antlr framework, which parses the pipeline definition and finds syntactic and grammatical errors.
4. **Definition translation.** The parsed pipeline definition is translated into an Antlr-independent, internal model.
5. **Pipeline generation.** The internal model is passed to the Freemarker templating system which uses elements of the model to generate the final code.

3.1   Pipeline Definition and the Pipeline DSL

Each pipeline requires a definition file, `pipeline.dsl`, containing pipeline DSL statements. The definition is comprised of a set of composited pipeline segments: pipeline, stages, and activities. Each of these segments can be associated with a variety of decorators: approvals, credentials, artifacts, gates, and properties.

Stages, Activities, and Event Scripts. Each *stage* in the pipeline is comprised of logical *activities*. The pipeline DSL is opinionated and allows only the configuration of a fixed set of stages and activities reminiscent of Humble [1]. One important aspect of this definition language is that the stages and activities are optional. By default an empty file will result in the same pipeline as that shown in Listing 1, that is, a pipeline with all stages and activities provided, but that doesn't perform any real work. By explicitly declaring the stages and activities, pipeline authors 'activate' those activities during pipeline execution. For example, a pipeline definition with only two activities declared will only perform those two activities; all of the other activities will be present, but will be skipped during pipeline execution.

The pipeline authors align the physical steps of their pipeline to the logical stages and activities, shown in Listing 1 using *script fragments*. Each activity invokes a corresponding *event script*. For example, the *build* activity invokes the `onBuild` script, the *setup* activity invokes the `onSetup` script and so on. Each event script is provided the names of the currently running activity and stage. This allows the pipeline authors to take different actions based on the stage in which a common activity is performed. For example, the *setup* activity might behave differently during the *functional, capacity, acceptance,* and *production* stages. Within the script fragments, developers can perform any required actions, such as compiling source code and running unit tests. SPaaS combines built-in, templated code with the script fragments provided by the pipeline author to produce the finished event scripts.

```
1   stages {                          19      capacityTest {...}
2     commit {                        20      teardown {...}
3       checkout {...}                21      promote {...}
4       build {...}                   22    }
5       package {...}                 23    acceptance {
6       publish {...}                 24      setup {...}
7       promote {...}                 25      smokeTest {...}
8     }                               26      acceptanceTest {...}
9     functional {                    27      teardown {...}
10      setup {...}                   28      promote {...}
11      smokeTest {...}               29    }
12      functionalTest {...}          30    production {
13      teardown {...}                31      setup {...}
14      promote {...}                 32      smokeTest {...}
15    }                               33      teardown {...}
16    capacity {                      34      promote {...}
17      setup {...}                   35    }
18      smokeTest {...}               36  }
```

Listing 1. Implicit stages and activities of the generated pipeline

Agents and Docker Images. By default, the event scripts are run on Jenkins agents with a compatible operating system. A definition configured to produce a Linux-based pipeline generates shell scripts whereas one configured for Windows produces Powershell scripts. If desired, activities can instead be configured to run within a Docker container. Listing 2 demonstrates this capability:

In this case, the *build* activity uses a Gradle docker image to perform its actions. The pipeline generator assumes that the image is available from DockerHub, but a different registry can be used if required. The `options` property allows further customization of the Docker container's execution.

```
stages {
  commit {
    build {
      docker {
        image    "library/gradle:4.8.0-jdk8-alpine"
        options "-v ${PWD}:/home/gradle/project"
      }
    }
  }
}
```

Listing 2. Build activity using Docker container

Properties. Properties are simple name-value pairs. They can be declared at the pipeline, stage, and activity scopes, as shown in Listing 3.

```
properties {
    NAME1 "pipeline-value-1"
    NAME2 "pipeline-value-2"
}
stages {
    commit {
        properties {
            NAME1 "build-value"
            NAME3 "build-value-2"
        }
        build {
            properties {
                NAME1 "commit-value-1"
                NAME4 "commit-value-2"
            }
        }
    }
}
```

Listing 3. Properties and their scopes

In Listing 3 the NAME1 property exists at all three scopes. The pipeline DSL exhibits the usual name-hiding rules where the value closest in scope to the activity will be used. Thus the NAME2 property is available to all activities within the pipeline, the NAME3 property is available to all activities within the *commit* stage, and the NAME4 property is only visible to the *build* activity.

All properties are exposed to their activities as environment variables. Several implicit properties are always provided to each activity including the current working directory, the current stage, and the current activity. This allows scripts that are invoked at multiple points in the pipeline (e.g. `setup`, `smokeTest`, and `teardown`), to determine the stage in which they are currently being invoked.

Gates. Gates are conditions that must be satisfied before an activity will be performed. If these conditions are not satisfied then the gated activities will be skipped although the pipeline will continue to execute. the DSL currently supports two kinds of gates: *skip* and *branch*. A *skip* gate unconditionally bypasses the gated activity. It is most often used for existing activities that should be temporarily ignored. An activity with a *branch* gate will only perform its work if the source code branch matches that of the gate. This is one way we can support more complex SCM workflows where one branch is used for feature-based work, another for release candidates, and a third for production releases. Consider the DSL snippet shown in Listing 4:

```
stages {
    commit {
        package {
            gates {
                skip
            }
        }
    }
    production {
        gates {
            branch 'master'
        }
    }
}
```

Listing 4. Gates and their scopes

In this example, there is a skip gate on the *package* activity of the *commit* stage and a branch gate on the entire *production* stage, which means that the gate will apply to each activity within that stage. It is possible to apply a gate at the pipeline scope, but it is rarely useful.

Approvals. Not all pipelines are completely automated. There are occasions when teams may want to control when activities occur or who performs them. For example, a project's QA team may want to restrict who can deploy code to the QA environment. Various compliance requirements often dictate a separation of roles between those who produce the software and those who deploy it.

Like properties and gates, *approvals* can be inherited from the pipeline and stage scopes down to the activity scope. However, unlike properties and gates, which are always applied to any activity within their scope, approvals are only applied to activities that explicitly declare that they require approvals. The DSL currently supports two kinds of approvals: *timer* and *approver*. To see how these types of approvals work, consider Listing 5:

```
approvals {
    timer 300
}
stages {
    production {
        setup {
            approvals {
                approver 'release-engineering'
            }
        }
    }
}
```

Listing 5. Approvals and their scopes

In this example, we declare a global `timer` approval, which restricts the amount of time that the pipeline will wait for approval before failing. When we look at the production stage's setup activity we see that there is an `approver` approval declared. This means that the activity can only be approved by an individual with the specified username or who is a member of the specified group. The `timer` approval inherited from the pipeline ensures that the `setup` approval must be provided within 300 s.

3.2   Plugin Configuration

The actual generation of the pipeline itself is driven by the Gradle plugin. In order for the plugin to know what kind of pipeline to generate, it must first be configured. The desired style of the generated pipeline is declared along with any additional information. The code in Listing 6 is for the plugin itself and declares that we want a Jenkinsfile-based pipeline that can be executed on a Linux-based Jenkins agent.

The generation process is initiated by invoking one or more Gradle tasks such as *generateJenkinsfilePipeline*. This causes the plugin to parse the pipeline definition file and perform the associated code generation. The version of the plugin to be used can also be declared within the Gradle build file. This allows the product teams to choose when to absorb updates to the code generator so that such updates can be scheduled and worked into the project plan as practical.

```
jenkinsfile {
    targetOS = 'linux'
}
```

Listing 6. Partial `build-pipeline.gradle`

3.3 Definition Parsing and Translation

During definition parsing the Antlr framework consumes the pipeline definition and constructs a parse tree. The parse tree passes through a series of visitors that convert it into Groovy objects. This internal model is a complete and independent translation of the pipeline definition and is passed to the final phase of processing. A sensible set of defaults are provided for any stages and activities that were not specifically included in the pipeline definition. This is part of what allows the pipeline structure to remain consistent across different product teams while allowing those teams to perform or ignore whichever activities make sense for their product.

3.4 Pipeline Generation

Pipeline generation is driven by a set of Freemarker templates and orchestrated by the Gradle plugin. For Jenkinsfile output, SPaaS uses a set of templates representing the major sections of the Jenkins Pipeline DSL.

```
environment {
  PWD = pwd()
  ${CURRENT_STAGE_VAR_NAME} = '${stage.name?lower_case}'
  <#if stage?? && !activity?? >
  <#assign allProperties = stage.allProperties()>
  <#else>
  ${CURRENT_ACTIVITY_VAR_NAME} = '${activity.name?lower_case}'
  <#assign allProperties = activity.allProperties()>
  </#if>
  <#list allProperties?keys as key>
  ${key} = '${allProperties[key]}'
  </#list>
}
```

Listing 7. Partial Freemarker template

Listing 7 defines one part of the overall Jenkinsfile template, specifically the `environment` clause, where environment variables are defined. When the generator invokes the template, it consolidates the properties from the pipeline, stage, and activity and exposes them as environment variables to the activity, where they can be consumed by the associated event scripts.

4   Discussion

This approach to pipeline generation itself is not entirely new. Domain-specific languages [9] and code generation for specific domains such as mobile applications [10,11], have been available for years. We can bundle common configuration into a Jenkins shared libraries [12], which was the implementation of an earlier evolutions of SPaaS. SPaaS is now completely independent of Jenkins and makes the pipeline definition language a first-class citizen. The approach is flexible enough that it can generate other pipelines beyond Jenkins, and, in fact, work is underway to extend SPaaS to produce AWS Code* [5] templates using CloudFormation [13] and Terraform [14].

SPaaS was influenced both by Jenkins shared libraries and the AWS Code* tool chain [5] including CodeBuild, CodeDeploy, and CodePipeline. Both Code-Build and CodeDeploy use a scripted model where developers provide custom scripts that are invoked during pipeline execution. However, AWS CodePipeline does not readily lend itself to reuse and there is no easy way to enforce common practices or governance policies. SPaaS combines the Jenkins-based and script-based models into a single approach.

SPaaS can use a variety of tools for the orchestration of its pipelines when those individual tools by themselves are too limited. For example, tools that enable "infrastructure-as-code (IaC)" such as CloudFormation [13] or Terraform [14] make up only a tiny portion of an overall software delivery pipeline, though that portion is unarguably important. Configuration management tools such as Chef [15], Puppet [16], or Ansible [17] again make up an important part of the pipeline, but are insufficient for representing the pipeline as a while. SPaaS' strength is that it can unify all of these tools, and any others for which there is a command-line interface or API, into a single pipeline. Spinnaker [18] provides the foundation for complete pipelines, but hides those pipelines behind a UI. Furthermore, while its pipeline definitions can be exported and stored within source code control, this is not its normal behavior, which makes it challenging to keep the pipeline definition in sync with the code that traverses that pipeline.

SPaaS provides many benefits centering on abstracting away common and challenging issues associated with developing pipelines across disparate technology platforms. For example, some teams have compliance requirements that each production deployment must be tied to an open, approved release request. While it is certainly possible for each product team to implement this logic in each of their pipelines, doing so takes time and resources. In contrast this logic can be included within the pipeline generator templates once and then an updated version of the generator published. As the product teams are ready to absorb the changes they simply re-generate their pipeline using the latest version of the generator plugin. Every impacted team will thus handle this aspect of the approval process the same way. Because the code is generated, it requires little effort to make the change, which allows it to be rolled out much more quickly.

SPaaS was only recently released[3] but its concepts have been greeted with enthusiasm and its implementation with a healthy degree of skepticism. SPaaS was submitted to and accepted for presentation at two regional conferences: AWS Chicago Summit [19] and the AWS Community Day Midwest [20]. We do not yet have sufficient hard evidence to draw reasonable conclusions, but anecdotal evidence suggests that savings numbering in person days of effort are likely.

While we believe SPaaS to be promising, there remain challenges. One obvious and significant example is that arbitrary scripts are being invoked during pipeline execution. If those scripts are executed with elevated privilege it opens the door to abuse. Proper approvals such as pull requests can help manage that risk as can regular security scanning of the code repositories.

Another challenge is one of pipeline evolution. One significant difference between the current implementation of SPaaS and its first evolutions is that the pipeline generation is now controlled by the product teams. Because the generated pipelines are now considered first-class assets of the project, the product teams can track changes to their pipelines in the same way as other source code. However, this also means that there is no way to ensure that changes to governance or standard practices incorporated into later versions of the pipeline generator are automatically incorporated into the pipelines themselves. Each time the pipeline logic changes, the product teams must regenerate their pipeline code. While the goal is that the product teams need not modify the generated pipeline code, it is not possible to prevent them from making such changes. Teams that make significant modifications to the generated code, will be hesitant to regenerate their pipeline.

A third challenge to this approach concerns ownership of the pipeline generator. For SPaaS to remain relevant, it must belong to a team that is vested in keeping it up to date, improving its efficiency, and addressing defects. Without a team to own it, SPaaS will rapidly begin to stagnate and it's capabilities will not keep pace with the needs of its users who will gradually find it simpler to build and manage their own pipelines, which regresses the organization back to a point when each product spent time on pipeline-related activities rather than capitalizing on economies of scale and centralized, shared logic. To address this concern, a new team was formed to own the pipeline generator and provide regular releases, bug fixes, and support.

Another challenge lies in maintaining the separation between the general pipeline definition exposed by SPaaS and the technology-specific elements required by the actual pipelines themselves. The needs of a Jenkinsfile-based pipeline are necessarily different than those required by AWS Code* because the implementations of those two technologies are very different. As such it can be difficult to take a generalized pipeline and provide the pipeline authors with the ability to represent these divergent technologies without building knowledge of those technologies into the DSL itself.

---

[3] The author is actively working with his employer to make SPaaS available as opensource.

A fifth challenge concerns testing the generated pipelines. Pipeline testing is difficult, both from a generator and a generated standpoint. We make use of the Jenkins Pipeline Unit Testing Framework [21] for testing the generated pipeline structures, however, we have observed some differences between the behavior within the unit test framework, and that from running within the actual CloudBees Jenkins environment, especially around the availability of and access to shared libraries. Products like Puppet and Chef can make the provisioning and testing processes simpler with associated tools like rspec-puppet [22] and Test Kitchen [23], which can also take advantage of rspec [24], respectively.

5   Conclusion

SPaaS is a pipeline generator that offers an opinionated view of what a software delivery pipeline should be. It exposes a set of predefined pipeline segments in the form of pipelines, stages, and activities. Each segment can be decorated with a collection of properties, approvals, and gates. SPaaS consumes this pipeline definition and generates a Jenkins-based pipeline. Pipeline authors can script and test their individual instructions for inclusion in the pipeline during key events by providing custom scripts that are incorporated into the final pipeline during the code generation process.

The use of code generation in software delivery pipelines can provide significant benefits to an organization. First, it helps ensure consistency in operation. Second, it helps provide a consistent structure, which facilitates measurement and continuous improvement. Third, it ensures that overarching governance and security practices are applied consistently. Fourth, it allows product developers to focus on those aspects of the pipeline that are unique rather than on those aspect that are common to most, if not all, such pipelines.

By ensuring consistency in structure, operation, and governance, we gain a degree of certainty that critical steps are not missing or bypassed. New capabilities can be added to the pipeline in a way that is comparatively transparent to the teams that use that pipeline. By generating the pipeline during execution, it is possible to incorporate structural changes to the generated pipelines each time they are executed. This in turn provides a means of measuring overall pipeline operation and reporting on its efficiency so that improvements can be identified and incorporated back into the pipeline, thus providing a valuable feedback loop against which an organization can gauge improvements to their processes. These factors encourage cross-team comparisons of pipeline activities to identify best practices and improvements, yielding cross-team efficiencies as an organization moves closer to continuous delivery and continuous deployment.

References

1. Humble, J., Farley, D.: Continuous Delivery: Reliable Software Releases Through Build, Test, and Deployment Automation. The Addison-Wesley Signature Series. Addison Wesley, Boston (2011)
2. Kim, G., Willis, J., Debois, P., Humble, J.: The DevOps Handbook. IT Revolution Press, Portland (2016)
3. CloudBees, Inc.: Jenkins and CloudBees (2018). https://www.cloudbees.com/jenkins/jenkins-cloudbees
4. IBM: Urbancode deploy - deployment automation, July 2018. https://developer.ibm.com/urbancode/products/urbancode-deploy/
5. Amazon Web Services: AWS developer tools, July 2018. https://aws.amazon.com/products/developer-tools/
6. Dockter, H.: Gradle, June 2012. http://gradle.org/
7. Parr, T.: ANTLR, July 2018. http://www.antlr.org/
8. The Apache Group: What is apache freemarker? July 2018. https://freemarker.apache.org/index.html
9. van Deursen, A., Klint, P., Visser, J.: Domain-specific languages: an annotated bibliography. SIGPLAN Not. **35**, 26–36 (2000)
10. Jones, C., Jia, X.: Using a domain specific language for lightweight model-driven development. In: Maciaszek, L.A., Filipe, J. (eds.) ENASE 2014. CCIS, vol. 551, pp. 46–62. Springer, Cham (2015). https://doi.org/10.1007/978-3-319-27218-4_4
11. Miravet, P., Marín, I., Ortín, F., Rionda, A.: DIMAG: a framework for automatic generation of mobile applications for multiple platforms. In: Proceedings of the 6th International Conference on Mobile Technology, Application & #38; Systems. Mobility 2009, pp. 23:1–23:8. ACM, New York (2009)
12. Alonso, J.: Centralise jenkins pipelines configuration using shared libraries, May 2017. https://dev.to/jalogut/centralise-jenkins-pipelines-configuration-using-shared-libraries
13. Amazon Web Services: AWS CloudFormation, October 2018. https://aws.amazon.com/cloudformation/
14. HashiCorp: Terraform, October 2018. https://www.terraform.io/
15. Chef: Chef, October 2018. https://www.chef.io/
16. Puppet: Puppet, October 2018. https://puppet.com/
17. Ansible: Ansible, October 2018. https://www.ansible.com/
18. Spinnaker: Spinnaker, October 2018. https://www.spinnaker.io/
19. Jones, C.A.: Software pipelines as a service. AWS Summit Chicago, August 2018
20. Jones, C.A.: Easing cloud migrations with software pipelines as a service. AWS Community Day Midwest, June 2018
21. Günalp, O.: Jenkins pipeline unit testing framework, July 2018. https://github.com/jenkinsci/JenkinsPipelineUnit
22. Sharpe, T.: RSpec test framework for your Puppet manifests (2017). http://rspec-puppet.com/
23. Chef: Kitchen (2017). https://docs.chef.io/kitchen.html
24. Baker, S., et al.: Behaviour driven development for ruby, July 2018. http://rspec.info/

Effect of Continuous Integration on Build Health in Undergraduate Team Projects

Suzanne M. Embury$^{(\boxtimes)}$ and Christopher Page

School of Computer Science, University of Manchester,
Manchester M13 9PL, UK
`Suzanne.M.Embury@manchester.ac.uk`

Abstract. We present the results of an analysis of the changing patterns of build health across three cohorts of undergraduate students, in a compulsory software engineering course unit. In the course unit, student teams were asked to make changes to a large open source software system, and to maintain clean release builds as they did so. Release build health (in terms of compiling code and passing unit tests) was explicitly included in the marking scheme for the coursework. We set up a continuous integration server to keep track of student build health. Initially, this was used only by TAs in marking student work, but for later cohorts we provided access to continuous integration results to all students from the early stages of each exercise. This has provided us with data on the changing patterns of student build health, with differing access to the CI server, giving an insight into how students learn to manage build health and the effects of allowing them access to CI results. We found evidence of a clear improvement in ability to manage build health when CI facilities are made available, but that some student teams were not making use of the facilities to much effect. The improvement effect was strongest on the build health of release builds, corresponding to the area of greatest marks in the marking scheme. The CI results also proved to be very valuable for academic staff, in making the problems with student builds visible.

Keywords: Continuous integration · Build health · Release quality · Software engineering education

1 Introduction

In recent years, the School of Computer Science at the University of Manchester has undertaken an extensive revision of software engineering teaching at undergraduate level. The focus was the level two compulsory course units in software engineering, taken by between 200 and 270 students each academic year. The course team for these units has a challenging goal. Some of our students have had little or no programming experience before joining us in their first year. Yet, after completing the second year, many will go on to undertake a year-long

© Springer Nature Switzerland AG 2019
J.-M. Bruel et al. (Eds.): DEVOPS 2018, LNCS 11350, pp. 169–183, 2019.
https://doi.org/10.1007/978-3-030-06019-0_13

internship in industry, acting as professional software engineers and often working on mission critical developments. The software engineering course unit must somehow bridge this gap, in just four contact hours per week.

To meet this goal, we designed a syllabus based on the use of an industrial strength toolkit, focussed on the kinds of brown-field software development tasks that form the bedrock of much software engineering practice. Turning our back on the more traditional document-oriented build-a-project-from-scratch approach, we asked our students to work with a large open source software system consisting of thousands of classes and many thousands of files. Students are asked to fix bugs, add features and refactor code to meet new non-functional requirements, while managing the quality of the code using an extensive test suite, code review, automated build tools and a continuous integration server.

The use of a continuous integration (CI) server has proven to be a key element of this approach. As well as providing students with experience of CI, the build health information provided by the CI server has given us an insight into how students learn about managing the quality of their builds, and the effects of introducing these tools on learning. In this paper, we describe how we have gathered data on build health from student coding teams across three cohorts, covering the work of around 700 students and around 10,000 builds. We use the data to compare how teams with access to continuous integration tools differ in their ability to release clean code (and to keep their development branch clean) with teams with reduced or no access to CI build results. The results indicate that embedding build health into marking schemes is not enough in itself to encourage students to maintain clean builds, even on key deliverables such as released code. However, our results suggest that CI facilities can help students to understand the importance of ensuring that code committed to team repositories compiles and passes all automated tests. The results had the additional benefit of providing a useful diagnostic tool for staff, in understanding how much ground we had to make up in our courses to help students develop the discipline and habits needed to deliver clean code in a professional manner.

The remainder of this paper is organised as follows. In Sect. 2, we examine how CI tools have been used in undergraduate teaching, as reported in the research literature. We then describe how we have used CI at the University of Manchester to support our undergraduate course units in software engineering (Sect. 3). The experimental design is outlined (Sect. 4) along with details of the data gathering pipeline we used to infer build health for cohorts where CI was not in place at the time of teaching (Sect. 5). The results of our analysis are presented (Sect. 6) and threats to validity are discussed (Sect. 7). Finally, we conclude and suggest some directions for future work (Sect. 8).

2   Literature Survey

With the increase in the use of CI (and related technologies such as continuous delivery) in industrial practice, there have been corresponding attempts by academic faculty to include CI within relevant course units. A common approach is to embed CI tools within a software engineering project, with the aim of giving students experience of working with this important class of software engineering tool [Wil01,LD11,MTU17]. Significantly, Süß and Billingsley demonstrated the ability of CI tooling to allow a small number of academic staff and teaching assistants to teach a project-oriented software engineering course for far more students than would have been practicable without it [SB12].

Others have set up CI infrastructure for use across multiple courses or projects. The work of Pedrazzini is an example [Ped10], in which the Team-City[1] CI tool is configured by staff for use by students, who then tailor the build script to suit the specific project being worked on. Pedrazzini notes the learning benefits obtained, including subject specific learning outcomes (such as increased understanding of release management, and of the value of regression testing) and transferable knowledge (such as the ability to track personal improvement over time using the CI reports).

Some proposals for the introduction of CI tools into undergraduate curricula have been motivated additionally by their potential to facilitate the automation of assessment. Heckman and King report on the *Canary Framework*, an infrastructure based on Eclipse, GitHub and Jenkins for automatically assessing software development exercises [HK18]. They found scaling benefits (particularly significant decreases in the time needed to mark work), and also note that the combination of software tools used in their project provides the opportunity to carry out learner analytics. For example, they looked at the relationship between submission times, submission frequency and grades, and found useful correlations. They mention requiring students to keep the release branch clean, though details of how this is converted into marks or assessment are not given.

Academics are increasingly turning their attention to approaches to teaching DevOps and related concepts [Chr16]. Eddy *et al.* proposed a pipeline using Jenkins and Docker to teach the concepts of continuous integration and continuous delivery [EWC+17]. They evaluated the resulting teaching materials with a cohort of 16 senior students, by taking them through an example set of exercises, and asking them to complete a survey afterwards. The results showed that the students appreciated the additional concepts they were able to learn through the approach, but also pointed to some areas for improvement.

We were able to find very few attempts to assess the effects of providing CI tools to undergraduates in terms of learning outcomes or skills gained. Most reports of courses using CI do not attempt to evaluate the usefulness of what was done, or else they rely on collating the results of surveys of learners, shortly after being exposed to the technology. Some attempts to be more systematic exist, such as the work of Billingsley and Steel, who compared two successive cohorts of a course unit, when improvements were made for the teaching of the second cohort [BS13]. Amongst the metrics compared between the cohorts are: number of commits made per week, and number of comments per issue tracker ticket. Bowyer and Hughes used a CI server as the basis for a course teaching test-driven development [Bec03]. They extracted a number of metrics from the

---

[1] http://www.jetbrains.com/teamcity/.

CI system: proportion of time with a failed build and number of overnight failing builds are two that are mentioned explicitly. However, these metrics are extracted for the purposes of assessing students in their proposal, and not to evaluate the usefulness of the course. Another very interesting proposal is the Prof. CI system, by Matthies *et al.* [MTU17], in which CI tools replace the more usual browser-based coding environments. Prof. CI is intended primarily to teach TDD, and while the authors have compared data from two cohorts in order to understand the strengths and weaknesses of the approach, they focussed on metrics relating to the number and quality of tests written, rather than on build health.

To the best of our knowledge, no work has yet attempted to assess students' ability to manage their build health, with and without the use of CI tools.

3   Continuous Integration at Manchester

Our first-semester second year software engineering course unit asks students to make multiple changes to a large open-source code base, using a number of best practice tools and techniques to ensure the code that is released has no obvious flaws. After consultation with the members of our School's Industry Club[2], we selected the following toolset, to be used by students during the course unit:

- A distributed version control system (Git, git-scm.com)
- An issue tracker (GitLab issue tracker, gitlab.com)
- An automated test tool (JUnit, junit.org)
- A code coverage tool (JaCoCo, jacoco.org)
- A code review tool (GitLab, gitlab.com)
- An automated build tool (Ant, chosen because the OSS we are using is based on it, ant.apache.org)
- A continuous integration server (Jenkins, jenkins.io)

In order to manage the risks inherent in introducing so many new technologies for use by large numbers of students, we elected to bring in the CI system gradually, across three consecutive cohorts. This gave us time to discover security and other set up problems before giving full access to students. Introduction of the CI tools into the coursework took place as follows:

- Cohort 1: for the first cohort, we set up CI builds for each student team, but did not make these visible to the undergraduates. They were used only by the course staff and teaching assistants, to help them assign marks to teams for their build health, and to provide feedback on build health problems.
- Cohort 2a: for the next cohort of students covered by this study, we set up the same pattern of build jobs for each student team, and allowed them to view the results just before the deadlines. This gave teams the option of making final changes to fix major build health problems before marking. These builds were also used by teaching assistants during the marking process.

---

[2] http://www.cs.manchester.ac.uk/employability/industry-club/.

– Cohort 3a: for the final cohort included in this study, we provided access to
the CI build job results to all teams, from early in each coursework exercise.
Most of the builds we provided are performing a continuous build and test
function, but for this cohort we also provided true continuous integration, by
setting up builds that merged feature branches with the development branch
and reported on the result.

For each team and for each coursework exercise, we set up a number of builds:

– A build of a tag which marks the starting commit for an exercise. This helps
teams to see if there are problems with the build at the start of the exercise
that they should fix before beginning work on the exercise itself. (Otherwise,
problems from earlier exercises can leach through to the current exercise, and
cause problems for the final release build.)
– A build of the release tag for the exercise. Students were asked to make sure
this build was compiled cleanly and passed all tests. Marks were lost if this
was not the case.
– A build of the development branch. Students were asked to keep this build
compiling cleanly and passing the tests, as far as possible but, since (for many
of our students) this was the first time they were required to consider build
health, they were not penalised for falling short of this provided release build
health was not impacted.
– A build of each feature branch. Students were asked to make sure feature
branches compiled cleanly and passed all the tests, but were only penalised
for falling short of this in terms of marks at the point where feature branches
were merged into the development branch.

We use the Jenkins continuous integration server in our course units[3]. Figure 1
shows an example of the build jobs that are set up for an exercise[4]. Figure 2
shows an example of the feature branch builds for an exercise with defined feature
branches. Later exercises ask students to manage their own feature branches; in
this case, a single build job is created that builds on any push to any feature
branch with a prefix set by the exercise.

The icons to the left of the build jobs in this figure show the status of the
most recent build. The exclamation-mark-in-a-circle icon indicates a *failed* build.
This means that some error prevented the build job from even creating any executable code. Compilation errors are the most common cause of this type of build
status amongst our students. The exclamation-mark-in-a-triangle icon indicates
an *unstable* build. Executable code was created and executed, but some quality
indicator has flagged up a problem. For our students, this quality indicator is
failure of one or more of the automated tests. Finally, the tick-in-a-circle icon
indicates a *successful* build; an executable could be created and all tests and
quality checks passed when run against it.

---

[3] jenkins.io.
[4] The Issue Revealing Builds folder contains builds set up to check that students are
working test-first. They are not relevant to the experiment carried out in this paper.

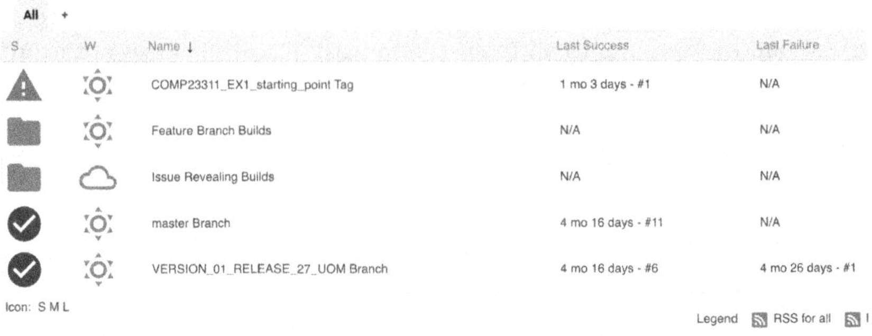

S	W	Name ↓	Last Success	Last Failure
⚠	☀	COMP23311_EX1_starting_point Tag	1 mo 3 days - #1	N/A
📁	☀	Feature Branch Builds	N/A	N/A
📁	☁	Issue Revealing Builds	N/A	N/A
✓	☀	master Branch	4 mo 16 days - #11	N/A
✓	☀	VERSION_01_RELEASE_27_UOM Branch	4 mo 16 days - #6	4 mo 26 days - #1

Icon: S M L

Legend RSS for all I

Fig. 1. Example build jobs set up for an exercise

S	W	Name ↓	Last Success	Last Failure
⚠	☁	COMP23311_EX1_fix_gardeners_greeting Branch	4 mo 17 days - #2	4 mo 22 days - #1
❗	🎐	COMP23311_EX1_improve_zone_description Branch	N/A	4 mo 22 days - #1
✓	☁	COMP23311_EX1_missing_scuba_quiz_info Branch	4 mo 17 days - #2	4 mo 22 days - #1
✓	☁	COMP23311_EX1_photographer_typo Branch	4 mo 18 days - #2	4 mo 22 days - #1
✓	☁	COMP23311_EX1_raise_joshua_quest_xp Branch	4 mo 19 days - #2	4 mo 22 days - #1
⚠	☀	COMP23311_EX1_slow_down_elder_dwarves Branch	4 mo 18 days - #3	4 mo 22 days - #1
⚠	☀	COMP23311_EX1_where_command_error_msg Branch	4 mo 22 days - #1	N/A

Icon: S M L

Legend RSS for all RSS fo

Fig. 2. Example feature branch build jobs

4   Experiment Design

It will be seen that the incremental introduction of CI tools into our course unit provides the set up for a *natural experiment* into the effects of giving CI facilities to UG students. In all three cohorts, release build health was factored into the marking scheme for the exercise (counting for around 10% of the marks for each of the three exercises). Build health of the development branch and feature branches at the point of merging was also included, though to a lesser degree. Student teams therefore already had a strong reason for doing their best to manage the health of their builds. However, teams in the earlier cohorts had to do this by remembering to check their code health by running the build script and tests on their own local repository before committing code to their Git repository. Students were asked to use an IDE for managing their code, and therefore should have had automatically generated warnings about compilation errors in their code, but other build errors and failing tests could only be found if students remembered to run the (simple to use and fully configured) automated build script before committing code to Git.

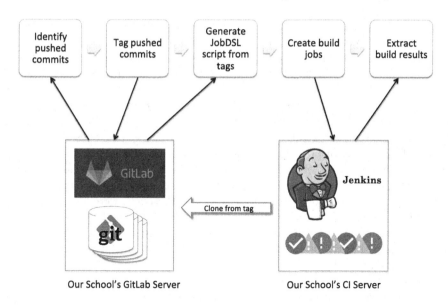

Fig. 3. The data extraction pipeline used to extract build health results from all cohorts.

In the latest cohort of the three covered by this paper, our CI server was set up to check build health on every push to the remote repository, and to provide student teams with a clear report on their build health at each stage. These students had to remember to log in and check the CI server results after pushing code, but had the advantage that build results from pushes by all individuals were visible to the whole team. Only one team member had to remember to check the results regularly for the whole team to have early warning of problems. The second cohort had access to the CI reports just before their deadline, giving them a final opportunity to manage the health of their release builds only.

By examining the different build health patterns across these cohorts, we hoped to be able to see correlations between the degree of access to CI build reports, and to understand whether the (not insignificant) effort involved in configuring and running the CI server for classes of more than 200 students was delivering useful educational benefits or not.

5   Data Gathering Pipeline

To understand the effects of introducing CI facilities for our students, we had to be able to compare the detailed build health records of cohorts that had access to CI with those that did not. Accessing the build health of teams in the third cohort was straightforward. The CI server we were using provided an easy-to-use API from which we could extract information about build jobs and their statuses programmatically. But for the cohorts that did not have CI in place throughout, we needed a way to reconstruct the build health reports these teams *would have seen* if CI had been running for their teams from the beginning.

Figure 3 shows the sequence of steps involved in extracting the build results for analysis. We first work out which commits would have been built by the CI server, if it had been set up at the time. These are the commits at the tip of each branch that was pushed to the remote Git repository by any team member. For some of our cohorts, we were able to extract this information from the *activity logs* maintained automatically by our School's GitLab[5] server. These logs record details of all the major operations performed on project managed by the server, including giving details of pushes to the repository. The activity log includes a time stamp for the push and the *HEAD* commit for the branch immediately after the push. But for some of the older cohorts, these logs were lost, as a result of a major system upgrade. By chance, the activity logs for the second cohort had been cached by the software we use for automatically marking part of the students' work. For the first cohort, we were able to reconstruct the pushes using timestamps on the objects in the Git database.

Having identified the pushed commits for all cohorts, we used a back-end script to create tags at each such commit. We used tags with the general form "SELA/<commit SHA>" to uniquely identify the point of each push. (SELA, here, stands for "Software Engineering Learner Analytics"). When the tags were created, we used a second script to read each repository, searching for the tags, and to create a script for each one using the Jenkins Job DSL[6]. This provides a means of creating a large number of Jenkins build jobs automatically, using a configuration-as-code approach. The Jenkins Job DSL script we generated created one build job for each commit across all cohorts with a tag with the "SELA/" prefix.

Since there were many builds to run (more than 20,000 in total, including builds for some cohorts not mentioned in this paper, due to space limitations), we ran the builds in stages. Once the builds for a cohort were complete, we ran a further script to extract the build results from the CI server (using the provided API) and load them into a spreadsheet for analysis.

6   Results

6.1   Ability to Manage Overall Build Health

We first examined the results to see how well teams in each cohort were able to manage the health of their builds overall. Figure 4 shows the total number of builds created by teams in each cohort, for each exercise. Builds are separated out into the various possible build results: primarily, failed builds, unstable builds and successful builds[7].

---

[5] gitlab.cs.man.ac.uk.

[6] jenkinsci.github.io/job-dsl-plugin.

[7] The small number of aborted builds in the final exercise for cohort 3 result from a feature of the exercise set, which caused GUI code which passed the tests successfully on a desktop machine to fail them when run on the headless server running Jenkins.

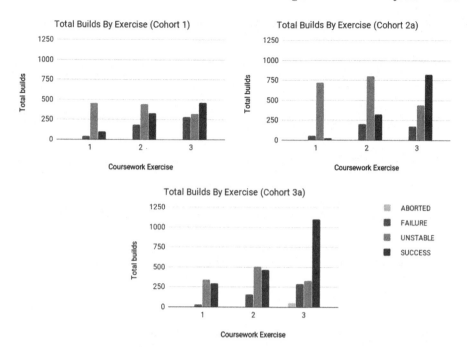

Fig. 4. Total number of builds of each build status, grouped by exercise, for the main cohorts.

Looking across the three cohorts, we can see several trends:

- The number of pushes being made increases across the semester, for all cohorts. This is most likely a factor of the exercises being attempted. In the first exercise, teams are asked to fix a number of small bugs, while in the second exercise they add small but complete features to the code base. In the final exercise, they re-factor a significant section of the code base. That is, the scale of the exercise set increases across the semester, leading naturally to increased commits and pushes. Increased student confidence with the use of Git for team coding could also be a factor.
- The proportion of successful builds increases throughout the semester in all cohorts, but the effect is most noticeable in the cohorts with at least some access to CI, and is most pronounced for the cohort with access to CI throughout. This is significant because students must manage the build health *before* seeing the results from the CI builds. Build health was increasing because students were learning to manage it better, and not just because they were reactively fixing problems reported by the CI server.
- A significant number of failed and unstable builds remain, even in the final exercises and in cohorts will full access to CI. This makes sense because CI tools can only detect failing builds when they have reached the remote Git repository. They make detecting such builds quick and easy, but they don't prevent them in the first place. And students have to remember and choose

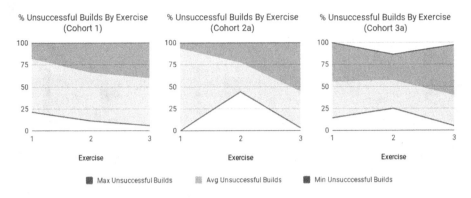

Fig. 5. Percentage of unsuccessful builds, grouped by exercise, for the main cohorts.

to access the CI build system reports. For the final cohort, we offered to set up e-mail notification for teams on unsuccessful builds, but only a handful of teams took us up on this.

6.2 Spread of Ability to Manage Overall Build Health

The figures for the total builds made of each status, given in Fig. 4, give an overview of how the cohorts were managing their build health across the semester. What they don't show is the spread of abilities across the cohort. Some teams may be managing their build health well, while others may be doing a much poorer job. We wanted to understand the spread of ability in this respect across our cohorts, to compare how the average teams were performing against the best teams, and against those teams that were struggling the most.

To understand this, we created the charts in Fig. 5. These show, for each cohort, information about the percentage of builds created by individual teams that were unsuccessful. Here, we define *unsuccessful* as meaning any aborted, failed or unstable build. The middle, orange, line in the charts shows the average percentage of unsuccessful builds across all the teams in a cohort. So, for cohort 1, in exercise 1, on average, around 80% of builds were unsuccessful. By exercise 3, this had dropped to approximately 60% of builds being unsuccessful.

The green line at the bottom shows the percentage of unsuccessful builds for the team that was managing their build health the best, and the red line at the top shows the percentage of unsuccessful builds for the team that was faring the worst in this respect. It will be noted that in all three cohorts, some teams made only unsuccessful builds.

Looking at the trends visible across the three cohorts, we can see an improvement for each cohort as the semester progresses: the average percentage of unsuccessful builds drops as the exercises progress, and students get more used to managing their build health (with or without CI). There is an improvement in the cohorts that had access to CI, but perhaps not as much as we had hoped. The average number of unsuccessful builds is around 50% or lower for cohort 3,

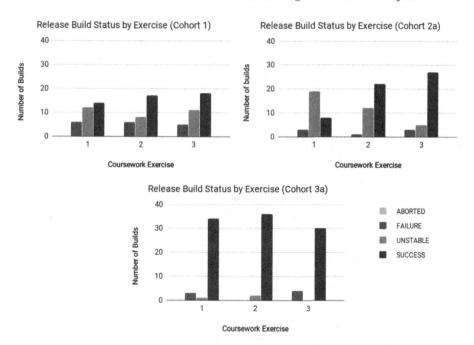

Fig. 6. Total release builds for each build status, grouped by exercise, for the main cohorts.

across all exercises, but that is still a lot of broken builds. And the best team is arguably not doing much better than the best team in cohort 1.

So, these figures show a small improvement in the ability to manage build health, but not the revolution in practice that we might have expected from the introduction of full CI.

6.3   Ability to Manage Release Build Health

The results presented so far show a somewhat mixed picture. CI tools seem to be helping our students to manage their build health, but there are still many unsuccessful builds being created. When we confine our attention to the health of the code released by students at the end of each exercise, however, the picture is somewhat clearer. The results in Fig. 6 show the total number of release builds for each build status, per exercise, per cohort. So, for example, for exercise 1, 6 cohort 1 teams released code that failed to compile, while 12 cohort 1 teams released code that failed some tests and 14 teams managed to release code that compiled and passed the quality checks.

When comparing across the cohorts in this case, we can see a marked improvement when CI facilities are made available compared with when they are not. While all cohorts included some teams that released broken code, the proportion of teams that were able to release a clean code base by the end of the semester was markedly improved when CI was available. For the third cohort, this was the case even from the first coursework exercise, while second cohort teams (who had access to CI only at the end of each exercise) appear to have taken longer to learn about the need to manage release code quality, and how the CI server can assist with this. However, by the end of the semester for the second cohort, the majority of teams have learnt how to release compiling code that passes all the tests[8].

7   Threats to Validity

This paper describes an opportunistic attempt to extract lessons from the data sets that happened to be available, rather than a properly designed controlled study. The difficulties of running such studies in an educational context are well known. As Holmboe, McIver and George have stated:

> "[...] there are obvious difficulties in empirically evaluating [teaching innovations] – aside from the expense of running two concurrent courses and comparing results, such techniques would be ethically dubious, potentially disadvantaging students in one course or the other. Where comparisons can be done across different years, the number of changes between the courses makes it difficult, if not impossible, to evaluate the effect of individual changes." ([HMG01], p. 4)

Many such differences occurred between the cohorts examined in this study, of which the most significant are probably:

- Differences in cohort sizes (ranging from 200 to 270), which go some way towards explaining the differences in number of pushes between cohorts.
- Differences in the exercises set. Since the use of Git means that any student can take and share a full copy of their team's solution to the exercise, we have assigned a different set of bugs to be fixed and features to be shared in each academic year the course unit is taught. A different aspect of the code was also chosen to be refactored. While we attempted to set work of a similar size aim each academic year, these differences could explain the differences in the number of pushes and the difficulty of making tests pass. (It was certainly a factor in affecting the number of aborted builds.)
- Differences in the open source code base used as the basis for the exercise. Since we aim to give students experience of working on a live code base, we update the open source code base used for our exercises every year. This means that each year we teach on a slightly larger and more complex code base, with new features added that are likely to be a little unstable in ways that are hard for us to predict. (Indeed, we exploit this feature in order to

---

[8] As part of the assessment process, we monitored whether teams disabled or deleted test cases, and found no teams that were doing this in an obviously fraudulent way. The builds released genuinely did pass the 1800 plus unit tests describing the required behaviour of the system.

find the bugs that the teams will fix.) Significantly for our analysis, each year the set of automated tests is slightly different, with different fragilities and defect finding powers. The high number of students releasing unstable builds in cohort 2a, for example, may have been affected by a particularly erratic test behaviour that was present in the code base used for that year.

– Differences in teaching approaches used. We learnt a lot about how to teach the use of these and related tools over the course of the three academic sessions covered by this paper, and have made significant changes to (and hopefully improvement of) our teaching materials and approaches. This could have affected our students' confidence with using Git as a tool for team coding. This could certainly be a partial explanation for the disproportionate increase in the number of pushes being made by later cohorts. How far students' increasing confidence and familiarity with the CI tools is a factor in this confidence with Git is hard to untangle with any precision.

8   Conclusions and Future Work

In this paper, we have examined data gathered on the health of builds produced by software teams, working to make changes to a large open source code base. For all cohorts, build health was a significant part of the marking scheme for the exercises the students undertook. We compared the statuses of builds produced by teams with no access to CI, limited access to CI and full access to CI. We were able to observe an improvement in the overall ability manage build health when CI facilities are provided, though the effect was only strongly visible in the release builds for the cohorts.

A significant unexpected benefit of introducing CI facilities into our course unit was that it raised the visibility of the fact that our students were struggling to form the habits needed to regularly commit clean code. For example, we had one team that never made a single clean build across the whole semester, and which pushed code 22 times for their solution to one exercise without ever pushing code that compiled. While not quite at this level, a significant number of other teams were discovered to be having difficulty in controlling the quality of the code they committed to their repository. This issue was formerly invisible to our students and (more importantly) to the teaching team. Now that we are aware of the issue, we can work on developing our teaching approaches to help guide students into better habits in this respect.

There are a number of further analyses we could carry out with the data we have collected from the cohorts in this study. We have been making use of the Jenkins Build Failure Analyser plug-in[9] to provide a more detailed characterisation of the causes of failing builds. This plug-in scans the console log for each build and classifies the build according to the types of failure it finds matches for in the log. It can therefore distinguish, for example, a failed build caused by a compilation error in code from a failed build caused by a run-time exception, from a failed build caused by a missing file. Using the data gathered by this

---

[9] https://github.com/jenkinsci/build-failure-analyzer-plugin.

plug-in, we will be able to perform intra- and inter-cohort analyses of the errors being made that lead to failing builds, and can design teaching materials that guide students to be aware of these common pitfalls.

We are also exploring ways in which we have configure our CI server to give students better tools for recovering from failed builds, and for preventing them in the first place. We will experiment with setting up e-mail notification of unsuccessful builds to all teams, rather than only for those that request it, as at present. The effect of this must be carefully monitored, however, as we would not want students to be deterred from pushing code because they are afraid of their errors being broadcast to their team. Other options are to design a GitLab sandbox, in which individual team members can apply their local commits to the team remote repository hypothetically, to examine their effects, before pushing them to the team repository. This would also allow CI to be applied to the hypothetical commits and merges, before any poor quality code reaches the other members of the team.

Acknowledgements. We are grateful to all the University of Manchester students who have taken the course units on which the work in this paper was based, for their willingness to engage with new approaches to teaching and for their (sometimes robust) feedback on our course units. We also thank the other members of the academic teaching teams we work with for their help in designing and running these course units.

References

[Bec03] Beck, K.: Test-Driven Development: By Example. Addison-Wesley Professional, Reading (2003)

[BS13]   Billingsley, W., Steel, J.: A comparison of two iterations of a software studio course based on continuous integration. In: Proceedings of the 18th ACM Conference on Innovation and Technology in Computer Science Education, pp. 213–218. ACM (2013)

[Chr16] Christensen, H.B.: Teaching DevOps and cloud computing using a cognitive apprenticeship and story-telling approach. In: Proceedings of the 2016 ACM Conference on Innovation and Technology in Computer Science Education, pp. 174–179. ACM (2016)

[EWC+17] Eddy, B.P., et al.: A pilot study on introducing continuous integration and delivery into undergraduate software engineering courses. In: Proceedings of 30th IEEE Conference on Software Engineering Education and Training (CSEE&T), pp. 47–56. IEEE (2017)

[HK18]   Heckman, S., King, J.: Developing software engineering skills using real tools for automated grading. In: Proceedings of the 49th ACM Technical Symposium on Computer Science Education, pp. 794–799. ACM (2018)

[HMG01] Holmboe, C., McIver, L., George, C.E.: Research agenda for computer science education. In: Proceedings of 13th Annual Workshop of the Psychology of Programming Interest Group (PPIG-13), vol. 13 (2001)

[LD11]   Baochuan, L., DeClue, T.: Teaching agile methodology in a software engineering capstone course. J. Comput. Sci. Coll. **26**(5), 293–299 (2011)

[MTU17] Matthies, C., Treffer, A., Uflacker, M.: Prof. CI: employing continuous integration services and Github workflows to teach test-driven development. In: Frontiers in Education Conference (FIE), pp. 1–8. IEEE (2017)

[Ped10] Pedrazzini, S.: Exploiting the advantages of continuous integration in software engineering learning projects. In: Koli Calling, p. 35 (2010)

[SB12] Süß, J.G., Billingsley, W.: Using continuous integration of code and content to teach software engineering with limited resources. In: Proceedings of the 34th International Conference on Software Engineering, pp. 1175–1184. IEEE Press (2012)

[Wil01] Wilson, D.: Teaching XP: a case study. In: XP Universe (2001)

Feedback from Operations to Software Development—A DevOps Perspective on Runtime Metrics and Logs

Jürgen Cito[1]([✉]), Johannes Wettinger[2], Lucy Ellen Lwakatare[3], Markus Borg[4], and Fei Li[5]

[1] University of Zurich, Zürich, Switzerland
cito@ifi.uzh.ch
[2] University of Stuttgart, Stuttgart, Germany
johannes.wettinger@iaas.uni-stuttgart.de
[3] University of Oulu, Oulu, Finland
lucy.lwakatare@oulu.fi
[4] RISE SICS AB, Kista, Sweden
markus.borg@ri.se
[5] Siemens AG, Vienna, Austria
lifei@siemens.com

Abstract. DevOps achieve synergy between software development and operations engineers. This synergy can only happen if the right culture is in place to foster communication between these roles. We investigate the relationship between runtime data generated during production and how this data can be used as feedback in the software development process. For that, we want to discuss case study organizations that have different needs on their operations-to-development feedback pipeline, from which we abstract and propose a more general, higher-level feedback process. Given such a process, we discuss a technical environment required to support this process. We sketch out different scenarios in which feedback is useful in different phases of the software development life-cycle.

Keywords: Software engineering · DevOps · Feedback

1 Introduction

A convenient perspective of software development is to view it solely as the practice of writing program code, in isolation from the reality of deploying the program to production systems. The DevOps movement challenges this perspective and aims on promoting cross-functional synergies between software development and operations activities [3]. One way to promote these synergies is to facilitate better communication between operations and development. When software is operated in production, it produces a plethora of data that ranges from log messages emitted by the developer from within the code to performance metrics observed by monitoring tools. All this data gathered at runtime serves as valuable *feedback* [1,5,8].

© Springer Nature Switzerland AG 2019
J.-M. Bruel et al. (Eds.): DEVOPS 2018, LNCS 11350, pp. 184–195, 2019.
https://doi.org/10.1007/978-3-030-06019-0_14

Feedback from operations can serve as the basis of decisions made by various stakeholders to improve the software itself and the process overall: Product owners can prioritize bugs and features based on usage. Software developers use stack traces to localize faults. Performance engineers use latency metrics to pinpoint slow execution and optimize performance. These stakeholders use feedback in different phases of the software development life-cycle, be it in system design, development, test or validation. Feedback from operations is an important vehicle in modern software development and vital to drive informed decisions. Modern software development approaches such as continuous deployment entail the capability of delivering new software updates continuously and in fast cycles as soon as code changes have been committed and successfully passed automated tests [9]. However, there are some challenges that organizations face when attempting to facilitate proper feedback channels between operations and the rest of the software development life-cycle. We argue that the challenges depend on the following key variation points: *organizational size, nature of business, presentation of feedback, and case-specific technical challenges.*

Organization Size. The challenges in feeding operations data back to development vary from organization to organization, and size is often an important contextual factor [7]. Smaller organizations (e.g. startups) can apply ad-hoc feedback processes simply because employees are located in the same site and know each other. However, global enterprises need more sophisticated feedback processes to effectively communicate across large geographical areas, organizational boundaries – and perhaps even with external business partners.

Nature of Software Business. The nature of business of an organization also has strong influence on the feedback mechanisms that can be implemented. The well-known Internet companies with established cloud infrastructure and a culture of extremely fast delivery life-cycles [14] are inherently more effective on communicating feedback. However, companies in traditional business, e.g. infrastructure management, utilities and factory automation, are strictly bound by regulations with regard to safety, industrial processes, certifications and data security [1,8]. In some cases, the feedback needs to be passed between different companies. For these organizations, feedback from operations to development has to take into account legal issues and business interests.

Presentation of Feedback. The wide availability of operational data in various formats challenges us to not only identify relevant data but how that data can be presented to the different stakeholders such that they are able to make decisions fast as required in a DevOps world. In addition, several challenges limit (or hinder) the availability of operational data to development organizations. Finally, for the operational data to have value, the feedback must be delivered with a user interface that can support the developers' decision making [12].

Technical Challenges. Regardless which type of organizations that are adopting DevOps practices, they face the same technical challenges in presenting operations data effectively to developers. Feedback coming from operations in raw format is often not actionable for many stakeholders. Different stakeholders, e.g. developers and product managers, need different views on collected feedback at different abstraction levels, presentation formats and tools. Well-designed visualizations of operations data, as a form of software visualization [11], can enable visual analytics, i.e. "analytical reasoning facilitated by interactive visual interfaces" [10].

To address these concerns, we recognize three important topics that are of interest both for research and industry, that we discuss in the following:

1. There is a need to model feedback processes that is somewhat representative across the different organizations. We present three case studies of companies in need of a process to facilitate feedback from operations to development. We abstract from their needs and present a possible feedback process that covers the concerns and needs of these organizations.
2. Given a more abstract, higher-level feedback process, there is a need to establish an organizational and technical environment where the process can be carried out. We present a suitable environment and tooling to enable the process.
3. We discuss *feedback phases* to capture a mapping of software development life-cycle phases to operations data. This helps to demonstrate what data and from what operations sources can be gathered and provided as feedback in suitable format to developers.

We conclude with a summary to our discussion and formulate questions for future work.

2   Case Studies

We characterize the feedback needs for three distinct company types to serve as case studies for further discussion of establishing a feedback process in our paper. This is by no means an exhaustive list and merely servers illustration purposes.

Startup/Small Company, Public Cloud. The startup is a B2C online platform that handles most of its transactions over its website that is operated in multiple geographical zones in a public cloud. Besides a frontend for their customers, it also offers additional online services for its partners, which are also hosted by the same public cloud provider. Generally, all engineers in the company (software and operations) are allowed to access any kind of data generated in production when they need it to solve design time problems. However, the partner services are perceived as more sensitive and production data is only given out after a screening step. The process is rather ad-hoc and decisions on the legitimacy of feedback requests are made on impromptu basis.

SME, Private Cloud/Data Center. The SME offers logistics and purchasing decision support system for retailers. The software is either deployed on a private cloud, for small to medium sized clients, or to a different data center location, for enterprise clients. Access to production data is only allowed for some operations engineers in the company. Especially for services hosted in the data centers, compliance is a very crucial topic. Engineers, data scientists, and product owners have to create a ticket in an issue tracking system to retrieve any kind of feedback from production systems.

Large Corporation, On-Premise. The large corporation offers factory automation solutions. A large portion of its software is deployed on the factory floor and control center on the client's plant. The software is often dependent on a specific hardware platform or connected to specific equipment. The whole system is vertically integrated to suite the needs of the factory in its specific industry, such as car production. Typically the client manages their own IT infrastructure behind a firewall, or even runs the factory automation solution in physically isolated networks. In this business context, solution providers and software providers are strictly excluded from accessing production data, which also includes software performance measures during production. Feedback is passed through business boundaries on the basis of legally binding agreements that require the processing and approval of multiple departments and multiple management levels in both parties.

Looking at the case studies, we can see that there is not one definite feedback process to rule them all. For companies doing most of their business online, both the development and operations are typically managed within the same company. However, for many large organizations the feedback from operations to development introduces cross-company concerns regarding data ownership and transactions. A common development context consists of three key activities: product development, solution development, and operations. While development mainly is managed with internal resources, tailoring a solution for a particular customer often requires external consultants to provide domain knowledge. Furthermore, the customer is typically responsible for the operations, i.e. it belongs to another company.

In a cross-company setting, several questions regarding feedback from operations to development arise. Who owns the operations data? How should it be made available to product development? Should solution architects, that act as mediators, have access to the same feedback? These issues are quite explicitly visible when it comes to cross-company boundaries in terms of operations feedback. It is more difficult to pinpoint these boundaries when they manifest in more implicit ways. In the case of the startup and SME in our case studies, operations feedback is, in theory, accessible within the same company or even division. However, in practice, the same questions of ownership and access of operations feedback arise. It is just that there is more potential for misuse and non-compliance when multiple companies are involved.

A feedback process is needed, along with legal requirements, to enable feedback loops in each of these contexts. There is a need for the customer on the operations side to have some form of feedback control (i.e. a filter) to explicitly toggle what kind of (operations data) logs, metrics, and usage data to expose to product development.

In Fig. 1, we attempt to model a feedback process that abstracts over the needs on a feedback pipeline that we extracted from our case studies. In the following, we briefly discuss the interactions in the process.

3   Feedback Process

Deployment. The process is initially kicked-off with deployment of software. Deployment can range from an automated, continuous delivery/deployment process to releasing a software unit that requires more complex (often manual) processes to roll out. In the former case, the process stays within a company's own organizational boundaries (public/private cloud or data center). Product development together with DevOps/operations engineers from the same organization (and often from the same team) are responsible for the operability. In the latter case, the process is delivered through consultants/solution architects as on-premise software (sometimes to multiple, geographically distributed client sites).

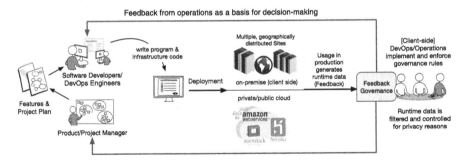

Fig. 1. Feedback process involving multiple stakeholders and organization boundaries.

Feedback Governance. In any grade between on-premise to full on cloud deployment, there needs to be control over which kind of operations feedback is available to which kind of stakeholder. This kind of governance should explicitly provide high-level rules on how data is handled either in organizations or as a cross-organizational concern. These rules are then implemented and enforced by the DevOps/operations engineers by filtering and controlling runtime data. The consequence of this part of the process is that privacy is being enforced and product development only has access to data that exhibits no threat of violations or non-compliance.

Decision-Making in Product Development. Once operations data passes through governance, it becomes valuable feedback to stakeholders in product development. Figure 1 illustrates two examples. Product/project managers can use runtime feedback to better plan their features and optimize their project plan. Software developers and DevOps engineers have a full picture of how users experience their software (e.g. performance metrics, usage counters) and can tweak program and infrastructure code to improve the overall experience. Here, the feedback loop starts again with deploying changes to software that were informed by better decisions through runtime feedback.

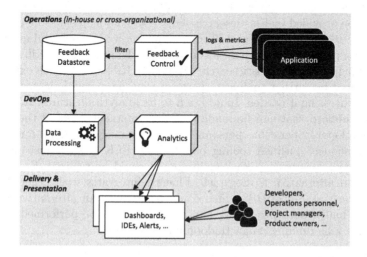

Fig. 2. (Technical) environment to facilitate feedback from operations to development.

4   Environment and Tooling

To enable efficient and fast feedback from operations to developers, a corresponding environment is required that follows the previously outlined feedback process. Figure 2 provides a high-level overview of how such an environment could be structured.

On the operations side, which may be in-house or part of another organization, the application itself produces diverse logs and metrics. These are filtered and preprocessed using a Feedback Control mechanism, e.g. to enable an external customer to define which logs and metrics are eventually stored inside the Feedback Datastore. This mechanism allows for fine-grained privacy control, i.e. deciding which data potentially leave the operations boundaries. The Feedback Datastore provides the foundation for a comprehensive interface exposed to developers and further stakeholders (project managers, product owners, etc.) that require feedback from operations. However, this datastore predominantly contains filtered raw data. To make this data useful, corresponding processing and analytics steps have to be performed to eventually present actionable information to the stakeholders such as developers. Such information can be delivered to the stakeholders in various ways, such as dashboards, context information in IDEs, or alerts such as e-mail notifications – as is discussed in research on recommendation systems for software engineering [12].

Various tooling options are available to implement such an environment. For example, an ELK stack (Elasticsearch[1] + Logstash[2] + Kibana[3]) could provide the technical foundation. Logstash is utilized to collect logs, events, and metrics from running applications. Additional tooling or custom extensions are required to implement the filtering as part of the Feedback Control. The Feedback Datastore could be provided by Elasticsearch, a distributed document store and search engine that exposes a RESTful API in conjunction with a powerful query DSL. Further data processing and analytics could be implemented using Kibana, which directly integrates with Elasticsearch. Of course, Kibana could be extended or complemented by further tooling to perform even more sophisticated analytics and data processing if needed. In addition to its analytics features, Kibana provides a dashboard that can be made available to stakeholders of the feedback such as developers, operations personnel, project managers, and product owners.

The previously outlined tooling based on an ELK stack is just one example of how the required feedback environment could be realized. For example, fluentd is an alternative to Logstash. Fluentd integrates with other database solutions, such as MongoDB, which could be used as an alternative to Elasticsearch. Finally, data processing and analytics could be performed based on MapReduce jobs running on an Hadoop infrastructure.

5   Feedback Phases

Feedback from operations data comes in different flavors and can be leveraged for different purposes. To make operations feedback actionable, it has to be viewed in the right context in the respective phase of development. Table 1 provides an overview of examples of how such a mapping of different kinds of metric/message types map to a phase in the software development life-cycle, with a purpose, and what possible ways there are to present the metric to a given stakeholder. In the following, we provide a brief overview of different relevant development phases and map the several kinds of operations data that might be relevant. *Note that,* neither the overview in the table nor the following text claim any completeness and are simply stated to illustrate the idea of feedback phases.

Operations data can be broadly categorized in three different categories:

1. System Metrics (e.g. CPU utilization, IOPS, memory consumption, process information)

---

[1] https://github.com/elastic/elasticsearch.
[2] https://github.com/elastic/logstash.
[3] https://github.com/elastic/kibana.

2. Application Metrics (e.g. exceptions, logs/events, usage)
3. Application System Metrics (e.g. method-level response time, load, garbage collection metrics).

Table 1. An exemplified list of runtime metrics that benefit different phases of the software development life-cycle.

Metric/messages	Phase	Purpose/stakeholder (examples)	Presentation
Metrics from instrumentation, Log message frequency	In-development	Informed refactoring/software developer	IDE, dashboard
System metrics	Post-CI, canary deployment	Non-functional and performance testing/DevOps or performance engineer	Reports, dashboards
Application (system) metrics	Post-deployment, Canary deployment	User behavior, Integration test in production/product owner, DevOps or performance engineer	Alerts, reports, dashboards

By metrics, we mean to cover any kind of messages (numerical or non-numerical) that represent the state of an application. These are created by either observing the system or by analyzing produced log messages. This list is not exhaustive and is only supposed to illustrate the categories. Next we discuss four phases in the development stage where feedback from operations are valuable: during software development, Post-CI (Continuous Integration), Canary Deployment, and Post-deployment.

5.1   In-Development

Application system metrics (response times and load) integrated into the IDE give developers an intuition about runtime specifics of their methods and identifies hotspots in context, i.e. when developers work with a particular set of code artifacts. This mapping from runtime metrics to code in the IDE has been initially explored in [6]. Further, we envision to map exceptions and application specific messages (logs) with their distribution at runtime to give an indication of number of exceptions and events in production.

5.2   Post-CI

After CI (Continuous Integration), applications can request feedback that might take longer to obtain, and thus is not justified to interrupt the software development flow. A good example of such feedback is performance testing. System metrics can serve as parameters to the testing approach or serve as a baseline to compare the performance results.

5.3   Canary Deployment

To reduce the risk of a change in production, a canary release only rolls out changes to a subset of users [15]. Application and system metrics are essential to detect deviations from the baseline and other forms of anomalies. Here, the primary purpose of operations feedback is to discover any mishaps and potentially roll-back or roll-forward with a fix.

5.4   Post-deployment

Similarly to canary deployments, in the post-deployment stage we observe application and system metrics. However, different stakeholders are involved in the analysis for different purposes that tend to be tied for more long-term goals. For instance, an operations engineer observes workload patterns to tune their self-adaptive controllers (e.g. load balancers), or a product owner investigates usage to plan upcoming releases and prioritize features.

6   Related Work

The topic under discussion is multidisciplinary covering activities in software engineering, software performance engineering and application performance management in particular. Achieving an holistic view of the activities, e.g. by integrating operations data, supports DevOps. This section briefly presents a few studies that have discussed feedback from operations to development in the context of modern software development specifically continuous deployment and DevOps contexts.

According to Bass et al. [2] there are other well known sources, namely standards, organizational process descriptions, and academic literature, that developers can use from an operational consideration to support them with activities such as deployment and designing of applications that are operations process aware. The latter facilitates the ability to determine additional application requirements and their verification in improving operations process. Their work provides complementary sources of feedback to developers in DevOps.

Several studies [1,4,6] acknowledge great value in giving timely feedback to developers from operations data to guide application design decisions. For instance, Brunnert et al. [4] point out the possibility of deriving performance models from IT operations for existing applications to enable architects and developers to optimize the application for different design purposes, e.g. performance and reliability. This is in addition to giving developers the ability to communicate performance metrics with operations whilst also ensuring certain level of application performance across the different development phases. However, some of these studies also note that gaining insights of the application performance (or operations data in general) by developers can be difficult. Brunnert et al. [4] mention several reasons including: *complex system architectures (implying geographical, cultural, organizational, and technical variety); continuous iteration between system life cycle phases (which means constant change in performance models); lack of access to monitoring data and developers' lack of knowledge in performance engineering.* To tackle the challenges, different automated approaches to support developers with performance awareness were proposed most of which relate to our work. For instance, as suggested by [4], during development, specifically unit testing, performance data of tests can be collected and integrated with performance regression root cause analysis into a developer's IDE. We add to this work by abstracting and modeling the feedback process and technical environment that is somewhat representative to different organizations.

Research on Recommendation Systems in Software Engineering (RSSE) [13] acknowledges the value of providing information, but also stresses that the abundance of information available is a serious threat to productivity – a typical developer is likely to experience information overload. To mitigate this problem, a well-designed system should deliver recommendations to developers in a timely fashion, i.e. when the information is actually useful. Murphy-Hill and Murphy [12] recommend information to be delivered with a user interface that (1) makes the user aware of the availability of a recommendation, (2) lets the user assess if the recommendation is useful, and (3) helps the user act on recommendations that is valuable. All three aspects are important also when delivering feedback from operations to developers. Five critical factors to be considered are suggested by the authors as: *understandability, transparency, assessability, trust and distractions.* These aspects give useful information that is to be considered when selecting presentation formats as well as the types of feedback. For instance, for DevOps feedback, rich information from the operational environment should be provided, letting the user explore it further if needed.

7   Summary and Discussion

We see DevOps as the cross-functional synergy between the software development organization and operations engineers. This synergy can only happen if the right culture is in place to foster communication between these roles. We investigate the relation between operations data produced or observed when the software is running in production and how this data can be used as feedback in the software development process. For that, we present three case study organizations that have different needs on their operations to development feedback pipeline, from which we abstract away and propose a more general, higher-level feedback process. Given such a process, we discuss a technical environment required to support this process. We sketch out different scenarios in which feedback is useful in different phases of the software development life-cycle. Finally, we set our work in contrast with related literature on the topic of feedback and recommendations in software engineering.

In future work, we plan to explore the following remaining issues in realizing a feedback process and pipeline:

– *Degree of Feedback in On-Premise Deployments*: We attempt to include scenarios of on-premise deployments in our discussion of feedback processes. The question is to what degree is such a feedback process doable? What are the constraints? Is "DevOps" possible in such a scenario?
– *Feedback delivery*: A DevOps approach opens up for numerous opportunities to aggregate data from operations to inform the development. However, a

developer cannot possiblly digest all available information – flooding developers with operations data would inevitably result in information overload. Rather, we stress on the need to customize the feedback delivery, considering both *what* feedback should be presented to *whom* as well as *when* it should be presented and *how* (i.e. in what format). This argumentation is in line with the research on how to develop recommendation systems for developers [12]. Thus, we see feedback delivery as highly contextual, depending on the task a developer has at hand. Future decision-support tools based on operations data should be designed accordingly.

- *Fast cycles in DevOps*: We observe challenges on how to determine a normal operative environment for detecting anomalies during software development phases such as testing. Additionally, the technical environment of the software development needs to be highly automated and integrated in order to supply timely feedback. How can we best design such an environment?
- *Process-clutter in large organizations*: Many challenges in implementing a feedback process might result from the size of an organization. Smaller companies can implement ad-hoc feedback processes to satisfy their feedback needs, whereas more sophisticated feedback processes need to be implemented for cross-organizational environments as they typically occur in the context of large companies. How can we overcome the bureaucracy of large organizations to implement an effective feedback process in a DevOps context?

Acknowledgment. This paper resulted from initial discussions at the GI-sDagstuhl Seminar: "Software Performance Engineering in the DevOps World" (seminar number 16394).

References

1. Barik, T., DeLine, R., Drucker, S., Fisher, D.: The bones of the system: a case study of logging and telemetry at Microsoft. In: Proceedings of the 38th International Conference on Software Engineering Companion, pp. 92–101 (2016)
2. Bass, L., Jeffery, R., Wada, H., Weber, I., Zhu, L.: Eliciting operations requirements for applications. In: Proceedings of the 1st International Workshop on Release Engineering, pp. 5–8 (2013)
3. Bass, L., Weber, I., Zhu, L.: DevOps: A Software Architect's Perspective. Addison-Wesley Professional, Boston (2015)
4. Brunnert, A., et al.: Performance-oriented DevOps: a research agenda. arXiv preprint arXiv:1508.04752 (2015)
5. Cito, J., Leitner, P., Fritz, T., Gall, H.C.: The making of cloud applications: an empirical study on software development for the cloud. In: Proceedings of the 10th Joint Meeting on Foundations of Software Engineering, pp. 393–403 (2015)
6. Cito, J., Leitner, P., Gall, H.C., Dadashi, A., Keller, A., Roth, A.: Runtime metric meets developer: building better cloud applications using feedback. In: Proceedings of the ACM International Symposium on New Ideas, New Paradigms, and Reflections on Programming and Software (Onward!), pp. 14–27 (2015)

7. Dybå, T., Sjøberg, D., Cruzes, D.: What works for whom, where, when, and why? On the role of context in empirical software engineering. In: Proceedings of the ACM-IEEE International Symposium on Empirical Software Engineering and Measurement, pp. 19–28 (2012)

8. Olsson, H.H., Bosch, J.: Post-deployment data collection in software-intensive embedded products. In: Bosch, J. (ed.) Continuous Software Engineering, pp. 143–154. Springer, Cham (2014). https://doi.org/10.1007/978-3-319-11283-1_12

9. Humble, J., Farley, D.: Continuous Delivery: Reliable Software Releases Through Build, Test, and Deployment Automation. Addison-Wesley Professional, Boston (2010)

10. Keim, D., Andrienko, G., Fekete, J.-D., Görg, C., Kohlhammer, J., Melançon, G.: Visual analytics: definition, process, and challenges. In: Kerren, A., Stasko, J.T., Fekete, J.-D., North, C. (eds.) Information Visualization: Human-Centered Issues and Perspectives. LNCS, vol. 4950, pp. 154–175. Springer, Heidelberg (2008). https://doi.org/10.1007/978-3-540-70956-5_7

11. Koschke, R.: Software visualization in software maintenance, reverse engineering, and re-engineering: a research survey. J. Softw. Maint. Evol.: Res. Pract. **15**(2), 87–109 (2003)

12. Murphy-Hill, E., Murphy, G.C.: Recommendation delivery. In: Robillard, M.P., Maalej, W., Walker, R.J., Zimmermann, T. (eds.) Recommendation Systems in Software Engineering, pp. 223–242. Springer, Heidelberg (2014). https://doi.org/10.1007/978-3-642-45135-5_9

13. Robillard, M.P., Walker, R.J.: An introduction to recommendation systems in software engineering. In: Robillard, M.P., Maalej, W., Walker, R.J., Zimmermann, T. (eds.) Recommendation Systems in Software Engineering, pp. 1–11. Springer, Heidelberg (2014). https://doi.org/10.1007/978-3-642-45135-5_1

14. Savor, T., Douglas, M., Gentili, M., Williams, L., Beck, K., Stumm, M.: Continuous deployment at Facebook and OANDA. In: Proceedings of the International Conference on Software Engineering Companion, pp. 21–30 (2016)

15. Schermann, G., Cito, J., Leitner, P., Zdun, U., Gall, H.C.: We're doing it live: a multi-method empirical study on continuous experimentation. Inf. Softw. Technol. **99**, 41–57 (2018)

A Lean and Devops Approach to Teach Lean Software Development

Vladimir Ivanov$^{(\boxtimes)}$, Dmitry Krasnikhin, Stanislav Litvinov,
Sergey Masyagin, and Giancarlo Succi

Innopolis University, Innopolis, Russia
v.ivanov@innopolis.ru

Abstract. This paper describes application of lean methodology in IT
education in a context of an undergraduate course on "Lean Software
Development" with a full devops pragmatics in mind. Strong connection
between software development and delivery processes can be build on
top of established lean practices. Which means that implementation of
end-to-end automation by devops approach needs good understanding
of lean principles and mindset. The course exposes students to the core
concepts underneath lean development in software engineering, beyond
myths and legends, emphasizing how it relates to the general principles
of Lean Development.

The principles behind Lean Management are crucial for the students,
but often even among senior managers lean is confused with the application of some lean practices, which actually can be applied in any context
even if they have been conceived inside a lean organization. So the goal
of course is to understand the core of lean to the point of being able to
understand its applicability in new software development environment.
To achieve this goal, our paramount idea has been to get the students to
"feel" what a lean approach is, therefore, we have decided to articulate
the class in a series of activities that aim at bringing lean into the class.

1 Introduction

This paper describes application of agile and lean methodology in IT education
in a context of an undergraduate course on "Lean Software Development" with
a full devops pragmatics in mind. The course exposes students to the core concepts underneath lean development in software engineering, beyond myths and
legends, emphasizing how it relates to the general principles of Lean Development. It discusses the different possible software processes, how they can be tailored, enacted, and measured. Strong connection between software development
and delivery processes can be build on top of established lean practices. Which
means that implementation of end-to-end automation by devops approach needs
good understanding of lean principles and mindset [1].

Understanding how the principles behind Lean Management is crucial for
the students – too often even among senior managers lean is confused with the
application of some lean practices, which actually can be applied in any context

© Springer Nature Switzerland AG 2019
J.-M. Bruel et al. (Eds.): DEVOPS 2018, LNCS 11350, pp. 196–204, 2019.
https://doi.org/10.1007/978-3-030-06019-0_15

even if they have been conceived inside a lean organization. We have recently conducted a survey in the Innopolis Special Economic Zone, Russia, and we have found that about 40% of the companies who claim to be lean, are actually companies who have a traditional process in place, or even no process, and that have institutionalized or just planned to implement some specific practices usually present in lean environments.

So the goal of course is to understand the core of lean to the point of being able to understand its applicability in new software development environment.

To achieve this goal, our paramount idea has been to get the students to "feel" what a lean approach is, therefore, we have decided to articulate the class in a series of activities that aim at bringing lean into the class.

In the course we emphase two reference principles of Lean Management introduced by Ohno [3] and widely described by Womack (alone and with co-authors) in his various books (1991, 1996, 1997) [4–6]:

(i) Elimination of waste;
(ii) Autonomation.

Elimination of waste refers to the careful analysis of all activities surrounding the production or the delivery of the service under the analysis and the determination whether:

1. They contribute to the goal, or
2. They are required by the environment for norms, regulations.

If an activity would not satisfy one of these two criteria, it would be eliminated, if needed, restructuring the remaining tasks.

Autonomation refers to the situation when the regulations (nomos in Greek are the regulations) are applied automatically, without any specific action or control to start them; it is what Janes and Succi (2014) [2] call "endogenous control."

Altogether, we have decided to articulate the course in a series of activities that try to be lean in themselves, such as:

– Paramount individual "grand challenges"
– Standard frontal lectures based on the textbook [2]
– Individual briefings
– Skype meetings with experts
– Immediate grading
– Frequent, formalized students feedback
– Meeting with students to assess the evolution of the course.

In this chapter, after some remarks on the overall architecture of the course (Sect. 2) we cover such activities. In Sects. 3, 4, 5, 6 and 7 we present methods applied in the course and discuss corresponding activities, from lecturing to learning by giving a talk and from immediate correcting and grading of student works to participation in Skype meetings with experts. The description of each part of the course is supplemented with an emphasis on our idea of using lean to explain lean concepts. Sample exercises are provided in Appendix. In Sect. 9 we summarize our approach, the outcomes of the course, and we draw the lines for our future research.

2   General Approach for the Course

As mentioned, the idea of the course is to teach students Lean Software Development using also a Lean approach, so to give them an even deeper understanding of the subject, which often get overseen, as it is evident in a research recently performed by the authors. In fact, our recent research in software companies has identified such discrepancies in software industry. A significant fraction of software companies claims that they are using Agile methodology while they do not implement it – we call them Quasi Agile. In practice, such companies become indistinguishable from those implementing "Waterfall" model.

Indeed, to know what is Lean and to apply it are two different things. Thus, in the course we teach students that following Lean approach implies ubiquitous application of core principles. The expected outcome of the course is getting students to think and act in a Lean manner. In our opinion, this outcome can be achieved by doing things according to Lean approach, rather just listening or reading about Lean. For instance, when students are applying Lean approach in various domains during the course, the organization and form of their learning activities in such exercises should be aligned with Lean as well. Otherwise, not only a significant number of students find many contradictions between the subject and the way of teaching, but the students might just miss the core idea of the course – a risk that is well evident also by simply analysing the status of the industry.

We have already mentioned that our two core reference principles that we wanted to apply to the class are:

(i) Elimination of waste;
(ii) Autonomation.

We have now to understand what they mean in an educational context.

The elimination of waste appears the easier principle to implement, which taken individually may look trivial, but properly contextualized and rationalized may help students perceiving the deepness of the issue. Referring to elimination of waste, we can consider a simple set of concepts and example that can help the students to perceive the matter at stake:

– Make the best possible use of the time in class;
– Develop and give assignments in the most productive way;
– Eliminate useless administrative burdens on the side of both students and instructor.

Autonomation has a broader and deeper implication. In a sense it should be the core of any educational endavour, because we would like every student to understand her/himself the progress s/he is making in her/his education, moreover, we would like any student to be the main actor of the education endeavour, the real protagonist of it. This may translate in the following course of action:

– Providing immediately the grading, even exposing to the risk of some lack of precision, but so there is the possibility of an immediate feedback
– Sharing assignments, so students can compare their solutions and grading with someone elses'.

These two concepts together lead to the development of the reference educational activities that have guided the development of the course, namely:

– **Reading and watching** (if video) home assignments regularly, to reason on the content of the course.
– **Grand challenges reports and presentations**, to empirically focus on the application of lean approaches to non traditional organisational context in a "pair study work", and report to the rest of the class in oral and written forms.
– **Briefings reports**, in which students study a new subject in software engineering, reviewing an assigned paper, preparing a presentation on it, then giving a presentation to the class.
– **Class participation and tests**, to enrich the discussion with of insights, relevant experiences, critical questions, and analysis of the material.

Students need minimal background to follow the course. The course can be delivered even to the first-year students with minimum knowledge of programming. In the following sections we present how the principles work in the context of concrete elements of the course.

3 Frontal Lectures

Frontal lectures are guided by the course instructor and in most cases the lectures are highly informal and experimental. Students are asked to participate intensively, give their presentations, and also, sometimes, take a leading role in the discussion, applying the ideas and explaining each other the subject, rather than by listening to a frontal explanation.

The topics of the frontal lectures included:

– Software metrics and non invasive measurement
– Taylorism, Fordism, and Lean Thinking
– Lean in Software Engineering
– Agile Methods
– Issues in Agile, the dark side of agile
– Toward Lean Software Development
– GQM+ and Experience Factory.

In general, the classes are organised as follows:

- The first 75 min are cross-reviews of previous lectures and presentations by the instructor;
- The second 75 min are composed by:
  - A quiz taken online and graded as a component of the final grade (see Sect. 4);
  - A presentation by a guest lecturer or from online videos (see Sects. 5 and 6);
  - A personal review of the progress of the grand challenges (see Sect. 7);
  - A final reflection on what has been learnt in the class.

Needless to mention, any distraction is eliminated from the lecture, so cell phones are not allowed in any open place in the class for everyone, including the instructor, and laptops are used exclusively when there is an activity requiring them.

Already here we notice the presence of autonomation and of elimination of waste:

(i) Elimination of waste: by the elimination of distraction of cell phones and laptop, by the elimination of wait for grading and feedback
(ii) Autonomation: by the oral recap of the lecturer at the beginning of the class, the automatically graded quiz, also at the beginning of the class, by the personal review of the grand challenges, and by the final reflection at the end of the class.

4   Immediate Collecting Corrections and Grading

The key point of any efficient learning activity is an immediate feedback. In courses such Lean Software Development this is of high demand, because many parts of the course could be considered as "fuzzy".

In such situation students may be confused about what is correct and what is not. Thus, activity related to assignments immediate corrections and grading are crucial. During each class assignment of the course students use Learning management system (Moodle) to upload their solutions. After that the instructor immediately started grading and the results of the grading were immediately available to students during the same class.

However, this is not the main reason to perform immediate grading. Rather, not letting any useless time to pass between the submission of an assignment or the performance of a task and its grading relates to the concept of elimination of waste and the positive impact it has on the overall organization. So, while we perform grading immediately, we encourage students to appreciate its value, the one discussed at the beginning of this paragraph, and then we clarify how we see it connected to the paramount principle of elimination of waste, along the line of the principles that are inspiring this course.

5   Briefings

Briefings are intended to broad the understanding of the subject, reading and presenting work related to lean software development. Particular emphasis is on empirical research, which is also one of the key tenet of lean, and on historical work that show the roots of existing technologies, explaining how they came into existence, and the reasons for specific constraints on them. During the briefings students:

- Study a new subject by reviewing an assigned paper,
- Prepare a 5 min short presentation on it,
- Give this presentation to the class, with 5 min of follow-up questions and answers.

Explicit requirement for each briefing was linking it to what has already been explained in class, to the overall theory of software development.

The deliverable of each briefing includes:

- A one page abstract of a presentation,
- At most 5 slides for a presentation.

The page limit of abstract and presentation is hard. Students were not allowed to overcome it lowering the standard font size, putting too much text in one slide, enlarging the standard paper size, etc. This requirement helped students to focus on value first, and to distinguish value of the deliverable from the size of the deliverable's text.

Grading criteria for the briefings include:

- Quality of the submitted documents and of the presentation,
- Originality of the understanding,
- Depth of the analysis and of the findings.

(i) Elimination of waste: short presentations and reviews are very useful for extraction of only significant ideas and concepts. As we want students to focus only on key points, it is unnecessary to ask them provide a comprehensive review and long talk. In these activities students can clearly see that very little time is needed to extract and to deeply understand main content.

(ii) Autonomation: endogenous control is enabled with 5 min of follow-up questions and answers. This activity is a natural conclusion for the presentation or talk. The Q/A session reveals the level of the analysis, and helps students learn which parts can be improved.

6   Skype Meetings with Experts

Each Skype meeting with expert was prepared in the following way. Students were asked to collect materials about an expert, find videos, papers, etc. Then a week before the meeting students were collectively collecting questions to the expert. This activity was done online in a shared document, edited by all students. The questions and topics of interest were available to an expert before the meeting. During the meeting an expert may answer questions from the very beginning, sometimes an expert made a short introductory talk. The list of experts includes: Dave Thomas, Alistair Cockburn, Ron Jeffrey, Kent Beck, Jim Highsmith, Robert Martin and others. The discussion between students and an expert was moderated by the course instructor. Each student was able to send a message with a question to instructor and then ask the question to an expert upon instructors request.

This type of eduction activity again reveal our two main points:

(i) Elimination of waste: topics and questions were collected and discussed before a meeting, thus eliminating of waste of time; collective editing reduces duplication, which is clearly leads to wastes in such activity;

(ii) Autonomation: sessions were guided by a primary instructor who properly structured a discussion and helped students to focus on interaction with an expert and his answers rather than selecting which question should be the next.

7   Grand Challenges

Grand challenges consist in applying the concept of lean software development to other knowledge intensive industry fields and to report the results in class. Their purpose is to determine:

– Goals of the industry under study,
– Specific measurement criteria to determine the satisfaction of a goal,
– Elaboration of strategies of such field,
– Identification of what "lean" would mean for such industry,
– Comparison with the techniques related to (lean) software development,
– Identification of what:
  • The industry under study could learn from (lean) software development,
  • (Lean) software development could learn from the industry under study.

Each grand challenge is undertaken by pairs or triples of students. The assignment of a grand challenge is in pull-style: students can create a group and pull assignment from the list of available grand challenges. To this end we use wiki as a platform for group edit and a FIFO policy for assigns. After a certain deadline grand challenges were assigned by instructor. Elimination of waste is clear here and it was appreciated by students.

Each grand challenge required a review of the existing material (books, scientific papers, articles in press, websites, news, etc.) with all such material duly collected, analysed and cited. At the next step a grand challenge required an empirical investigation also involving interviews with key experts of the field, if needed.

The outcome of grand challenge is a deliverable, which need to be supplied through the wiki as well as a comprehensive report of the grand challenge of at most 10 pages, and a presentation of at most 10 slides.

Grading criteria for the grand challenges were clearly stated:

- Quality of the submitted documents,
- Originality of the findings,
- Breadth of the sources used to perform the analysis,
- Depth of the analysis and of the findings,
- Clear evidence of the rational deduction of the findings from the (empirical) analysis.

However, students were also informed that to get the best grade they were expected to apply the principles discussed in this course about handling uncertainty, irreversibility, wicked projects, etc.

8 Connection Between the Lean Approach and the Devops Approach

It was mentioned in Sect. 1 that implementation of end-to-end automation by devops approach needs good understanding of lean principles and mindset. Here we show the relations and differences between Lean and Devops approaches. Clearly, application of devops approach needs autonomation, which is one of two pillars of the Lean approach. Indeed, autonomation leads to automatic application of the regulations, when they needed, without any specific action or control. For instance, live grading strongly connects two processes: (i) development of the solution (by a student) and (ii) testing and accepting of the solution (with possibility of discussing and improving the solution). Thus, it shows to students a clear example of connection between development and operations (grading) as two stages of the same (learning) process. In this sense, the Lean approach provides a key to understand main idea behind the Devops approach.

9 Discussion

In this paper we have discussed the principles that have inspired our approach to teach lean software development, which are centered on the idea of having student experiencing a lean organization while learning lean software production. We have aimed at providing ways to help students to define a suitable lean process for a new organization, a process to introduce and institutionalize it, and an approach to measure the outcome of such introduction and institutionalization. Moreover, we have put a significant effort in teaching students how to identify what "lean" would mean for a given organization, with specific attention to software development.

This work it is at start, we are now progressing our experimentation and we hope to find other institutions interested in replicating our approach. We are ready to share our entire experience to any interested instructor.

Acknowledgments. We thank Innopolis University for supporting our activities and for letting us experimenting fully our lean approaches to teaching.

Appendix

Sample Assignments of the Lean Software Development Course

Sample Assignment
Part 1: In at most 100 words describe a wicked project in which you got involved during your life (it does not need to be in software engineering) and explain in details why it is wicked.

Part 2: In at most 100 words describe on aspect of uncertainty discussed in the paper you read that struck you attention and explain why it got you interested.

Sample Assignment
Describe in at most 50 worlds a key concept of this courses that you have learnt so far, that you have never heard before the beginning of this course, and that has struck your attention. Explain the reason for your choice in at most 50 words.

References

1. Ebert, C., Gallardo, G., Hernantes, J., Serrano, N.: Devops. IEEE Softw. **33**(3), 94–100 (2016)
2. Janes, A., Succi, G.: Lean Software Development in Action. Springer, Heidelberg, Germany (2014). https://doi.org/10.1007/978-3-642-00503-9_11
3. Ohno, T.: Toyota Production System: Beyond Large-scale Production. CRC Press, Boca Raton (1988)
4. Womack, J.P.: Lean Thinking. Simon & Schuster Limited, New York City (1997)
5. Womack, J.P., Jones, D.T.: Lean Thinking: Banish Waste and Create Wealth in Your Corporation. Lean Enterprise Institute, Simon & Schuster (1996)
6. Womack, J.P., Jones, D.T., Roos, D.: The Machine That Changed the World: The Story of Lean Production Harper Perennial Modern Classics. HarperCollins, New York City (1991)

DevOps' Shift-Left in Practice: An Industrial Case of Application

Miguel Jiménez[1(✉)], Luis F. Rivera[2], Norha M. Villegas[2], Gabriel Tamura[2], Hausi A. Müller[1], and Pilar Gallego[3]

[1] University of Victoria, Victoria, British Columbia, Canada
{miguel,hausi}@uvic.ca
[2] Universidad Icesi, Cali, Valle del Cauca, Colombia
{lfrivera,nvillega,gtamura}@icesi.edu.co
[3] Carvajal Organization, Cali, Valle del Cauca, Colombia
pilar.gallego@carvajal.com

Abstract. DevOps aims at unifying software development and operations to improve products and deliver value to customers. However, many organizations adopt DevOps mainly from a traditional perspective, that is, going forward from development to operations. In this paper we present a case of study that illustrates how Carvajal Technology and Services, a software development organization, improved the design of a family of its software products by exploiting operations data. This case of application constitutes a first incursion of the organization into DevOps, exemplifying how the community and companies in industry can also go backwards from operations to development and design, thus realizing the DevOps *shift-left* concept. The main contributions of this paper are: (i) the analysis of the industrial DevOps application, for which the deployment automation mechanism is crucial to realize the shift-left concept effectively; and (ii) AMELIA, the DSL we developed for deploying the different (re)designs to put into operation and gather feedback data rapidly. To evaluate the approach, the organization analyzed this incursion in both directions: from development to operations, on the benefits of deployment automation; and from operations back to development, by improving the throughput of the original design by a factor of five.

Keywords: DevOps · Shift-left in DevOps · Software deployment · Deployment automation

1 Introduction

In recent years, the need for delivering added value to end-users as soon and as frequently as possible, even due to small changes, has increased the adoption of DevOps and continuous delivery processes [1]. Several frameworks and tools have been proposed to address this urgency of faster and more frequent software releases. In general, these frameworks recognize the deployment as an independent phase in the software development life cycle. Given its crucial importance

© Springer Nature Switzerland AG 2019
J.-M. Bruel et al. (Eds.): DEVOPS 2018, LNCS 11350, pp. 205–220, 2019.
https://doi.org/10.1007/978-3-030-06019-0_16

for achieving continuous software delivery, there is a need for a better under-standing of the various deployment uses and roles it can adopt for realizing the versatile DevOps principles in both, the forward and backward directions.

On the one hand, many organizations adopt DevOps from a traditional point of view, that is, focusing on deployment as a checkpoint going forward from devel-opment to operations, considering it as an end for that purpose. On the other hand, from a wider DevOps perspective, automated deployment is a crucial phase for instance to explore, in the operations setting, different design implementa-tions, enabling the collection of data efficiently. This data, used backwards, is key to improving development, and in this process, deployment serves as a medium rather than as an end. Achieving DevOps requires to find ways of traversing development and operations processes in both directions, and the shift-left con-cept enforces especially its backward application.

The goal of this paper is to present an industrial application that uses auto-mated deployment as a fundamental mechanism to enable the organization to systematically conduct experiments to collect data from the software opera-tions and improve the design of its reference architecture. This is an example of how organizations can realize the backward application of DevOps, centered on automating the deployment phase. We developed this application in the con-text of an industrial-academic partnership between Carvajal Technology and Services, and Icesi University. Carvajal is a multinational organization with IT and software development as one of its business units and over 1,200 software developers.

Concretely, for the experiments conducted, we employed and combined dif-ferent design patterns to produce several architectural configurations. However, the number of configurations to be deployed and executed raised several chal-lenges, such as the repeated deployment and re-deployment of the resulting con-figurations instantiations, which requires its automation to enable the efficient gathering of performance measurements. We addressed these challenges follow-ing the DevOps principles. Solving them required the development of AMELIA, a domain-specific language (DSL) for automating deployments. The analysis and evaluation results confirmed the critical role of AMELIA for achieving the dual-direction of the DevOps application—especially the shift-left concept.

This paper is structured as follows. Section 2 presents the background and relevant DevOps concepts for this work. Section 3 presents AMELIA, our language for deployment automation. Section 4 presents the methodology used to apply and evaluate AMELIA in a dual deployment strategy to address this industry application, and discusses the evaluation results. Finally, Sect. 5 concludes the paper.

2   Background

This section introduces DevOps principles and relevant concepts of continu-ous delivery upon which the subject application is built, and where automated deployment is crucial.

2.1 DevOps Adoption Paths and Principles

IBM proposed four paths and respective foci of concerns for adopting DevOps: (i) *steer* continuous business planning; (ii) *develop/test* continuous integration and testing; (iii) *deploy* continuous release and deployment; and (iv) *operate* continuous monitoring [2]. We follow the *deploy* adoption path, on which most of the DevOps inherent concepts and capabilities were originated, including the definition of the delivery pipeline. This pipeline enforces continuous deployment of software to quality assurance and then to production, efficiently and in an automated way.

Similarly, IBM consolidated the main principles developed in the evolution of the DevOps movement [2]. Humble *et al.* played an influential role in advocating the practices supporting these principles [1,3–5]. These principles are: (i) develop and test against production-like systems, the main premise of the shift-left concept moving operations toward development; (ii) deploy with repeatable and reliable processes, for which automation is essential; (iii) monitor and validate operational quality, based on functional and non-functional software characteristics; (iv) amplify feedback loops, reacting and producing changes more rapidly. For the development of our industrial case study, we followed these principles in the context of the deployment adoption path.

2.2 Continuous Delivery

Continuous delivery is a software engineering approach—aligned with the Devops principles and the *deployment* adoption path—that promotes to deliver added value to end-users as soon and as frequently as possible, by deploying successful releases of a subject software system [1]. The major benefits of this approach are the empowerment of teamwork between development and operations, the injection of fewer bugs (therefore reducing costs and risks), generation of less pre-release team stress, and a more flexible deployment process. To achieve these benefits, a software provider must promote a culture of collaboration between all teams involved in the delivery process, the sharing of knowledge and tools among participants, the establishment of measurement metrics, and the gathering of regular feedback for continuous improvement. That is, software providers must subscribe to DevOps principles to acquire continuous delivery benefits [4] and guarantee a repeatable and reliable process for releasing software, the automation of deployment and operation activities, the automation of integration, testing, and release processes, and the definition of an effective quality assurance process [1].

2.3 The Deployment Life Cycle

Deployment has been characterized by the Object Management Group (OMG) and others as "the process composed of interrelated and evolving activities that comprise the lifecycle of a particular system to be brought into—and out of—service" [6–9] as depicted in Fig. 1.

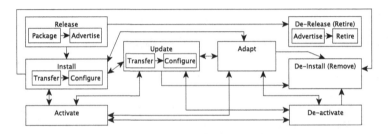

Fig. 1. Deployment process adapted from Carzaniga *et al.* [7]

We now describe the main activities of the deployment lifecycle as outlined in Fig. 1. *release* is the bridge between development and deployment. It comprises all necessary tasks to prepare, package, and provide (*e.g.*, via its publication) a software product for deployment into consumer sites. *Installation* encompasses all configuration operations and assembly of the resources to prepare the software system for activation. Installation involves the transfer of the software components from the producer site to the consumer sites. *Activation* allows the consumer to actually use the software. It is usually realized through the creation of a command for executing a binary component of the application. In the case of complex software, it involves several components that must be executed in a particular sequence. *Deactivation* means to stop any running component of the software system. *Update* is a special case of installation triggered by the release of a new version of the product or of any of its components. However, it may require the deactivation of the software (or the component to be updated) before executing any operation. *Adaptation* is similar to the update activity, in the sense that both modify a previously installed software system. However, an adaptation is triggered by context changes with the goal of assuring the accomplishment of properties or requirements in the deployed system. An adaptation may be performed autonomously in the form of self-adaptation while the subject system is running. *Deinstallation* is the activity performed when the deployed software system is no longer required at the consumer site. *Derelease* (retirement) is the process of finishing the support for a software system or a given configuration of a software system. Retiring a system makes it unavailable for future deployments.

3   Shifting Operations Left by Automating Deployment

This section presents our subject application and addressed challenges, and illustrates how we realized the shift-left conceptual movement of operations toward development. For this realization, the key enabler for exploiting operations results back into design, effectively, was the automation of the deployment phase. We performed this automation with AMELIA, a domain-specific language (DSL) we developed for expressly this purpose.

3.1   The Industrial Case of Application

The case of application mainly answers the question of how to satisfy the performance requirements of the core engine of a software product family that processes large XML files for different application domains, established as a product's quality attribute by a set of corporate clients. Of course, this is a problem of design, critical for a reference architecture that affects an entire family of products. Nonetheless, despite a design problem, its effective solution requires to move operations toward development.

Post-deployment tests on the infrastructure showed serious performance limitations. At this point, the organization decided to look for alternatives, and our research group at Icesi University joined Carvajal for their first incursion into DevOps.

As an exemplar of the product family, we selected a concrete product that Carvajal developed for the Colombian National Agency for Overcoming Extreme Poverty (ANSPE—initials corresponding to the Spanish name[1]) to allow census workers to collect demographic data in mobile devices offline (*i.e.*, in regions with no access to telecommunications). After days or weeks, hundred of workers synchronize the collected census data with a centralized server, from around the whole country. This synchronization suffered from severe delays and timeout errors, due to the large number of requests overloading the central server.

3.2   Addressed Challenges

Processing XML files is a common, IO-intensive task that supports core business processes in different domains, ranging from plain data transmission and transformation to full data interoperability, for all of which there are several existing libraries and processing strategies. However, it is non trivial to decide which strategy and libraries to select in a large-scale solution design space, whose primary requirement is performance, given the combined implications they have on this quality attribute. Moreover, these decisions must be considered in distributed processing scenarios, such as the one illustrated in Fig. 2. As a result, most of the challenges we addressed are referred to as deployment issues, as follows:

Variability in Architectural Configurations and Instantiations. In addition to the number of XML processing strategies and libraries, there are also a number of domain-specific design patterns to consider among those for improving performance, such as Producer/Consumer, Master/Worker, Reactor, among others. These design patterns' components, along with the application's software components can be deployed in different processing nodes (*cf.* Fig. 2 for example), yielding several architectural configurations and variations. That is, for each architectural configuration, several instantiations are possible (*e.g.*, varying the number of slave processing nodes). Each of these instantiations implies

---

[1] Agencia Nacional para la Superación de la Pobreza Extrema.

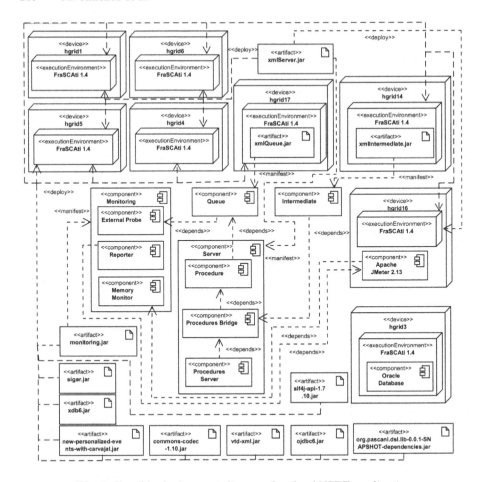

Fig. 2. Possible deployment diagram for the ANSPE application

a corresponding deployment and execution process to test on operations, whose variations are intricate and their combinations large in number.

Dependency Management. Dependencies exist in all of the deployment variations, and along all the deployment process phases, both among software components, and among software and hardware components.

Coordination Control. The execution of the deployment tasks and phases, not only within a particular processing node but also among all of them, must be coordinated and controlled along all consumer sites, especially in the case of distributed software systems such as the ANSPE. This coordination and control must observe the deployment dependencies of each particular application.

Modularity and Composability. Deployment tasks and phases should be specifiable in independent but composable modules. Specification encapsulation and modularity should allow abstraction scalability and factoring out common and repeatable deployment tasks in separate modules, each having well defined interfaces and internal specifications, and enabling the integration of other specifications. However, composability increases the complexity of dependency management through the entire deployment life cycle.

Reusability. Deployment specifications should be reusable in different deployment workflows. These specifications could be provided as part of a catalogue to facilitate deployment design and specification. Reusability also increases the complexity of dependency management.

Extensibility. Refers to the functional ability to easily override or extend the behaviour of an existing deployment specification. Without adequate extensibility capabilities, a deployment specification must be either modified in place or duplicated to adapt it to be used in a different deployment context, which reduces reusability.

3.3   The AMELIA DSL for Automating Deployment

Automatically deploying, configuring and executing scalable software-intensive systems, whose components are distributed in several processing nodes and feature runtime dependencies among them, is not a trivial task. For instance, even in systems such as Docker [10], the way to resolve runtime dependencies in a distributed software deployment and execution scenario is left to the developer—checking for them in the application's subsystems source code, which is not appropriate nor possible in all scenarios. Therefore, we adopt the following lean strategy for automating deployment. Instead of using heavy-weight and multifunction systems like Kubernetes [11] and Apache Mesos [12], which were originally invented for cluster management (*i.e.*, not exactly focused on deployment automation), we designed and developed AMELIA, a compact DSL tailored for specifying and executing deployment workflows for distributed software systems. AMELIA contains both declarative and imperative statements that facilitate coordinated control of the overall deployment process, and at the same time, offer granular control over all of the executed operations. AMELIA is fully integrated with the Java type system. This integration allows not only to reuse existing Java code, but also to extend the Java's base library.

An AMELIA file specification can be written as either a subsystem description or a deployment strategy. The first one is a modular unit representing the overall structure of the (sub)system to deploy and corresponding deployment operations; a subsystem description is composed of, and dependent on, other subsystems, thus supporting modularity, dependency management, composability and reusability. The latter is an execution flow specification that dictates how to perform the deployment operations, thus supporting coordination and control. For example, AMELIA allows to retry tasks upon encountering a failure, or systematically repeat the same deployment procedure, which is useful for instance to "warm up" a system before running performance tests. The current implementation of AMELIA can be used as a standalone compiler or as an

Eclipse plug-in. From a specification file, the compiler generates an executable Java application that automatically resolves the subsystem dependencies and (sub)module inclusions while logging the results of deployment task execution.

Language Structure and Concepts. Listing 1.1 is an example of a system description for the deployment of the ANSPE `Monitor` subsystem.[2] An AMELIA specification is comprised of a package declaration section, an optional Java import section, an optional extension section, and a type declaration section (*cf.* respective highlighted regions ❶, ❷, ❸, ❹ in the listing). The characteristics of each section are as follows.

Subsystems. A `subsystem` collects and encapsulates the sets of variables, parameters, and execution rules for a software subsystem to be deployed. Local variables within a subsystem may control the execution flow (*e.g.*, variable `compileMonitor` in Listing 1.1). Parameters are used to configure a subsystem according to a deployment strategy. They are included in the subsystem's constructor in the same order they are defined. In Listing 1.1, the (implicit) constructor of the `Monitor` subsystem includes the given name for the monitor, the communication protocol, and the target architecture. Execution rules group commands that describe the deployment lifecycle of a subsystem; that is, they represent the various phases of a subsystem's deployment. The deployment of the `Monitor` subsystem is described as follows: *initialization* checks whether the monitor's source code must be compiled; *compilation* generates an executable artifact by compiling the monitor's source code; and *activation* executes such artefact passing the corresponding arguments.

There is no main entry point or main function in a subsystem specification where the deployment execution starts. Instead, the execution flow is expressed and controlled by rules and their dependencies. Thus, any rule not depending on any other rule is triggered immediately upon deployment execution. For example, in Listing 1.1, the `compilation` rule depends on the local rule `initialization`; that means that the first command from the former will be executed after the last command from the latter. A group of commands within an execution rule is executed sequentially. A rule (*i.e.*, its commands) is executed on at least one host and may depend on a Boolean expression (*e.g.*, line 44 in Listing 1.1). Conditional expressions may be placed next to the host(s) to guard the execution of a set of rules on a host. In case the Boolean expression is false, the set of rules is not executed and the dependent rules are released from the dependency.

AMELIA has built-in support for five commands: transfer files, change the working directory, compile FRASCATI [13] components, run FRASCATI components, and execute other commands (*e.g.*, line 41 in Listing 1.1).

---

[2] The complete versions of all examples discussed in this paper are available in the AMELIA evaluation repository https://github.com/unicesi/amelia-evaluation.

```
❶  1  package co.edu.icesi.driso.amelia.carvajal.xml.large
   2
❷  3  import java.util.concurrent.atomic.AtomicBoolean
   4  import co.edu.icesi.driso.amelia.carvajal.xml.large.CommProtocol
   5  import static extension examples.Util.warn
   6
❸  7  includes co.edu.icesi.driso.amelia.carvajal.xml.large.CommonSpecification
   8  depends on co.edu.icesi.driso.amelia.carvajal.xml.large.ApacheServer
   9
  10  // A Subsystem for the monitoring component.
❹ 11  subsystem Monitor  {
  12    // The name of the monitor
  13    param String name
  14
  15    // The protocol used for communication among components
  16    param CommProtocol protocol
  17
  18    // The target architecture
  19    param Arch arch
  20
  21    // Activation variables.
  22    var String component = "memory-monitor"
  23    var String service = "startMemoryMonitor"
  24    var String method = "startMemoryMonitoring"
  25
  26    // Whether to compile the monitor
  27    var AtomicBoolean compileMonitor = new AtomicBoolean
  28
  29    // The classpath used for compiling the monitoring component
  30    var String[] _classpath = #[
  31      'org.pascani.dsl.lib-0.0.1-SNAPSHOT-dependencies.jar',
  32      'new-personalized-events-with-carvajal.jar',
  33      'slf4j-api-1.7.10.jar',
  34      'sigar.jar']
  35
  36    // The libpath used for activating the monitoring component
  37    var String _libpath = classpath + #[component]
  38
  39    on CommonSpecification.host {
  40      initialization: CommonSpecification.changeDirectory;
  41        (cmd 'ls')
  42          .fetch[compileMonitor.set(!it.contains('«component».jar'))]
  43
  44      compilation ? compileMonitor: initialization;
  45        compile CommonSpecification.actionFolder component -classpath _classpath
  46
  47      activation ? protocol == CommProtocol.RMI ||
  48                   protocol == CommProtocol.REST: compilation;
  49        (run component -libpath _libpath -s service -m method -p #[name, arch])
  50          .warn('Executing the Monitor, could take several minutes...')
  51    }
  52  }
```

Listing 1.1: A subsystem specification to deploy a monitor in ANSPE

```
 1 package co.edu.icesi.driso.amelia.carvajal.xml.large
 2
 3 import java.util.Map
 4 import org.amelia.dsl.lib.descriptors.Host
 5 import org.amelia.dsl.lib.util.Hosts
 6 import org.amelia.dsl.lib.util.RetryableDeployment
 7 import examples.ubuntu.Arch
 8 import co.edu.icesi.driso.amelia.carvajal.xml.large.CommProtocol
 9
10 includes co.edu.icesi.driso.amelia.carvajal.xml.large.Monitor
11
12 // Deployment of a monitor component.
13 deployment DeploymentMonitor {
14    // Load all hosts and then filter
15    val Map<String, Host> hs = Hosts.hosts("hosts.txt").toMap[h|h.identifier]
16    val executionHosts = #[hs.get("hgrid1"), hs.get("hgrid4"), hs.get("hgrid5")]
17    for(i: 0..executionHosts.size - 1)
18      add(new Monitor("monitor/src", 'mntr«i»', CommProtocol.RMI, Arch.amd64))
19    val helper = new RetryableDeployment()
20    helper.deploy([ start(true) ], 2) // Deploy everything & retry if it fails
21 }
```

Listing 1.2: A deployment strategy for the ANSPE Monitor subsystem

The extension section of a subsystem allows expressing subsystem dependencies and inclusions. In the former case, the execution of all the subsystem's rules depends on the successful execution of the rules defined within the subsystem's dependencies. In the latter case, both parameters and execution rules from the included subsystems are made part of the including subsystem. This means that its constructor is modified to accept the included parameters, and that included rules are dependent on local rules. In Listing 1.1, CommonSpecification.host refers to a parameter defined in subsystem CommonSpecification. In the same way, the local rule initialization depends on the changeDirectory rule defined in subsystem CommonSpecification. In this case, the dependency uses the rule's qualified name to avoid a name collision with a local rule.

Deployment Strategies. Deployment strategies are simpler than subsystems and their purpose is twofold: (i) to configure subsystem instances; and (ii) to determine how many times, and including which subsystems, must the system be deployed.

Listing 1.2 presents the monitoring deployment strategy in detail. Line 18 shows how to instantiate the subsystem Monitor. To make a subsystem available for deployment, the subsystem must be included in the extension section.

An invocation to the static method start initiates the deployment execution. Notice that it can be invoked more than once, always blocking until the deployment finishes. Line 21 features a utility class that invokes a lambda function as many times as specified if its execution throws an error. In this case, if the deployment fails this helper will retry exactly one time.

Extensions. AMELIA supports two Java-based extension mechanisms. The first one allows creating new commands by instantiating a `CommandDescriptor`—a Java class defined in the Java runtime library. The second mechanism allows augmenting a command by extending its behaviour. For example, `fetch` (*cf.* line 42 in Listing 1.1) is an extension that implicitly imports a static method that returns a new command; that is, a `CommandDescriptor` instance wraps another `CommandDescriptor`. Thus, the extension retrieves the output from the input command and passes it to a lambda function. Extensions can be chained together.

3.4 Automated Deployment Execution

Performing the deployment of the various architecture configurations and variants is a demanding task, even with automated tools. It requires specifying the deployment of each architectural configuration, whose variants and instantiations requires repeating the same portions of the specifications. AMELIA addresses this problem by allowing parameterised and reusable modules and procedures to specify different configuration instantiations. Each specification comprises the deployment and configuration operations required to deploy and execute each of the software components. Of course, some of these specifications are reusable to the extent to which the deployment language or mechanism supports modularity and encapsulation. For example, the Master/Worker design pattern is deployed ·by creating two types of specification, a master and a worker component, whose computing node is a parameter. Encapsulation is critical to avoid side effects. In AMELIA, these specifications are subsystems, which define explicit instantiation parameters and a clear interface based on the deployment operations.

Furthermore, systematic deployment execution can be further exploited in AMELIA. Each execution cycle may comprise from configuration and deployment to measurement gathering and metrics storing. In fact, new deployments can be stopped when a previous instance already presents better metrics. AMELIA's deployment strategies allow this by providing granular control over the deployment start and end, tight integration with the Java programming language, and control over first-class deployment concepts, such as subsystems and their parameters.

4 Evaluation

This section presents the analysis and evaluation of the subject industrial application, aimed at demonstrating how to exploit automated deployment in the DevOps process chain, not only in the forward (*i.e.*, traditional), but also in the backward direction.

4.1 Qualitative Analysis

In the forward direction, going from development to operations, we performed a qualitative evaluation of the language effectiveness for specifying the deployment of different architectural configurations of the ANSPE software system.

For this evaluation, we designed an evaluation protocol that was applied by six Masters students, some of them members of the Carvajal engineering staff. They developed several AMELIA specifications from UML deployment diagrams representing some ANSPE architecture configuration variants. These were variants of two design patterns: Producer/Consumer and Reactor; all variants used RMI as the communication protocol and executed on the same middleware. The first configuration required four processing nodes, while the second required twelve; in both cases, only one Consumer component was deployed on each processing node. Then, the participants completed a questionnaire regarding their experience. Based on their answers, we evaluated the language effectiveness using FQAD, a Framework for the Qualitative Assessment of DSLs [14], which refines a subset of quality characteristics defined in the ISO/IEC 25010:2011 standard. Carvajal participated in the selection of the quality characteristics to evaluate: functional suitability, usability, reliability, productivity, and expressiveness, as defined in the standard.

In summary, AMELIA as a DSL for deployment automation was evaluated having either "full support" or "strong support" in all of these characteristics. Given the space restrictions in this paper, we omit the details of the evaluation protocol and its execution. Nonetheless, the evaluation files are available in the AMELIA evaluation github repository.[3] This repository also contains a comparison of AMELIA with alternatives from the state of the art and practice. Among the characteristics, functional suitability (i.e., the degree to which the DSL supports completely and appropriately the specification of scripts to automate the deployment of distributed software) along with productivity and reliability, are most important in gathering evidence to demonstrate deployment automation benefits for the organization.

4.2 Quantitative Analysis

This section presents the quantitative evaluation of AMELIA as the vehicle that enables the shift-left realization (i.e., the backward direction of the DevOps application). For this evaluation, we took advantage of the qualitative evaluation results, that is, by directing the Masters students to refine and complete the deployment scripts specified for that evaluation, and executing them to finally obtain a design that satisfies the performance requirements.

The quantitative evaluation follows a four-step experimental design approach. First, we started by selecting a set of domain-specific design patterns for improving performance, suitable for our case. Second, we defined several architectural configurations, variations and corresponding instantiations that result from the incorporation of the selected design patterns to the ANSPE's reference architecture, and finally adapted and completed the corresponding AMELIA deployment scripts. Third, we prepared a hardware infrastructure as close as possible to the organization's one, with controlled conditions, and executed the experiments by running the deployment scripts for each of the architectural instantia-

---

[3] https://github.com/unicesi/amelia-evaluation.

tions. From these executions, the metrics of system performance were collected. Finally, we compared the performance metrics to arrive at the best architectural configuration.

In the following sections, we explain the experimental design, its execution and the analysis of the results.

Experimental Design. The experimental design involved the generation of combinatorial instantiations of architectural configurations and factors, where the objective was to measure the performance of these configurations instatiations. The experimental unit encompassed the different system architectural configurations systematically. The response variable under study was performance (throughput) in the number of XML files processed per minute. The controllable input factors included (i) the set of XML files with CRUD operations to update the census and demographic status of families; (ii) the design patterns relevant for distributed processing (*e.g.*, Producer/Consumer (P/C) and Reactor); (iii) the communications protocol used; and (iv) the number of working components that were deployed on each slave processing node (*i.e.*, consumers in P/C, controllers in Reactor). The uncontrollable input factors comprised the clock synchronization issues among the processing nodes,[4] and the indispensable operating system processes. Table 1 summarizes and abstracts the experiment design,[5] for XML files of 1 Mb of application operations, and 12 processing nodes (*i.e.*, computers with 1 quadcore CPU).

Table 1. Factors instantiated for the experimental design

Design pattern	Communications protocol	No. consumers/controllers
P/C	RMI	12
P/C	RMI	48
P/C	RMI	96
P/C	Ice	12
P/C	Ice	96
Reactor	RMI	12
Reactor	Ice	12

Experiments Execution. The experiments were executed in an infrastructure equipped with 22 computers configured with one CPU Intel i7 quadcore, and 16 GB of RAM running Linux Fedora 25, although not all computers were used at

---

[4] We used the Precision Time Protocol (PTP, IEEE 1588).

[5] The complete version of the experiment design comprises a set of 324 configurations resulting from the following number of instantiations: 4 patterns × 3 numbers of consumers/controllers × 3 numbers of processing nodes × 3 communication protocols × 3 sizes of input files. We present a subset because of space restrictions.

the same time in any of the experiments. As part of the configuration process in the deployment specification, all useless and non-critical operating system services were stopped before executing the experiments.

The steps for performing the deployment of the architectural configuration instantiations included an important point in the pre-requisites of execution: the database required to be restored with data backed-up exactly to replicate the XML files to be synchronized. This implied that, previous to executing any experiment, restoring the database was necessary.

The deployment and execution of each of the configurations of the experimental design was repeated at least three times, and the performance metrics averaged. This means that a total of 21 deployments and executions were performed for the subset of the experiments outlined in Table 1. The role played by AMELIA for developing and executing these experiments was really critical,[6] especially because AMELIA's reuse features allowed sharing code among all architecture variants.

Analysis of Results. The reference throughput baseline given was of 1 XML file every 32 s (that is, 1.87 XML files per minute). Thus, we present the quantitative results of the experiments in Table 2 in this form.

Table 2. Execution results of the experiment

Experiment configuration	Throughput
P/C, RMI, 12 components	1 file/11.35 s
P/C, RMI, 48 components	1 file/6.9 s
P/C, RMI, 96 components	1 file/6.7 s
P/C, Ice, 12 components	1 file/11.51 s
P/C, Ice, 96 components	1 file/6.1 s
Reactor, RMI, 12 components	1 file/21.95 s
Reactor, Ice, 12 components	1 file/20.51 s

According to these results, the best architectural configuration uses the Producer/Consumer design pattern with Ice as communication protocol, distributing 96 consumers in 12 processing nodes, for a throughput of 1 file every 6.1 s, around five times better than the reference baseline.[7]

In addition, it is worth noting two other points: first, that Producer/Consumer is consistently and significantly better than Reactor, and second, that even though Ice is in general better than RMI, the difference is not that significant.

---

[6] In the complete experiments set, a total of 972 deployments and respective executions were performed.

[7] In fact, this configuration was the best among the 324 in the complete experiment.

5   Conclusions

Conveying good design practices into actual architectural configurations with the purpose of guaranteeing specific quality metrics can be performed more effectively when having access to gathered evidence from experimentation with systems in operation. Automated deployment is crucial for performing this experimentation for an architect to select, for instance, the most appropriate design pattern. Thus, we believe that, in the context of DevOps, realizing automated deployment as presented in this paper, is important to make informed decisions in the development process based on factual data gathered from operations.

In this paper, we reported on an industrial case study regarding the dual use of automated deployment in the both directions of a DevOps setting: from development to operations and also in the inverse direction, effectively realizing the shift-left concept. To this end, we illustrated how our AMELIA DSL facilitates the automation of the deployment process for various architecture variants and configurations, following the DevOps principles and the *deployment* adoption path.

We applied FQAD to evaluate five quality characteristics in AMELIA, confirming its effectiveness for deployment automation. For the quantitative evaluation, we used AMELIA to specify and deploy 324 architectural configurations and variations in a set of experiments. We used the experiments results to redesign the reference architecture of our industrial subject system and improve its throughput by a factor of five. One of our findings in this case study is that the Producer/Consumer design pattern is consistently better than Reactor with respect to throughput.

Acknowledgments. This work was funded in part by the National Sciences and Engineering Research Council (NSERC) of Canada, IBM Canada Ltd. and IBM Centre for Advanced Studies (CAS), the University of Victoria, Universidad Icesi (Colombia), and Organización Carvajal SA (Colombia).

References

1. Humble, J., Farley, D.: Continuous Delivery: Reliable Software Releases Through Build, Test, and Deployment Automation. Addison-Wesley (2011)
2. Sharma, S., Coyne, B.: DevOps for Dummies. 3rd Limited IBM edn. John Wiley & Sons (2017)
3. Humble, J., Farley, D.: Continuous Delivery: Reliable Software Releases Through Build, Test, and Deployment Automation, 1st edn. Addison-Wesley Professional (2010)
4. Humble, J., Molesky, J.: Why enterprises must adopt devops to enable continuous delivery. Cutter IT J. **24**(8), 6–12 (2011)
5. Kim, G., Debois, P., Willis, J., Humble, J.: The DevOps Handbook: How to Create World-class Agility, Reliability, and Security in Technology Organizations. IT Revolution (2016)
6. OMG, Deployment: Configuration of component-based distributed applications specification–version 4.0. Object Management Group (2006)

7. Carzaniga, A., Fuggetta, A., Hall, R.S., Heimbigner, D., Van Der Hoek, A., Wolf, A.L.: A characterization framework for software deployment technologies. Technical report, DTIC Document (1998)
8. Hall, R.S., Heimbigner, D., Wolf, A.L.: A cooperative approach to support software deployment using the software dock. In: Proceedings of the 21st International Conference on Software Engineering, ICSE 1999, pp. 174–183. ACM (1999)
9. Dearle, A.: Software deployment, past, present and future. In: 2007 Future of Software Engineering, FOSE 2007, pp. 269–284. IEEE Computer Society (2007)
10. Willis, J.: Docker and the three ways of DevOps. Technical report, Docker Inc. (2017)
11. Burns, B., Grant, B., Oppenheimer, D., Brewer, E., Wilkes, J.: Borg, omega, and kubernetes. Commun. ACM **59**(5), 50–57 (2016)
12. Hindman, B., et al.: Mesos: a platform for fine-grained resource sharing in the data center. In: NSDI, vol. 11, p. 22 (2011)
13. Seinturier, L., Merle, P., Rouvoy, R., Romero, D., Schiavoni, V., Stefani, J.B.: A component-based middleware platform for reconfigurable service-oriented architectures. Softw.: Pract. Exp. **42**(5), 559–583 (2012)
14. Kahraman, G., Bilgen, S.: A framework for qualitative assessment of domain-specific languages. Softw. Syst. Model. **14**(4), 1505–1526 (2015)

DevOps'18 Education Panel
Teaching Feedback and Challenges

Jean-Michel Bruel[1]([✉]) and Miguel Jiménez[2]

[1] University of Toulouse, IRIT, Toulouse, France
`bruel@irit.fr`
[2] University of Victoria, Victoria, Canada

Abstract. DevOps is increasingly becoming a *de facto* standard in the industry. Every year, more and more software companies report improvements on their development process and ability to deliver value-added services. The role of Software Engineering professors, teaching boards, and program committees is to take a step back and think over about the skills requirements in the industry and strategies to teach these skills. As a first exercise to discuss DevOps as part of the university curriculum, the DevOps'2018 workshop organized an educational session and a discussion panel. This paper presents the organization of this panel and the discussions that occurred there.

Keywords: Education · DevOps

1 Organization

For this panel, we put on stage the presenters of the workshop who addressed educational issues: Alfredo Capozucca, Christopher Jones, Manuel Mazzara and Sebastien Mosser. Besides, we decided to invite Benoit Combemale, Professor at the University of Toulouse. He has been kind enough to come earlier than just the panel to participate and to attend the presentations that the panelists did earlier in the afternoon (*cf.* the teaching session in the proceedings). The panel was animated by Jean-Michel Bruel, and this report was written together with Miguel Jiménez. As Combemale had no occasion to talk or present anything, he was the only panelist allowed to give a short presentation[1].

This report is organized as follows. Section 2 introduces and describes the preliminary questions planned for the panel. Section 3 summarizes and comments Combemale's invited talk. Section 4 summarizes and comments the various discussions held around the prepared questions. Section 5 concludes this paper.

---

[1] The slides of this presentation are available here: https://smart-researchteam.github.io/slides/2018-03-06-DevOps-combemale.pdf.

© Springer Nature Switzerland AG 2019
J.-M. Bruel et al. (Eds.): DEVOPS 2018, LNCS 11350, pp. 221–226, 2019.
https://doi.org/10.1007/978-3-030-06019-0_17

2   Expected Outcomes

Like the other panels and discussions in this workshop, we adopted a dynamic and agile organization.[2] The moderator had prepared a few questions for the panelists to start the discussion and attract more questions from the attendees. The moderator presented those questions at the beginning of the panel, right before the invited talk. Next, we list and describe the preliminary questions.

Q1. *How would you define DevOps?*
   We found out during the previous sessions of the workshop that there was no consensus on the definition of DevOps. To avoid the trap of spending too much time defining what DevOps is, the expected answer was not a typical book definition, but the one the panelists explain to their students.

Q2. *Could you share some tips on teaching DevOps?*
   Panelists were asked to share some tips or nice, short stories of either good or bad teaching experiences. Something they would like to share with other teachers. For example, during the Education session, one of the presenters recommended not to grade commits because there may be unexpected side effects.

Q3. *What do you think about the prerequisite skills to learn DevOps?*
   Curriculum often talks about the expected skills the students will acquire and prerequisite courses, but not that often in terms of competencies.

3   Invited Talk by Benoit Combemale

After the usual acknowledgments for the invitation, Benoit Combemale started his invited talk by reinforcing that he was previously a professor of Software Engineering (SE). He also made emphasis on the fact that his experience is on the Dev part rather than the Ops part, as already mentioned during the workshop. Combemale provided his understanding of the state of the practice in DevOps. He highlighted the differences between the current practices, both in teaching and also with all of his industrial partners. According to Benoit, what is called DevOps is mostly the automation of what was done by hand previously regarding build, deployment, test, monitoring and so on. In other words, it is mostly about tools for an automation approach.

   In his view, DevOps is the future of the development process as a whole. His practice, in terms of DevOps, is usually divided into two parts. The first one, which takes almost half of the time of the course, is a regular literature survey. Most of our students are undergrads, which means that they may need more internships in the industry to fully understand why DevOps is so important for the IT industry, said Combemale and continued: so, starting by looking at current and practical articles from the web, is really a way to show them the scalability that is needed in a real-world environment. The second part is addressed throughout actual code development. This part is driven by projects,

---

[2] In potentially both classical meanings of *agile*: very smart or very messy.

which means that the lectures are not given per se but are raised by the need during the organization of each project.

In his course, Combemale relates to many topics he has seen in previous courses, including programming, testing, configuring, and deploying software, and also courses related to system configuration and visualization. His observation is that the requirements for the students are similar: to have good skills in software development (*e.g.*, design, programming, testing, among others). A question then arises: is DevOps something that leverages on previous skills that are coming from software development or can DevOps help us to learn how to program efficiently in the modern world? Rephrasing this question, an open issue towards teaching DevOps is whether or not it should be taught by itself or integrated into a larger SE course. His opinion is that DevOps should be a proper course in the curriculum. Benoit also underlined the benefit, as a teacher, of using tools that students can access anywhere (*e.g.*, school, home or even at work). This benefit makes DevOps courses *pretty fun* for the students, as stated by Combemale.

Of course, some teaching challenges remain. He chose to insist on the lack of a proper and sound theory of DevOps. For example, for the composability of the different artifacts or the different pipelines that are defined, what is the correctness or how to validate these pipelines? Or even, how to orchestrate correctly these pipelines? The scientific community should work about it in the future, said Combemale.

Another teaching challenge is the number of tools, techniques, and languages that are used, implying a tooling overhead and unsupported heterogeneity. It is very difficult to ensure interoperability, synchronization, and other properties among the different artifacts.

To conclude, Combemale shared two main observations. The first one is that he is convinced that DevOps needs to be taught with practical labs as confirmed by the afternoon session talks. The difficulty is to find realistic enough projects that students can still handle. These projects are necessary to illustrate the need for DevOps. The second observation is that, even if the course is project-driven, students need personal assistance.

4   Discussions

The panel discussion started with the question raised by Combemale: should DevOps be taught as a course by itself or as part of a regular SE class? In other words, and in order to relate this question to the one about DevOps' definition (*cf.* Q1 in Sect. 2): can we define DevOps as something that needs to be mastered as a specific course or is it only a set of assembling techniques that are already there?

To start discussing this point, Manuel Mazzara made the parallel with how programming was taught at the beginning in universities as part of mathematics or physics curriculum. At some point, someone must have started such a course as an elective one, maybe in the last year of the mathematics or physics program.

Then programming became fully part of the curriculum until finally programming was an important part of a dedicated Computer Science curriculum. For those who advocate that DevOps be a dedicated course, they might hence need to be patient, even to simply avoid useless tensions with the teaching board.

Sebastien Mosser discussed two options that, in his opinion, need be addressed: First, either DevOps is not a course, which implies that it does not deserve a particular focus, but raises the question of where it should be taught to students (i.e., as part of which course or courses). Second, it does require a course by itself, which raises two more questions then: who should attend such a course, and what should be the focus, Dev for Ops or the contrary? Mosser is convinced that he cannot answer the question without having matured those two questions. One of the attendees made a parallel with object-orientation, which was at some point important enough to have its own dedicated course, but is nowadays commonly included in introduction to programming courses. Another argument for having a dedicated course on DevOps is that it helps students to make the connection among other fundamental courses, such as programming and systems administration.

Christopher Jones mentioned that DevOps is a very specific label that practitioners attach to process improvement, within the context of software development. Nevertheless, according to him, nothing is inherently new about DevOps, it is simply recognizing that there are sources of friction in the development process, and finding ways of alleviating those sources within a particular context.

For Alfredo Capozucca, DevOps comes from Software Engineering. In his University, it is introduced in the context of methodology processes. According to Capozucca, the marketing name today is DevOps but why not calling it "Software Engineering 2.0?"

Switching to the question about prerequisites for attendees of a DevOps course (cf. Q3 in Sect. 2), a first discussion starts based on some outputs from the afternoon Education session: the interest of a holistic mindset for students, the importance of communication skills, and the ability to work on development projects.

Benoit Combemale's DevOps course takes place at the end of the curriculum. The course's requirements for the students are: to be good in coding, with some skills in databases and other complementary technologies. Combemale wondered whether DevOps could also be used for teaching how to code and, therefore, taught a lot earlier. Capozucca added that it would be good if more courses were based on project-based learning; from the viewpoint of both the students and teachers. Students will be ready for the DevOps course by the time they take it. Teachers would share experiences, frameworks, and other means.

An attendee mentioned that we cannot talk about students requirements for a course without defining the associated teaching methodology. Indeed, DevOps is the ideal candidate for non-traditional ways of teaching, such as peer instructions, flipped classroom, problem-based learning, among others.

Another attendee pointed out that the discussions from the panel had been focused on the Dev part of DevOps, and the Ops part was slightly touched. How does a practitioner become part of the operations staff? University programs, in general, do not teach this specifically. We can even wonder whether any operations people come from University programs. An important question to address would be: what are the teaching requirements for an operator (*e.g.*, a systems administrator) to become more DevOps akin?

The discussion then turned around the Ops people. An attendee mentioned, based on his own experience at one of the GAFAM company, that the company's "site reliability engineers" are, basically, the programmers who did not make it as programmers. Joke apart, operations people often have skills, such as problem-solving, and knowledge developers do not have. Thereby, in this transitional period, where DevOps is still new, it is normal to have dedicated DevOps courses. In the long term though, a good reason for not having a dedicated course is that if DevOps is important, it should be included in courses teaching fundamental concepts. As such, in an SE course, DevOps could be addressed through two forms: the first form is treating DevOps as a different kind of development (*i.e.*, with continuous integration and other agile practices). This form could happen early in the course, where almost no additional background is required. The second form emphasizes the Ops part, which is not typically addressed by SE teachers. And so, in terms of prerequisites, this is what SE teachers could improve in themselves. Most of SE teachers, at least before venturing into teaching DevOps, do not know much about that part. This is really something that SE teachers need to learn in order to be able to teach it to students.

On the question of sharing good experiences (*cf.* Q2 in Sect. 2), apart from the already mentioned project-based approach, numerous people pointed out that students' motivation is crucial for a successful DevOps course. One way to achieve this is by making the course optional so that students who register in the course are truly motivated. Another good practice that was mentioned several times turns around "small steps". Most reported courses started, basically, with a little, easy to achieve step (*e.g.*, a small task where students do not start from scratch), and then make things complicated.

Another good advice is to try, as much as possible, to bring industry partners into the course. It can be through the presentation of their own DevOps context, or through support on the Ops part, especially on the activities related to the computing infrastructure. One attendee shared about the homework he assigns to his students: they have to find an organization that claims to be successful in practicing DevOps or one that tried and failed. Then, the students have a big round table at the end of the term to identify common characteristics and things that proved to work or fail.

5   Conclusion

As usual, the panel brought more questions than answers. Some of the raised points and good practices were not specific to DevOps of course, and the main challenge, especially from the very software-oriented audience, was to find ways of emphasizing the Ops part of the approach. It seems that we are starting to have some feedback on the beginning of teaching DevOps and that the future will bring more insights very soon.

Acknowledgements. The authors would like to thank the panelists and the DEVOPS'2018 workshop attendees for their valuable contributions.

Author Index

Printed in the United States
By Bookmasters